Responsibility from the Margins

Responsibility from the Margins

David Shoemaker

OXFORD
UNIVERSITY PRESS

OXFORD
UNIVERSITY PRESS

Great Clarendon Street, Oxford, OX2 6DP,
United Kingdom

Oxford University Press is a department of the University of Oxford.
It furthers the University's objective of excellence in research, scholarship,
and education by publishing worldwide. Oxford is a registered trade mark of
Oxford University Press in the UK and in certain other countries

First Edition published in 2015

Impression: 1

Published in the United States of America by Oxford University Press
198 Madison Avenue, New York, NY 10016, United States of America

British Library Cataloguing in Publication Data
Data available

Library of Congress Control Number: 2014953533

ISBN 978–0–19–871567–2

Printed and bound by
CPI Group (UK) Ltd, Croydon, CR0 4YY

For Glenna

Preface

Oddly, I cannot remember when I first read P. F. Strawson's "Freedom and Resentment," the primary inspiration and motivation for this book. It had to have been when I was in graduate school at the University of California, Irvine, sometime in the early 1990s, but other than that, I unsurprisingly draw a blank, as my graduate years were ones of both sensory and philosophical overload. I likely didn't understand it anyway. I do, however, recall rereading the paper many times over subsequent years, as well as teaching it in several graduate seminars and then even, once, to a group of precocious freshmen at Tulane. It has become my favorite philosophical paper, one that several of my bemused colleagues have heard me pronounce the "greatest philosophical paper of the twentieth century." There is plenty of room to deny that grandiose claim, but there is no room to deny the paper's thoroughgoing influence on contemporary philosophical research on free will and responsibility. Much like Rawls' *A Theory of Justice* in political philosophy, it set up a powerful new agenda, one with which, whether one likes it or not, one at least has to reckon.

This book is my attempt to develop as fully as possible a *Strawsonian* theory of responsibility, although the final result is rather different from Strawson's. I take quite seriously three central features of Strawson's account. First, he urged an approach to discovering the nature of responsibility that starts with and leans on an investigation into our deeply human interpersonal responses and practices as given, as opposed to viewing those responses and practices as afterthoughts or as requiring some justification external to those practices, such as antecedent facts about responsibility or social efficiency. Second, he opined about what a pity it was that philosophers no longer seemed to want to talk in terms of the *moral sentiments*, and how useful such talk could well have been in putting forward his view. Third, Strawson's theory about all of our responsibility responses and practices was that they were unified in taking as their object agents' *quality of will*, so that agents were on the hook for the full range of attitudes when a certain quality of will was displayed in their behavior, and off the hook—excused or exempted—when no such quality of will was implicated.

I take on board to some extent all three of these features. But there are serious problems with the last, quality of will, feature, which are revealed by our widespread ambivalence to cases of what I call *marginal agency*. There are many marginal agents among us, including those at the high-functioning end of the autism spectrum, those in the mild to moderate stages of Alzheimer's dementia, those with mild intellectual disability, those with clinical depression, those from poor formative circumstances, psychopaths, and more. These are agents who often strike us as ineligible only for *some* subset of responsibility responses while nevertheless being fully eligible for others. If we are to take our responses seriously in investigating the nature of responsibility, then it looks as if no single quality of will approach can handle these cases, for these look to be agents who do have quality of will in some sense even when they are off the hook for (some) responsibility responses. That is, it looks as if our responsibility responses, when appropriate—and so responsibility itself—are not about (only) agential quality of will after all.

My response to this problem drives Part I of the book, in which I develop what I call the *tripartite theory of responsibility*, a pluralistic approach to the nature of quality of will. There is not just one single quality of will, in other words; rather, there are three: quality of character, quality of judgment, and quality of regard. These are the *qualities* of will revealed by our ambivalence in the marginal cases, as they are what those cases prize apart. Investigation into the conditions for each type of quality of will ultimately yields three distinct types of responsibility: attributability, answerability, and accountability. In Part II, I test the theory by looking individually at several marginal cases, investigating whether, when the empirical details are filled in, the tripartite theory yields the most plausible verdicts about the specific kind of ambivalence at work in each. I also discuss the kinds of *practical* payoff a theory like mine has, both for the treatment of marginal agents and the counseling of their caregivers. To explain, most other theories of responsibility deliver the verdict that agents are either responsible or they are not. To the extent that certain responsibility responses nevertheless linger in the caregivers of some marginal agents generally deemed non-responsible, though, guilt or shame often follows (and would seem appropriate, were the up-or-down approach to responsibility the right one). On my more nuanced theory, however, such lingering responses may be quite appropriate, vindicating some of the feelings of these caregivers. The theory also has the resources to provide counsel against the feelings of some otherwise responsible marginal agents who beat themselves up inappropriately.

Writers of fiction are often counseled to "Write what you know." I have taken this advice to heart in my philosophical writing. My interest in marginal agency derives from the many marginal agents who populate my life, a general population with which I have no doubt readers of this book will also be intimately familiar. Indeed, it is hard to live a life without engaging with or being someone who is clinically depressed, has dementia, is autistic, and so on. Several members of my own family, both immediate and more distant, have Alzheimer's disease. Another family member has a mild intellectual disability. And another is a psychopath. I also have several close friends with clinically depressed or autistic spouses or children. These are people about whom (*sans* the psychopath, anyway) I care dearly. As a result, my appeal to marginal agency is not clinical or anthropological; rather, it is deeply personal. It matters to me that I represent such agents as they really are, as fellow humans, and as (at least partial) members of our moral responsibility communities.

A standard approach in the philosophical literature on agency and responsibility is to appeal to science fiction examples to test the limits of our theories. Thus we often get stories about people whose values are replaced wholesale by another set of values in an instant; or people who exist for only a minute, perform an action, and then die off; or people whose decisions are manipulated by evil neuroscientists, etc. I do not want to discount the value of such examples. But we have plenty of real life examples at hand that can also do significant work in developing and testing the limits of our theories of responsibility, so why don't we look to them more often (or at all)? After all, don't we want a theory about *human* responsibility, a theory about *us*? This book is in part an attempt to illustrate the power of this appeal.

And now it is time to get down the business of thanking the many people who have helped me write this book. I want to begin with my intimates, the people I love who make my life outside of philosophy worth living. Thanks go, first and foremost, to my wife Marie Lantz, whose patience and support throughout my philosophical career have been unwavering, especially during the writing and rewriting of this book, which took place part or all of nearly every day for a two-and-a-half-year period. She was often subject to my complaints and struggles with the material, and she never stopped believing in me and providing encouragement, sympathy, and helpful advice. I am ever grateful for her love and support.

Thanks also go to my elder stepdaughter, Kristin Hearns, for preventing me from making an egregious error in my discussion of one of the disorders in the book, and for providing lots of helpful material and bibliographic references. Her own interest in and knowledge of marginal agency informed my own. I am also grateful to my younger stepdaughter, Ashley Castillo, for inspiration and insight. And I am grateful to my grandsons Parker and Cohen for hours of creative playtime and quiet talks. I always look forward to my time with them and they recharge my philosophical batteries.

I also want to thank my parents, Mel and Glenna Shoemaker, for their support, inspiration, encouragement, and (often unfitting) pride. With my mother now going through the ravages of Alzheimer's disease and my father as her caregiver, I have learned more than I ever wanted to know about this heartbreaking disease. Thanks go as well to my brother Daniel, a remarkable man who has become a true friend, and whose discussion with me about some of these marginal agents (without his knowledge, at least until now) was very helpful in my thinking about them.

Finally, I am grateful to my dog Cooper. There was a moment early on in the writing of the book where I thought I had hit a complete dead end and that the project was unworkable. Crushed, I took Cooper for a long walk, and during that walk the problem sorted itself out. There were plenty of other less dramatic walks in which smaller problems were worked out, but I will never forget that day, that walk, and that dog.

Turning to my philosophical comrades, I want to begin with someone in whose debt I will forever remain. Gary Watson was my dissertation advisor at UCI, a valued mentor, and is now someone I am lucky to call a friend. I did no work on agency or responsibility for seven years after I got my Ph.D. (my dissertation and early publishing was on personal identity and ethics), in part because I thought that Gary had already dealt handily with all the main issues. Gradually I began to see some elbow room for the non-Watsons among us, and so I began, ever so quietly, to write about the issue from a different perspective. But Gary's influence on me, both personally and philosophically, remains profound, and I am grateful for it.

When I did begin writing (poorly) about agency and responsibility, another excellent philosopher, Paul Russell, was kind enough to read some early drafts and provide me with generous comments and helpful advice. I contacted Paul out of the blue as a fan after reading his outstanding book on Hume and Strawson, *Freedom and Moral Sentiment* (the one and only philosopher I have done that with), and we began a correspondence that turned into a friendship. He has been a champion of my work and I am deeply appreciative. But I am also grateful for the inspiration provided by his excellent paper, "Responsibility, Naturalism, and 'the Morality System'," which he presented at the first New Orleans Workshop on Agency and Responsibility (NOWAR) and then published in *Oxford Studies in Agency and Responsibility* (*OSAR*) in 2013. It is from this presentation and paper that I began to understand the need to take seriously a type of responsibility that could not be situated easily within the world of second-personal demands and obligations. This opened my eyes to the way in which a pluralistic approach to responsibility might have great explanatory power with respect to the wide variety of ways in which human responsibility responses have functioned both in the past and across cultures. Russell's paper finally(!) led me to Bernard

Williams' *Shame and Necessity*, a seriously underappreciated book amongst responsibility theorists and another inspiration for the present work (although I disagree with Williams in the end).

A third point of inspiration came from Dan Jacobson, who also presented an outstanding paper at the first NOWAR, called "Regret, Agency, and Error" (which was also subsequently published in 2013 in the first *OSAR*). Dan's paper actually gave me the idea of how one might lean on different *sentiments* in articulating the different types of responsibility, and his discussion of how regret evaluates decisions turned the tide in my thinking about answerability. I was then able to take seriously a sentimental approach to all three qualities of will, and from there I was led to Dan's and Justin D'Arms' work on rational sentimentalism, which I find very plausible, and I have drawn much from it, and discussions with both of them, throughout this book.

As should be obvious, NOWAR (a biennial workshop I organize) and *OSAR* (a series I edit) have wound up being enormously influential on my own work, and I am fortunate to be a part of both ventures and talk shop with some of the best in the business. I could not have put NOWAR together, however, without the support of the Murphy Institute at Tulane University, and especially its director, Steve Sheffrin. Steve's support of the many projects on agency and responsibility I have proposed has been remarkable, and deeply appreciated. And I could not be a part of *OSAR*, nor have my favored forum for the publication of this book, without the ongoing support and encouragement of Peter Momtchiloff, at Oxford University Press. Peter championed the idea of *OSAR* right away, and he has been amazingly supportive during my writing of this book, giving me the freedom early on to work on it with the peace of mind of knowing that it would have OUP as its home. I am ever grateful for that.

The book occasionally draws snippets from some of my previously published papers. The basic idea of responsibility from the margins was sketched in my 2007 *Ethics* paper, "Moral Address, Moral Responsibility, and the Boundaries of the Moral Community." I refined some of those ideas in "Responsibility and Disability" (*Metaphilosophy* 2009), and some of that material now appears in Chapter 6. The tripartite theory of responsibility first appeared (although not under that label) in my 2011 *Ethics* paper "Attributability, Answerability, and Accountability: Toward a Wider Theory of Moral Responsibility," and some of its material appears in Chapter 2. The tripartite theory was updated quite a bit, with a motivation explicitly connecting it to our ambivalent responses to marginal cases, in my 2013 paper "Qualities of Will," originally published in *Social Philosophy & Policy*. This was the breakthrough paper that let me know how my book could be motivated and structured, and material from it appears in the

Introduction, Chapter 2, and a paragraph of Chapter 3. I developed the *Ecumenical Deep Self* theory in my paper "Ecumenical Attributability," forthcoming in an OUP volume on the nature of responsibility edited by Randolph Clarke, Michael McKenna, and Angela Smith, and material from that paper appears in Chapter 1. Material from my paper "Moral Responsibility and the Self" (in the 2011 volume *Oxford Handbook of the Self*) appears in Chapter 1 as well. Material from my paper "Remnants of Character," just out in a volume for OUP edited by Justin D'Arms and Daniel Jacobson on the science of ethics, appears in Chapters 1 and 7. I first presented my critique of the moral/conventional distinction and task in "Psychopathy, Responsibility, and the Moral/Conventional Distinction" in 2011 for a Spindel Supplement to the *Southern Journal of Philosophy*, and material from it appears in Chapter 5. Finally, David Faraci and I first discussed our survey results about Susan Wolf's JoJo case in our 2010 paper "Insanity, Deep Selves, and Moral Responsibility," published in *Review of Philosophy & Psychology*, and material from it appears in Chapter 7. I am grateful to all the publishers of this material—John Wiley and Sons, University of Chicago Press, Oxford University Press, and Cambridge University Press—for granting their permission for my use of it here.

I began writing the book in May 2012, at the beginning of my sabbatical year away from Tulane University. I am grateful to Tulane University for that opportunity, and I am also grateful to the state of Louisiana for awarding me an ATLAS grant, which enabled me to take the entire year off from teaching and administrative duties. I wrote the bulk of the book during that sabbatical, something I otherwise could not have done (or at least it would have taken much longer). Thanks also to my chair at the time, Ronna Burger, for allowing me to take that sabbatical the same year as two other faculty members in our department.

During that sabbatical year, I spent a month in Tucson, Arizona, as a guest of the Freedom Center. My thanks to David Schmidtz, Carmen Pavel, Michael McKenna, Steve Wall, and Guido Pincione for their help in arranging that trip. I wrote most of Chapters 1 and 2 while in residence.

Victor Tadros, Matt Talbert, and Mikhail Valdman read very early drafts of a few chapters, and they provided me with helpful comments. My thanks to them.

I completed a very rough first draft of the entire book in January 2014, and a reading group at Tulane was formed to work through it. As I can now recognize, that reading group had to slog through a mess: the master argument was not yet clear, the organization was poor, and the role of marginal agency was not sufficiently highlighted. I am *extremely* grateful to that group of guinea pigs, er, readers, who somehow simultaneously held nothing back in their criticisms while doing so with grace and aplomb. They saved me from a torrent of errors and also taught me how to write a *book* in the process. The book was completely rewritten in light of their comments, and I cannot thank them enough. The group included Tulane faculty and graduate students, as well as all three of the Murphy Institute's Faculty Fellows for 2013–2014. Among the attendees were Nathan Biebel, Gwen Bradford, Bruce Brower, Christian Coons, Alison Denham, Oliver Sensen, Nathan Stout, Bas Van der Vossen, and Frankie Worrell. My deep thanks to them all.

After making massive changes to the manuscript in light of the Tulane reading group's comments, I was fortunate to be able to workshop the book at two other locations. First, Mark Timmons arranged a workshop for me at the University of Arizona in March 2014. Among the discussants were Hoi Yee Chan, Keith Hankins, Terry Horgan, Yael Loewenstein, Michael McKenna, Shaun Nichols, Hannah Tierney, Mark Timmons, Chad Van Schoelandt, Steve Wall, and Brandon Warmke. My thanks to them all for a very lively and helpful two days. Second, a workshop was arranged at Georgia State in May 2014, with assigned lead discussants for each chapter. I am deeply grateful to all the lead discussants for their detailed and helpful comments—in order of presentation, Eddy Nahmias, Randy Clarke, Angie Smith, Jeanette Kennett, Nicole Vincent, Stephen Kearns, and Katrina Sifferd—as well as to the other discussants in attendance, Andrew I. Cohen and George Rainbolt. Both workshops were extremely helpful, and I spent three solid months rewriting the manuscript yet again in light of attendees' comments.

I presented some of this material in many forums, including a 2012 conference on the science of ethics at the University of Michigan, the 2012 Wake Forest conference on the 50th anniversary of "Freedom and Resentment," a 2013 colloquium at Richmond University, a January 2013 conference on new directions in moral philosophy at the Freedom Center in Tucson, a conference on the Ethics of Lobbying at Georgetown in Fall 2013, and the 2014 NOISE conference. I am grateful for the invitations to all of these events and to the audiences at them for their questions and comments.

For the idea of the tripartite profile chart, I am grateful to Gwen Bradford. For the idea of the marginal ambivalence chart, I am grateful to Walter Sinnott-Armstrong. For asking me the question—"Who is your audience?"—that forced me to reconceive the Introduction, I am grateful to Bruce Brower. For pressing upon me the importance of a discussion of second-personal reasons, I am grateful to Bas Van der Vossen. For many enjoyably beery discussions about Strawson and the naturalness of the reactive attitudes, I am grateful to Tamler Sommers. For helpful discussion about some of the details of the tripartite theory, I am grateful to Justin D'Arms. For many enlightening discussions about this material over golf, I am grateful to Sean Foran, a brilliant, underappreciated philosopher. For numerous helpful discussions on these topics and for being my NOISE-making partner in crime, I am grateful to Steve Wall, who does philosophy right. I am also grateful to my other NOISE-making fellows—David Sobel, Janice Dowell, Jeff Moriarty, Eric Cave, Elizabeth Brake, Dale Dorsey, Connie Rosati, Jon Quong, Pamela Hieronymi, Simon May, and the others already thanked or soon to be—for their discussion with me about various aspects of this book. And for discussion about many of these issues over many years—most of our professional lives!—I am grateful to my good friend Doug Portmore.

Several people have given me detailed written comments on the entire manuscript. I took these very seriously, and they invariably made the book much better than it otherwise would have been. These included two anonymous reviewers for OUP, Gwen Bradford, Eddy Nahmias, Walter Sinnott-Armstrong, and Frankie Worrell. Also included is Angie Smith, who not only gave me comments on the whole manuscript, but who has also served as the friendliest of foils over many years now. She makes many appearances in this book as someone whose own views are opposed to mine in many respects, but she could not be nicer or more generous about it. She is also one helluva critic, and I have had to adjust many arguments in the book because of her penetrating insights and objections. I am very grateful for our many conversations and e-mail exchanges over the years, and I am proud to call her a friend.

My final thank yous go to two people who went so far above and beyond in their help on the book that they must be singled out for praise. The first is Christian Coons. He was relentless, merciless really, in his oral comments during the Tulane reading group, and he then provided me with detailed, handwritten notes on every single page of the manuscript. These included everything from major worries about the arguments to nit-picky copy-editing suggestions. I have literally changed some part of every page due to these comments. He was just right 99 percent of the time. He caught things no one else caught time and again, he made suggestions about how to improve various arguments that I repeatedly took on board, and his notes about wording invariably made things much clearer. Christian is a formidable philosopher, and I am deeply grateful that he was really on my side all along, and that he took such time to help me with the manuscript. It would have been a much worse book without his help.

Finally, words cannot express the gratitude I have to Michael McKenna. For those who know Michael, this will not be a surprise: he is as generous and kind a person as there is, and his support and encouragement throughout the duration of the project have been unstinting and unwavering. He has had the burden of reading two very different versions of the manuscript from start to finish and he has provided detailed and extremely helpful comments on both. He did this while in the midst of his own nonstop barrage of work. He has saved me from numerous errors. He has offered many excellent suggestions to bolster my arguments (reflected in the many footnotes mentioning him throughout). He provided comments on my "Quality of Will" paper that enabled me finally to begin structuring the book project properly. He was a key force in getting me to Arizona for the month of January 2013, during which we had a ton of helpful conversations (along with Steve Wall) about the book. He has touted the book publicly. He has patiently answered all of my pestering e-mail questions. And he has become in the process a true friend. Thank you, Michael.

I obviously could not have written this book without the support and advice of many people. Any errors which remain, however, are theirs, as they should have caught them as well.

July 2014

Contents

Contents

Introduction

PSYCHOPATHY—As a boy, Skip loved to blow up frogs. He had begun his adventures with frogs by merely stabbing their stomachs and watching their eyes go cold as they died, but he eventually found that it was much more fun to see them explode. So he would steal cash from around the family home to buy fireworks, which he would light and put in their mouths. Once, he invited his sister to watch. She screamed and ran off, horrified. To Skip, that was icing on the cake.

As an adult, handsome and brilliant Skip charmed his way through college and into a job at a large mining equipment company. Through his relentless lying and manipulation, he managed to secure several enormous contracts for the company. The founder of the company, who Skip privately called a "fool," gave Skip a Ferrari. He became known as "Super Skip." He then married Juliette, the daughter of a billionaire, and made sure Juliette's father thought of him as the charming and clever son he had never had. He also made sure his new wife never found out about his ongoing random sexual encounters with other women. A week before the wedding, Skip's own mother, wearily familiar with his behavior over the years, asked him why he had to marry her, why he had to do this to Juliette's life. Tempted to ignore her at first (as usual), Skip smiled and said, "We both know she'll never know what hit her."

Skip was eventually made president of the international division of the company. He was extremely valuable to them, so valuable that the company repeatedly had to pay significant amounts of money to settle the cases of many female employees who sued them in response to Skip's sexual assaults or harassment. Skip broke one woman's arm when trying to force her to sit in his lap. He said of this woman, "She's insane. She broke her own arm. She struggled with me, the stupid bitch. Why the hell did she put up such a fight?" In 2003, the Securities and Exchange Commission accused Skip of fraud (drawn from Stout 2005, 36–43).

AUTISM—From Naoki Higashida, a thirteen-year-old Japanese boy with autism who learned to communicate by pointing to letters on a grid:

Q13: Do you prefer to be on your own? No, for people with autism, what we're anxious about is that we're causing trouble for the rest of you, or even getting on your nerves. *This* is why it's hard for us to stay around other people. This is why we often end up being left on our own.

The truth is, we'd love to be with other people. But because things never, ever go right, we end up getting used to being alone, without even noticing this is happening. Whenever I overhear someone remark how much I prefer being on my own, it makes me feel desperately lonely. It's as if they're deliberately giving me the cold-shoulder treatment.

Q20: Why do you make a huge fuss over tiny mistakes? When I see I've made a mistake, my mind shuts down. I cry, I scream, I make a huge fuss, and I just can't think straight about anything anymore...

It must be hard for you to understand why this could make me so unhappy. And even to me, I know really that it's not such a big deal. But it's almost impossible for me to keep my emotions contained. Once I've made a mistake, the fact of it starts rushing toward me like a tsunami. And then, like trees or houses being destroyed by the tsunami, *I* get destroyed by the shock.... To get away, I'll do anything. Crying, screaming and throwing things, hitting out even...

Finally, finally, I'll calm down and come back to myself. Then I see no sign of the tsunami attack—only the wreckage I've made. And when I see that, I hate myself. I just hate myself. (Quoted from Higashida 2013)

DEMENTIA—From a patient with Alzheimer's disease:

Theologian Martin Buber was concerned that... [w]e were treating each other as if we were objects rather than human beings. This dynamic occurs in the relationship between caregivers and Alzheimer's patients. It is happening to me. As the weave of the lace curtain becomes thicker, as the wind blows away even the most recent of memories, people do not have time to explain to me over and over again, things that I don't understand. They tire of telling me the same things over and over. They cannot depend on me to remember the simplest of instructions.... The trust relationship between husband and wife, father and son, grandfather and grandchild is breaking. Not because we do not love each other as much as in the past, in fact now it is even more. It is strained to the point of breaking by the symptoms of Alzheimer's disease.

So how do you relate to a Thou who does not act or think like Thou? Inevitably, I will become an It. I will look, smell, and walk like a Thou, but I will not think and act like a Thou. It's no one's fault this happens. It just does. The Thous start lying to the It because they are tired of arguing with It. "The car has been sold," when in reality it's in the garage and we just don't trust It to drive. "The accountant is writing our checks" when in reality we just do not want to argue over the fact It cannot manage the family money. We still love Thou, but for its own safety and our own peace of mind we treat Thou as an It. I don't have a solution. I don't want it to happen to me. I don't know how to avoid it. (unpublished communication of Professor Richard Taylor, quoted in Snyder 2006, 272–3)

POOR FORMATIVE CIRCUMSTANCES—On July 5, 1978, Robert Harris shot and killed two young men and then calmly ate the fast food they had just ordered. He joked to his horrified brother that they should pose as police officers and inform the boys' parents that their sons had been killed. Harris was caught and sent to death row, where his loathsome personality was loathed by guards and even his fellow inmates. As the Deputy Attorney General said of him, "If this isn't the kind of defendant that justifies the death penalty, is there ever going to be one?"

Harris's upbringing, however, was unimaginably terrible. His parents were alcoholics who repeatedly terrified, beat, and abused him. At 14, he was sentenced to a youth detention center, where he was regularly raped and beaten. He attempted to commit suicide twice. By the time he was 19, it is no wonder that he had begun killing and torturing animals. His adult criminal life had begun (drawn from Corwin 1982; Watson 2004, 235–42).

Are any of these people *responsible agents*? One time-honored way to think about this question is to ask whether any of them are worthy of a certain range of responses, typically glossed as praise or blame. Call these our *responsibility responses*. So are the agents in our four cases worthy of such responses?

My own reaction, and the reaction of others who have written about such cases, is a profound unease. This is not, however, the unease of uncertainty. Rather, it is the unease of *ambivalence*. The reaction, in other words, is that these agents seem worthy of some responsibility responses but not others, which suggests that they are responsible in some ways but not in others.

Consider the cases in reverse order. As Gary Watson writes of the Robert Harris case, when we hear just about what he did, "We respond to his heartlessness and viciousness with moral outrage and loathing" (Watson 2004, 238). Once we hear of his terrible upbringing, though, "this history gives pause to" a range of our emotional responsibility responses known as "reactive attitudes" (Watson 2004, 242). Yet "our response to the case is not the simple suspension of reactive attitudes that this diagnosis would lead one to expect, but ambivalence" (Watson 2004, 243). We may still respond with full-on contempt to Harris, given that he is a moral monster, but in coming to appreciate the way in which his upbringing contributed to his becoming that monster, we may think blaming attitudes of another sort—angry remonstrance, say—are off the table, or at least ought to be significantly dampened.

The case of dementia hits much closer to home for many of us, and Taylor's description surely resonates with family members and caregivers of those with Alzheimer's disease. These are agents who are off the hook for a range of responses to their forgetful or incompetent actions, say: resentment, indignation, disapproval, and criticism all seem inappropriate. But if their inner lives are anything like the one expressed by Taylor, the appropriateness of some other responses is left intact, such as admiration or esteem. What fortitude he has, we may think, what bravery! Alternatively, some of those with dementia may remain as nasty as they ever were. They might thus still be the appropriate targets of our disdain, even if they get off the hook for a variety of other responses, such as resentment and so forth.

Many of us would likely have a variety of ambivalent responsibility responses to Naoki Higashida as well (once we know the relevant details of his disorder). On the positive side, admiration for his general concern for others, or for his aiming at avoiding mistakes, feels appropriate. We may also be with him to a very limited extent when it comes to the evaluation of his mistakes, thinking yes, perhaps some negative responses (on his and our parts) are appropriate when he makes them, albeit nothing remotely on the magnitude of his own volcanic response. We may also feel as if he just is not an appropriate candidate for anger or its ilk in any event.

Turn finally to Skip, who lacks both empathy and conscience. Stipulate that we come to know these details about him. What would our responses tend to be? He seems profoundly lacking in a key aspect of humanity. It feels *pointless* to rail at him indignantly; he will only give us a cold smile in return. Yet he is also, it seems, quite cruel, a horrible person. Disdain and contempt for that cruelty still feels right.

There are other cases in which we tend to feel ambivalence as well. The clinically depressed may make terrible decisions, and we may tend to respond to them negatively when they do (say, with disapproval or disappointment), while nevertheless withholding other sorts of negative responses, such as disdain or resentment. And we sometimes get from caregivers a different sort of ambivalence to mildly intellectually disabled adults, to whom resentment and indignation sometimes apply, while general moral disappointment or disapproval do not.

These are all cases of *marginal agency*, cases at the boundaries of our interpersonal community where agents tend to strike us as eligible for some responsibility responses but not others. But to what extent does taking seriously our ambivalent responses to them tell us anything about the *nature* of responsibility?

Furthermore, what specific agential features generate our ambivalence to them, and are such responses actually appropriate? These are the two questions I will attempt to answer in this book.

My subject here will primarily be a subset of *non-institutional responsibility*, marked by the informal responsibility assessments, responses, and treatments "between us," that is, those not governed or dished out by some institution or other. Institutional responsibility (think here of legal or criminal responsibility) is a subtly but importantly different beast from non-institutional responsibility, due in part to the fact that the relations that obtain between institutions and their subjects are different from those that obtain "between us," and so it would confuse matters considerably to include a discussion of it here (see Shoemaker 2012a and 2013b). Nevertheless, the non-institutional variety contains many domains of responsibility: moral, aesthetic, athletic, epistemic, prudential, and more. Because of our greater familiarity with it—both from the many philosophers who have discussed it and from its importance in our interpersonal lives—I will most often discuss *moral* responsibility, but I will also discuss the other domains much more than is customary (at least in the philosophical literature).[1]

Furthermore, my primary topic will be the nature of responsible *agency*, that is, I will conduct an investigation into the conditions that must be met by agents in order to be eligible targets for the appropriate deployment of responsibility responses. I will say more about this notion below, but for now I want to make explicit that I will not (primarily) be investigating those conditions that make a generally responsible agent responsible or not *for some specific action or attitude*. Rather, the focus of my investigation is prior: What makes someone have the status of being a responsible agent in the first place?

So how shall we identify the conditions of responsible agency? One way would be to examine clear-cut paradigm members of the responsibility community[2] and then try to figure out what it is about them that makes them members. But this approach would be too indeterminate, providing us no reason to think that any particular feature is more or less relevant or important than any other for membership. And it would also be unhelpful to examine agents far outside the community, such as fish or fowl, as it would be indeterminate what relevant or important features they would be missing given their vast agential differences from paradigm members.

[1] Although see Russell 2008 for an insightful comparison between the aesthetic and moral domains of responsibility.

[2] I will use the phrases "responsible agent" and "member of the responsibility community" interchangeably throughout.

A more promising way to identify the conditions of responsible agency, then, would be to look at agents who are much more akin to paradigm members of the responsibility community than fish or fowl yet who are nevertheless outside of it. Presumably, then, we could examine what precisely is different about them and so isolate the feature(s) most relevant to their outsider status in a way that reveals more determinate necessary conditions for full membership. This method should sound quite familiar, for it has been deployed by responsibility theorists stretching back to Aristotle. We begin with its most influential contemporary advocate.

Strawson and Pure Quality of Will

P. F. Strawson, in "Freedom and Resentment," examined the specific sorts of pleas that, when successful, allegedly serve to exempt agents from the realm of what he called the participant reactive emotions, the range of attitudes to which we are susceptible within interpersonal relationships. These attitudes include "gratitude, resentment, forgiveness, love, and hurt feelings" (Strawson 2003, 75). He was motivated to examine these attitudes and their suspension in order to reconcile the two main disputants about freedom and moral responsibility, those whom he labeled optimists and pessimists. Optimists are those who believe that the facts as we know them do not show determinism to be false, yet these facts are nevertheless sufficient to ground the application of the concepts of moral obligation and responsibility, as well as justify their associated practices of blaming, praising, and so on. The optimist's basic move is to point to the efficacy of such practices for social regulation. Pessimists are those who, while agreeing that the facts as we know them allow for the possibility of determinism's truth, also believe that these facts are insufficient to ground the responsibility concepts and practices. They maintain that appealing to social regulation to do so leaves out an essential element of these concepts and practices, namely, *desert*, and making sense of desert requires going beyond the facts as we know them by appealing to the existence of something like libertarian agency.

Strawson's strategy in reconciling these two positions was to examine closely the nature of our practices, and in particular our interpersonal reactive attitudes. As he put it:

> [T]o speak in terms of social utility alone is to leave out something vital in our conception of these practices. The vital thing can be restored by attending to that complicated web of attitudes and feelings which form an essential part of the moral life as we know it, and which are quite opposed to objectivity of attitude. Only by attending to this range of attitudes can we recover from the facts as we know them a sense of what we mean, i.e. of *all* we mean, when, speaking the language of morals, we speak of desert, responsibility,

guilt, condemnation, and justice. But we *do* recover it from the facts as we know them. We do not have to go beyond them (Strawson 2003, 91; emphasis in original).

The key, then, was to get the pessimist to concede to the optimist that we could accomplish this "recovery" project without going beyond the facts as we know them, just as long as the optimist made a radical but crucial modification to her account by acknowledging that our responsibility responses are genuine expressions of our nature, of our moral attitudes, "and not merely devices we calculatingly employ for regulative purposes" (Strawson 2003, 93). When we take seriously our responsibility responses, we will quickly see, first, that they involve much more than social regulation (contra the optimist), but we can also see that these deeply human responses are still sensitive to certain accessible, perceivable features of agents' moral psychologies and not (as the pessimist would have it) to inaccessible features such as those seemingly required by libertarian free agency (e.g., agent causal powers or contracausal freedom). To defend the first point, he noted that reactive attitudes like resentment, indignation, and guilt are predicated on our beliefs about others' attitudes toward us, not on any beliefs about what their deployment will contribute to social efficiency. Our susceptibility to them is just constitutive of our being in interpersonal relationships, those connections with others we cannot for long live without. To defend the second point, Strawson surveyed various types of pleas we regularly deploy to get off the hook to enable us to see that the features to which our responsibility responses are actually sensitive remain among the facts as we know them.

So what are these facts to which our responses are sensitive? As he famously put it, "The reactive attitudes... are essentially reactions to *the quality of others' wills* towards us, as manifested in their behaviour: to their good or ill will or indifference or lack of concern" (Strawson 2003, 83; emphasis mine). To achieve his aim of getting the pessimist to concede to a more robust and "vital" optimist view, he thus advanced the first version of what I call a *Pure Quality of Will* theory of responsibility. Such a theory puts forward "quality of will" as exclusively filling its two central roles: (a) as the sole object of our appropriate responsibility responses, and (b) as the sole unifying explanation of nonresponsibility. To understand (a), focus on resentment as a paradigm responsibility response. Suppose that we are standing in a crowded subway together and your foot suddenly lands on mine, causing me great pain. Consider two variations. In the first, the subway car jerks hard, and as you lose your balance your foot lurches forward onto my foot. In the second, you stare right at me with a nasty smile and press your foot down on mine. Resentment is inappropriate in the first variation, appropriate in the second. But the movements of your foot and the subsequent pain you caused were identical in both. So what is the difference? In the first case, the "fact of injury was quite consistent with the agent's attitude and intentions being just what we demand they should be" (Strawson 2003, 78).[3] In the second, you had a poor quality of will. So my resentment targets you for your poor quality of will in stepping on my foot. And this reaction could be appropriate even if you did not hurt me at all (perhaps I had on my steel-toed boots).

To understand (b), consider the first variation. When the subway car jostled your foot onto mine, it was an accident. On the *Pure Quality of Will* theory, this excuses you from responsibility—from appropriate resentment—precisely because your quality of will was not poor after all, despite the injury you inflicted. In addition to accidents, epistemic limitations may also excuse, and when they do it is for similar reasons: "I didn't know!" begs off from resentment because it disconnects what one did from any bad quality of will. And one may get off this particular hook even without any excuse, as when one is justified in causing the injury. The plea "They left me no alternative!" reveals that one "had reluctantly to cause the injury for reasons which acceptably override [one's] reluctance" (Strawson 2003, 78). So excuses and justifications—what are often called "Type 1 pleas"—tend to suspend our reactive attitudes for some particular injury in virtue of blocking any connection between their agents' behavior and their qualities of will.

But there is another way to get off the hook, namely, one might be *exempted*. When one is excused or justified, on the Strawsonian picture, reactive attitudes are appropriately suspended to one with respect to one's specific injury, given that one's quality of will was not poor in that instance. But one remains susceptible to deployments of the reactive attitudes in other cases, for one is still, in general, a responsible agent with the *capacity* for a quality of will. When one is exempted, however, reactive attitudes are generally suspended to one *qua* agent, and on a *Pure Quality of Will* theory it would have to be in virtue of one's lacking the capacity for a quality of will altogether. Here some of the exempting pleas—what are often called "Type 2 pleas"—include, "He's not himself," "She's been under great strain lately," "She's only a child," or "He's a hopeless schizophrenic." In Type 1 pleas, the agents are normal but the circumstances are not. In these exempting, Type 2, pleas, the circumstances may be normal but the agents are not (Strawson 2003, 78–9). In either Type, though, nonresponsibility is purportedly explained exclusively in terms of quality of will.

[3] We also need to assume here that, in the first case, you had taken due care not to lose your balance and so forth, so that it really was an unexpected accident.

For Strawson, a successful *Pure Quality of Will* theory would have two huge payoffs. First, it could account for *all* of our (appropriate) responsibility responses (and so capture all we mean by "responsibility," "desert," and so on). These seem to be all the relevant data for any theory of responsibility to explain. And, second, it could sidestep the long-standing worries about determinism that seem to lead either to objectionably dehumanizing consequentialist treatments of responsibility or to the "panicky metaphysics of libertarianism" (Strawson 2003, 79). If all that matters to ground the robust range of responsibility responses is the actual, occurrent quality of one's will, then we have no need to wonder about whether that will was *free*, that is, to wonder about alternative wills one could have had or whether one was the ultimate source of that will.

This second argument is very ambitious, and its critics have been plentiful.[4] For instance, it looks as if some of Strawson's own excusing pleas might indeed be generalized in ways that raise the specter of determinism again (e.g., "He couldn't help it"), and, for some, quality of will itself may still have to include a free will component in order to explain our sensitivities to it.[5] For instance, if having a quality of will requires, at a minimum, some kind of control, and the control relevant to moral responsibility is all that free will amounts to, then quality of will would have to require free will. Consequently, in this book I will set aside the second purported advantage of Strawson's argument—and the attendant metaphysical questions about free will—to ask just about the first: *Could a theory of responsibility appealing exclusively to quality of will do justice to the entire range of our responsibility responses in both their deployment and their suspension?*[6]

Strawson's own positive answer to this question founders on some important exemptions. Watson makes the point succinctly: "A child can be malicious, a psychotic can be hostile, a sociopath indifferent, a person under great strain can be rude, a woman or man 'unfortunate in formative circumstances' can be cruel" (Watson 2004, 228). In other words, these agents still exhibit a poor quality of will *in some sense*, even though resentment seems inappropriate to them generally, so reactive attitudes must not just target quality of will; they must "depend as well upon a background of beliefs about the objects of those attitudes" (Watson 2004, 228). Indeed, many theorists seem to have taken this position as gospel, requiring instead of, or in addition to, quality of will complicated amalgams and algorithms of additional agential features like authenticity, autonomy, agential

[4] Including Strawson's son, Galen Strawson 1993. For others, see Russell 1992, 287–302; Wallace 1994; Wiggins 2003; Watson 2004, 219–59; and McKenna 2012, esp. Chapters 2–3.

[5] In addition to those just cited, see McKenna 2005.

[6] I will discuss the ideas of free will and desert in the conclusion. Until then, however, I will say no more about them.

history, control, and/or epistemic standing. But as Watson remarks, if we must appeal to additional features like this, the *Pure Quality of Will* theorist's enterprise "is doomed" (Watson 2004, 228).[7]

Nonetheless, other responsibility theorists have advanced or suggested versions of *Pure Quality of Will* theories that seem tailor-made to avoid this worry. In the next section I will survey three such possibilities. In the section that follows, I will explain why a version of Watson's worry will still generalize to any such theory, no matter how it is tailored.

Three Qualities of Will

The very first question one must address in trying to advance a *Pure Quality of Will* theory is, "What *is* a quality of will, precisely?" Strawson himself does not help much, for he does not explain exactly what he means by a good or ill *will*. Three possible interpretations of "will" have emerged in the literature.[8]

The first theorist to attempt to characterize "will" in a way that it could carry the burdens of a *Pure Quality of Will* theory was T.M. Scanlon, in "The Significance of Choice" (Scanlon 1988).[9] As his analysis is intended to dovetail with his larger moral theory, its content is explicitly contractualist: quality of will refers to the way in which one governs oneself, which is a function of the degree to which one attends and adheres to the standards produced by contractualism's nonrejectability procedure within the system of co-deliberation.[10] The will whose quality is to be assessed is thus the agent's *judgment* (or lack thereof) about the worth of relevant reasons for actions and attitudes. On Scanlon's treatment,

[7] I should note that some theories appealing to these features could still be perfectly consistent with Strawson's proposal. With respect to them, therefore, Strawson's proposal could perhaps be taken as establishing their fundamental unifying condition, where they serve to provide more fine-grained versions of the basic quality of will theory, accounts that are also drawn from interpretations of our actual responsibility practices. Thanks to Michael McKenna for urging me to note this point. For my part in this book, I intend to remain agnostic on whether more fine-grained theories are needed. Instead, I really just aim to reveal the force, scope, implications, and conditions of a robust, foundational quality of will theory.

[8] Some of the material that follows borrows from and expands on Shoemaker 2013c.

[9] Wallace 1994 later offered a similar view, targeting "quality of choice" (see 124–33). In recent years, Nomy Arpaly has advanced a *Pure Quality of Will* view as well that cashes out the notions of good and ill will in terms of responsiveness to moral reasons, so falls, I think, under the general will-as-judgment rubric I develop in the text, even though the notion of "judgment" might be too "conscious" for her. See Arpaly 2003, 2006. For ease of exposition, and because it is the most fully developed account, I will focus solely on Scanlon's view. Nevertheless, he, Wallace, and Arpaly disagree on key points and I will note some of these when they arise.

[10] The contractualist thesis is that "an act is wrong if its performance under the circumstances would be disallowed by any set of principles for the general regulation of behavior that no one could reasonably reject as a basis for informed, unforced general agreement" (Scanlon 1998, 153).

judgment is the relevant agential feature that is *up to us*, and so we can be properly "held responsible" for any attitudes that are sensitive to judgment "in several central senses of that phrase: they can be properly attributed to us, and we can properly be asked to defend them—to justify the judgment they reflect" (Scanlon 1998, 22). Negative responsibility responses are thus warranted for (judgment-sensitive) attitudes in virtue of their reflecting either defective or absent judgment, what Scanlon labels "faulty self-governance" (Scanlon 1988, 268). Call this the *Pure Quality of Judgment* theory.

So how does it offer a unifying explanation of Types 1 and 2 pleas? To view agents as blameworthy, on this account, is to believe there to be a gap between the way they governed themselves and the relevant standards of judgment. Successful excuses and justifications reveal that the agents governed themselves without fault, despite initial appearances. Accidents excuse, for example, because they sever any connection between agents' judgments about reasons and their bodily movements. And what of exemptions, the Type 2 pleas Strawson had difficulty explaining under the rubric of quality of will? Essential to the *Pure Quality of Judgment* story are agents' capacities for "critically reflective, rational self-governance" (Scanlon 1988, 174). If you are incapable of governing yourself in this way, you lack quality of judgment because you lack the *capacity* for judgment; your self-governance is not faulty, it is just nonexistent. Exemptions apply to agents in virtue of their lacking this capacity, and the set of incapacitated agents includes young children and the insane. Both Type 1 and Type 2 pleas may thus be unified solely by appeal to quality of judgment, and there is no need to look beyond facts about this quality to account for either the deployment or suspension of our responsibility responses.

The second interpretation of "quality of will" is much more consciously Strawsonian, and it has been most fully developed recently by Michael McKenna (2012, Ch. 3).[11] On McKenna's understanding, quality of will consists, not in judgment, but in the worth of the "regard or concern one has for others (or oneself), and toward the relevance of moral considerations, as manifested in one's conduct" (McKenna 2012, 59). This regard is "*exhibited* in the reasons for which one acts, the intention with which one acts, or the choices one makes" (McKenna

[11] McKenna himself does not advocate a *pure* Quality of Will theory, for one, because he allows that there are multiple types of responsibility, namely, attributability and accountability, and the latter is the only one to which he applies the quality of will treatment. Nevertheless, it's not clear even with respect to accountability alone that he's offering a *Pure Quality of Will* theory. That's because, while he thinks quality of will is *necessary* for accountability, it may not be sufficient (he remains agnostic on this point). See, e.g., McKenna 2012, 61.

2012, 59; emphasis mine), but it may not necessarily be found *in* any of these, given that they could each be morally innocuous. Regard is construed as a kind of attitude or stance one takes toward others or morality, not a judgment about reasons.[12] Call this version, then, a *Pure Quality of Regard* view.

So how would this view theoretically explain and unify Type 1 and Type 2 pleas? The story is structurally similar to the one told on the *Pure Quality of Judgment* view. One is worthy of negative responsibility responses to the extent that one has expressed insufficiently high regard for others (or oneself) or for moral considerations in her actions or attitudes. For example, if you disregard me by deliberately knocking me down, you are worthy of my resentment. Successful excuses and justifications reveal, though, that what was initially thought to be poor regard actually was not: when you knock me down by accident, for example, there was no connection between your actual regard for me and your behavior.

To see how exemptions might work in terms of the *Pure Quality of Regard* view, note that McKenna draws from Watson the idea that the reactive attitudes are communicative, their function being to express the basic demand for good will (Watson 2004, 226–33). McKenna then builds on this view to require the capacity not just for understanding the basic demand but for *participating* in the practices of holding responsible, which itself becomes the key capacity for having quality of regard. It is not just that those in the exempted class cannot understand the communication of others; it is also that they cannot communicate themselves within the practices. This means that if you are incapable of understanding the basic demand for good will as expressed via the reactive attitudes, then you are "incapable of acting from a will with a moral quality that could be a candidate for assessment from the standpoint of holding responsible" (McKenna 2012, 78). Exempted agents are thus "incapable of acting from a will that *could* have the relevant kind of moral quality" (McKenna 2012, 78). The fact that they lack this capacity for regard would thus be the real explanation why, for example, children and the insane are exempt.

A third way of understanding "will" has been floated by Jeanette Kennett and Nicole Vincent. In a recent presentation, "Folk Psychology, the Reactive Attitudes, and Responsibility,"[13] they introduced what I will call the *Pure Quality of Character* view, according to which quality of will is about "character traits,

[12] In Shoemaker 2014c, I argue that the most defensible version of McKenna's view is one according to which regard consists, not in an attitude, but in a perceptual stance, akin to the account of regard I lay out here in Chapter 3.

[13] Presented at the September 2012 conference at the College of William and Mary for the 50th anniversary of P. F. Strawson's "Freedom and Resentment," and currently a paper-in-progress.

personality, temperament and behavioural dispositions." Kennett and Vincent themselves do not defend such a theory, but one easily might. We do seem to respond to people's characters in a responsibility fashion (e.g., by feeling contempt, disdain, or admiration for them), so it might well be that they are responsible for only, or most fundamentally, the qualities of their character, as opposed to the qualities of their judgment or regard.[14] Type 1 pleas would thus be successful in virtue of referring to actions that actually did not reflect a poor quality of character. Accidents, again, for example, would not do so.[15] And on a *Pure Quality of Character* view, Type 2 pleas would apply to agents who lacked the capacity for some kind of full-fledged character in the first place. This would be the real reason why children and the insane, for example, would be exempt (assuming, of course, we had a fleshed-out theory of the nature of character).

The Generalized Watsonian Challenge

Each of these possible *Pure Quality of Will* theories attempts to build a comprehensive theory of the nature of responsibility by purporting to account for all of our responsibility responses (and their objects), and so explaining why some agents are excused, justified, or exempted from those responses. They also might seem to have the tools to avoid Watson's specific counterexamples to Strawson's version. To continue considering just the first two (as I have been doing above), even if children and the insane could be said to express poor quality of will in some sense, nevertheless the *right* sense—the sense around which our responsibility responses are properly organized and unified—generates exemptions for them without our having to appeal to any facts beyond facts about quality of will. After all, a malicious child or a hostile psychotic would tend to generate only recoils, of either the repugnant or fearful variety, but these are not what we would think of as *responsibility* responses; rather, they would merely be aversive reactions. Consequently, any of these theorists could agree that children might have a poor quality of will in *some* sense (the sense generating mere recoils), but insist that that is not the sense implicated in our responsibility responses and so is not the one relevant to the conditions for responsible agency, conditions which instead are drawn from these theorists' own favored interpretations of "will."

[14] See, e.g., Eshleman 2004. David Hume also held a view along these lines.

[15] So-called 'out of character' actions might seem to pose a problem for a *Pure Quality of Character* view, but I think there are ways to respond that I won't detail here. For some possibilities, though, see Arpaly and Schroeder 1999, esp. 182–4.

Nevertheless, none of these individual theories can be right, nor could any other *Pure Quality of Will* theory, and that is because a version of Watson's worry generalizes to each. The fundamental flaw, in each case, is the monistic interpretation of "will" they espouse, a monism which prevents them from providing an adequate explanation of our *ambivalent* responsibility responses to several marginal cases. As we have seen, some of our fellows are neither easily nor obviously full-on members of or full-on aliens to the community of responsible agents; rather, we tend to have very mixed reactions to them, responding to them in ways suggesting they are included in some ways but excluded in others. But there is no room for such mixed reactions on any of the *Pure Quality of Will* variations that we have thus far discussed.

To see this point, note again that the only Watson examples I have thus far discussed are children and psychotics, and our reaction to both is fairly *un*ambivalent: all of our responsibility responses to them tend to be suspended, even in the face of our recognition of a kind of hostility on their part.[16] But at least two of his other (Strawsonian) examples—psychopaths[17] and those from poor formative circumstances—do not yield such single-minded responses at all.[18] Instead, as already noted, our responsibility responses to such agents tend to be deeply *ambivalent*.

I will illustrate this point here just with psychopathy, as the extension to the other cases should be fairly obvious and I will discuss them anyway in the chapters to come. Recall our earlier responses to Skip. He is like many other psychopaths, who tend to be manipulative, selfish, greedy, cruel, and all-around jerks. But it is not as if we simply make these judgments about them and have merely aversive emotional responses, as we tend to do with young children and psychotics; rather, we would tend to respond to psychopaths with disdain or contempt. These are clear-cut responsibility responses. In addition, psychopaths seem capable of rational calculation, and they may judge our interests are not worth respecting, so we may be morally disappointed, disapproving, irritated, critical, and the like in response (see, e.g., Kennett 2001, 212). These

[16] While it might seem controversial to apply this point to children, we can avoid any controversy by thinking here primarily in terms of fairly *young* children.

[17] Watson uses the term "sociopath." The terms "psychopath" and "sociopath" have come to mean essentially the same thing, however, and as "psychopath" has become the term favored in the relevant psychological and philosophical literature, I will use it instead throughout the book.

[18] His third example, recall, is "a person under great strain" who "can be rude" (Watson 2004, 228). I think this case probably falls under a rubric similar to that of children and the psychotic, namely, as one to which we unambivalently tend to suspend (or reduce) our responsibility responses across the board, despite the application of a kind of *aretaic* predicate. I thus will not be including it in my discussion of marginal cases.

too are clear-cut responsibility responses. But other sorts of responsibility responses to psychopaths, like resentment and indignation, have seemed to many people to be pointless or inappropriate, once we are fully aware of certain psychological details.[19] Psychopaths have significant incapacities—empathic, emotional, and/or normative—that prevent them from having much or any moral concern for others (Fine and Kennett 2004). But if this story about our ambivalent responses to psychopaths is right, then there just is no single *Pure Quality of Will* story that can satisfactorily account for all of our responsibility responses. Each of the *Pure Quality of Character* and *Pure Quality of Judgment* views implies that, insofar as psychopaths have the capacity for, respectively, character or judgment—both of which they do seem to have—they are not exempt from our responsibility responses. But they also seem exempt from some such responses, as we have just seen. If anything, their incapacities suggest they lack the ability to *regard* us properly. Now this might seem to give a *Pure Quality of Regard* view a leg up on the others, for it could explain why psychopaths are exempt from resentment and indignation in a way the others could not, namely, because psychopaths lack quality of regard. But then how might a *Pure Quality of Regard* theorist explain—solely in terms of quality of regard—why psychopaths seem fully susceptible to some of our *other* negative responsibility responses, e.g., disdain, contempt, condemnation, disappointment, disapproval, and so forth?

Again, it should be evident how this problem generalizes to all the other marginal cases. The bottom line is this: if each—or any—*Pure Quality of Will* theory purports to explain, all on its own and in virtue of its favored interpretation of "will," the exemption conditions of *all* our responsibility responses, and so the conditions of paradigm responsibility membership from them, it will fail. This is because, in the marginal cases, we actually have what we take to be appropriate responsibility responses to more than quality of character alone, or quality of judgment alone, or quality of regard alone. Once again, then, it may seem that we are forced to appeal to facts beyond those just about quality of will, the sorts of facts (e.g., about history, control, knowledge, and so on) that *Pure Quality of Will* theories have been constructed to avoid or replace. To the extent that this is the case, the *Pure Quality of Will* project is, once more, "doomed."

[19] There are those who disagree with this assessment, including Smith 2012 and Talbert 2008, 2012a. One of the aims of this book is to show them (and others who agree with them) how the kinds of negative responses they may think are appropriate for psychopaths actually conflate several distinct responses, some of which are appropriate and some of which are not.

I believe that we are not forced in this direction at all; indeed, such a move concedes the game far too quickly. Instead, I propose that we can still get the elegant advantages of a pure quality of will approach by incorporating *all three* interpretations of "will" as occasional objects of our responsibility responses. But given that each interpretation implicates different exempting conditions, our responses in each case are going to be best construed as picking out different, albeit noncompeting, *types* of responsibility—what I call attributability, answerability, and accountability.[20,21] This is the *tripartite theory of responsibility*.

I will argue for this theory by taking much more seriously than has been done before the full range of our responsibility responses (a range we identify from our ambivalence in the marginal cases), what their appropriateness conditions consist in, and, as a result, what the capacities of their agential targets must include. If we can account for the fact of our ambivalence in marginal cases by going down this route, then we can undermine the motivation to explain the nature of responsibility by appealing to something external to our three *qualities* of will.

The Wide Array of Responsibility Responses

Here is where we are in the argument. Our best method for determining the necessary conditions of responsible agency is to look at exemption cases—cases in which agents much like paradigm agents are nevertheless not the appropriate object of our responsibility responses—and then try to figure out what relevant differences such agents manifest (as opposed to paradigm agents). The most elegant contemporary adoption of this method is Strawson's, according to which

[20] I use the term "types," not "conceptions," as I have in the past (Shoemaker 2011b, 2013c), given that "conceptions" has, as part of its philosophical lineage, an indelible *competitive* component. As Rawls uses it, for example, different conceptions of justice are rivals: the perfectionist conception of justice is different from, and a competitor to, that of the Two Principles or utilitarianism (Rawls 1971, e.g., 5; he is following Hart 1961, 155–9 in his deployment of the concept/conception distinction). The three types of responsibility I will delineate, however, are noncompetitors: only one, just two, or all three may apply to agents at any given time. The idea, then, is that the most basic *concept* of responsibility applies to agents in virtue of their being appropriately eligible for some subcategory of the responsibility responses, where these responses are categorized in terms of the type of responsibility they characteristically pick out. I am very grateful to Terry Horgan for raising the issue and to Steve Wall for discussion about it.

[21] Many readers are surely familiar with Gary Watson's "Two Faces of Responsibility" (in Watson 2004, 260–88), which distinguishes attributability from accountability. I am, obviously, deeply indebted to this insightful paper. However, I disagree with Watson on a number of fronts. For just two examples, I think he runs together the key features distinguishing attributability from answerability (namely, quality of character and quality of judgment), and he also has a view of accountability that is sanction-based, a view to which I no longer adhere. I will spell out our various disagreements throughout the next three chapters where appropriate.

what accounts for the suspension and deployment of all of our responsibility responses is a *Pure Quality of Will* story. But what counts as "will" is vague, and anyway it looks as if there are several cases where our responsibility responses are suspended but agential quality of will is not. We can thus either abandon the *Pure Quality of Will* story for a much more inelegant and complicated theory or we can attempt to flesh it out and thwart the purported counterexamples. There were, we saw, three ways to take up the latter approach, by interpreting quality of *will* as referring either to character, judgment, or regard. But none of these monistic attempts could individually account for all of our responsibility responses, a fact revealed by our ambivalence in the marginal cases. So once again, we can either abandon the *Pure Quality of Will* approach or seek a way to preserve it, refine it, and thwart the counterexamples. My position is that we should take the latter approach and go *pluralistic* in our understanding of quality of will. In order to best account for all of our responsibility responses, we have to allow that they may take multiple objects: some target character, some target judgment, and some target regard.

So what are all of these alleged responsibility responses? By "responsibility" I have in mind a very thin, inclusive concept, something essentially defined and delimited by those responses that plausibly fall under the wide rubric of "praise" and "blame." Responsibility responses only target agents. But these agents must also be responsible *for* things. And our responses must be rendered appropriate in *virtue* of things. So together these three relational features of responsibility are captured in the following very abstract formulation:

To be a responsible agent is to be <u>worthy of</u> X <u>for</u> Y <u>in virtue of</u> Z,

where *X* refers to some kind of "praising" and "blaming" responsibility responses, *Y* refers to something like actions or attitudes, and *Z* refers to the responsibility-maker, be it, for example, one's capacity for reasons-responsiveness, one's capacity for having and expressing one's deep self, or, as Strawson would have it, one's capacity for having a quality of will.[22] As we go through the book, I will fill in the variables for each of the three types of responsibility.

So what goes into the *X*-slot for general responsibility? Let us begin by surveying our negative responsibility responses. No one doubts that these include the Strawsonian trinity of resentment, indignation, and guilt. But Strawson mentions other reactive attitudes that are regularly ignored but that nevertheless

[22] For examples of formulations adopting something like this general template, see Eshleman 2009; Fischer 1986, 12; Fischer and Ravizza 1998, 7; McKenna 2012, 2; Nelkin 2011, 7; Pereboom 2007, 86; and Wallace 1994, 91.

implicate responsibility too, namely, hurt feelings (Strawson 2003, 75), and sometimes shame (Strawson 2003, 85). And beyond Strawson there are other sorts of negative reactive attitudes that are clearly part of our responsibility-response arsenal, including disdain, disesteem, contempt, abhorrence, hatred, revulsion, irritation, disapproval, regret, condemnation, embarrassment, frustration, and disappointment. And it is equally important, albeit less often recognized as such, that we include the wide range of *positive* responsibility responses. The primary one that Strawson mentions is gratitude. But beyond gratitude there may be admiration, awe, esteem, forgiveness, elevation, pride, veneration, approval, appreciation, approbation, gratification, or warm feelings.[23]

These emotional responses also typically have behavioral or motivational manifestations to which we point in identifying and differentiating them (McKenna 2012, 69–70).[24] While I will say much more about what these are in subsequent chapters, I will now simply point out familiar examples: guilt typically motivates something like the repair of relations, regret typically motivates changing one's decision-making policies, admiration typically motivates emulation, and shame typically motivates hiding from the gaze of others. But there are many other behavioral or motivational manifestations of our responses, which may include not only the sanctioning treatments most often associated with blame—shunning, criticizing, haranguing, socially isolating—but also less retributive responses, such as withdrawing friendly greetings, modifying dispositions for trust and cooperation, quietly ending friendships, and so forth.[25]

What I have argued thus far is that, given our ambivalence to marginal agents, our responsibility responses cannot target only one of the types of will—character, judgment, or regard—on the table. For even when these agents lack the capacity for one of the types of will and a certain subset of responses to them seems inappropriate as a result, they seem to remain eligible for some *other* responsibility responses regardless. What I have proposed is that we do not have to abandon or go beyond a quality of will theory of responsibility to explain this

[23] There may be those who insist that it is only *expressions* of these sorts of emotions that properly fall under the rubric of praising or blaming. This might be true. But it ought to be clear in such cases that the expression itself is not what matters to its counting as praise or blame. Rather, expression is just a blaming or praising delivery device. Expressions of the truth to someone, after all, or expressions of one's horror at a person's ugly scar, do not count as praise or blame. Rather, it is the specific psychological state being expressed that determines the rubric under which the expression falls, and so I will focus only on such states, in particular our emotional responsibility responses. Talk of "expression" is still very important to theorizing about responsibility, however, and I will take up this task in Chapter 3.

[24] I am grateful to Michael McKenna, as well as to Justin D'Arms and Daniel Jacobson, for helpful discussion on this point.

[25] These last are included under Scanlon's capacious rubric of blame (Scanlon 2008, Ch. 4).

phenomenon; rather, we could adopt a pluralistic understanding of "will" in order to do so. On this understanding, different subcategories of our responsibility responses would appropriately take as their objects different types of wills. But do we have any positive reason to believe this is the right approach? To answer this question, we need a better idea of what these subcategories would be and what their appropriateness conditions would consist in (the *Z*-variable in the general formulation above). But before we can delve into these matters, I first need to say something more about the relation between our responses and responsibility.

Sentiments and Sentimentalism

> It is a pity that talk of the moral sentiments has fallen out of favour. The phrase would be quite a good name for that network of human attitudes in acknowledging the character and place of which we find . . . the only possibility of reconciling these disputants to each other and the facts. (Strawson 2003, 92)

What precise role should our responses play in an investigation into the nature of responsibility? There are two traditional answers to this question.[26] The first maintains that our responses are most fundamentally our best epistemic trackers of the attitude-independent facts about responsibility. In other words, there is an objective, antecedent fact of the matter about whether agents are responsible, and our responses are primarily "*evidence* about when to hold people responsible, but not something that constitutes them being responsible" (Brink and Nelkin 2013, 287; emphasis in original). Responsibility responses are thus appropriate for agents only in virtue of their (antecedently) being responsible agents (see also, e.g., Smith 2007). The second tradition, by contrast, maintains that our responses most fundamentally help constitute what it is to be responsible, such that the facts about the nature of responsibility are in some robust way attitude-dependent, and so regarding people as responsible just consists in being prone to respond to them in these ways (Watson 2004, 220). Consequently, the appropriateness of our responses, on this second view, is not a matter of their being justified by facts about agents' antecedent responsibility; instead, it must be a matter merely of how the responses somehow *fit* with their objects.

[26] McKenna 2012 (50–5) attempts to chart a course between them, offering what he calls a modest metaphysical interpretation of responsibility. I have some sympathy for this moderate position, although I will not discuss it here.

The issue here is one of metaphysical basicness: Which is more metaphysically fundamental, we want to know, being responsible (something to which our responses answer) or holding responsible (something of which being responsible is a function)? An advocate of the former follows in what I will call the *B-tradition*, whereas an advocate of the latter follows in what I will call the *H-tradition*. While I myself follow in the H-tradition, I want to remain officially neutral about the issue in this book. Both traditions have to take seriously our range of responsibility responses, after all; they just have different ends in mind by doing so. Those from the B-tradition take the responses seriously primarily as epistemic markers, whereas those from the H-tradition take them seriously primarily as metaphysical constituents. In either case, though, it makes perfect methodological sense to start with those responses, as I will. One may then take my theorizing about the nature of responsibility from there to take one's favored traditional route: either these responses may be taken to *reveal* or they may be taken to *constitute* the contours of the different types of responsibility I will lay out. And I will occasionally adopt either or both ways of talking.

It is my decision to talk in terms of the *sentiments* throughout the book, however, that might stir some anxiety in adherents of the B-tradition. Strawson is widely interpreted, by adherents of both traditions, to have effectively begun the H-tradition (see Wallace 1994, 19; Watson 2004, 220–59 and Forthcoming; Deigh 2011; McKenna 2012, Ch. 2; and Brink and Nelkin 2013, 287). As the quality of will construal of responsibility begins with him, I will develop my theory as he longingly wishes he could have done in the epigraph above, namely, in terms of the "moral sentiments."[27] One might worry, though, that doing so begs the question against the B-tradition, as sentimentalists about value tend to advance an analog of the H-tradition, holding that some values are a function of human sentiments. For example, the fearsome, on one contemporary sentimentalist view, is just whatever merits fear in humans, or the funny is just whatever merits our amusement (see, e.g., D'Arms and Jacobson 2000, 2003, 2006b). But while, again, I do believe that something like this is true of responsibility, I want to remain officially neutral on the issue in this book. And this can be accomplished if we just think of what I will call the *responsibility sentiments* as the

[27] In doing so, I am indebted to the important discussion of Strawson and the moral sentiments in Russell 1995 (esp. Ch. 5). Wallace 1994, while making reference to the moral sentiments in the very title of his book (*Responsibility and the Moral Sentiments*), focuses only on the negative subclass of reactive attitudes—resentment, indignation, and guilt—only one of which (guilt) is even arguably a *sentiment*, as we will see in Chapter 3. It is, as Russell notes, "a striking fact... that the Strawsonian/Humean element of moral sense plays no role in Wallace's Kantian account of moral agency..." (Russell 2004, 293).

relevant data points in our theorizing, for whether they *reveal* or *constitute* the nature of responsibility, it is just that nature that theorists from both traditions are ultimately after.

So what are sentiments, precisely, and what do we actually gain by appealing to them in theorizing about responsibility? "Sentiment" has more or less been a philosophical term of art, yet it has a rich history. As a theory of value, sentimentalism has its roots in the Hume/Smith tradition, according to which value "depends on some internal sense or feeling which nature has made universal in the species" (Hume 1740/1975, 172). Now Hume's way of putting it makes it sound as if sentiments are just emotions, but they are perhaps more accurately thought of as *dispositions* to various bouts of emotion. I will generally ignore this distinction, often talking about sentiments as if they were simply subsets of human emotions. But there are two crucial differences between sentiments and emotions that we cannot ignore. First, sentiments are pan-cultural (sometimes referred to as "basic emotions" although there is some controversy in the psychological literature on this score; see Ortony and Turner 1990, and Eckman 1992), and, second, they are encapsulated from judgment. There is great value to a theory that can capture both features.

Regarding the first distinguishing point, emotions generally have a characteristic triple syndrome of feeling, thought, and action tendency (see, e.g., Frijda 1986; D'Arms and Jacobson 2006b). But various aspects of the syndrome, for some emotions, may be missing or vary wildly from culture to culture. As examples, the action tendency of grief differs across cultures: sadness, in Tahitians, is typically somatized as illness or fatigue (Parkinson, Fischer, and Manstead 2004); and pride, in China, is often more associated with thoughts about achievements benefiting others than one's own accomplishments (Stipek 1998; Eid and Diener 2001). And some other emotions are just culturally bound. In (only) the West, there is existential angst (Wierzbicka 1999). In the East, Japan specifically, *amae* characterizes an "indulgent feeling of dependency" (Prinz 2004, 7; Doi 1973), and *oime* characterizes a feeling of indebtedness (Prinz 2004, 7; Markus and Kitayama 1991). Sentiments, by contrast, are generally taken to refer to pan-cultural emotional syndromes, those emotions instantiated universally with roughly equivalent feelings, thoughts, and action tendencies (see, e.g., D'Arms and Jacobson 2000, 2003, and 2006b). My aim is to explore the possibility of a theory of *human* responsibility, which will be much more interesting and ultimately rewarding, I think, than a theory of responsibility just about *us*, that is, us Westerners, or us philosophers, or some other restricted range of agents. Focusing on the sentiments is thus our best bet for constructing such a universal theory. (I will address skeptical challenges to this universalistic approach in the conclusion.)

The second distinctive feature of sentiments is that they, unlike many other emotions, are at least partially encapsulated from judgment. Justin D'Arms and Daniel Jacobson, the leading contemporary advocates of sentimentalism about value, point out that we need to view some emotions in this "sentimental" way in order to have a plausible explanation for two familiar psychological phenomena. First, some emotions (i.e., the sentiments) are *stably recalcitrant*, that is, they sometimes persist even in the face of contrary judgments. I may persist in fearing a spider, after all, despite judging it not to be dangerous (D'Arms and Jacobson 2003, 129). Relatedly, trying to type-identify various sentiments by some constitutive judgment invariably leads to counterexamples. For example, suppose one thinks, as Philippa Foot did (and as many other have), that for an emotion even to count as pride, it must reflect what the proud agent believes to be some achievement or status of his (Foot 1978, 20). What this implies, implausibly, is that what the football fan feels about his team is never pride. The sentimentalist can say about him, more plausibly, that what he feels is pride, albeit irrationally.[28] "The phenomenon of recalcitrance reflects the epistemic aspect of the sentiments' partial encapsulation from our beliefs and desires . . . " (Jacobson 2013, 103). This is in contrast to other "cognitively sharpened" (and nonsentimental) emotions, which do contain some essential judgment and so do disappear with the disappearance of that judgment. If resentment is partially constituted by the judgment of having been wronged, then once one realizes one has not been wronged, what one feels is no longer resentment, *even if it is still anger* (D'Arms and Jacobson 2003, 143).

The phenomenon of *unthinking action*, on the other hand, "reflects the motivational aspect" (Jacobson 2013, 103) of the encapsulation of sentiments from judgment. The flash of anger one drunken denizen of the bar feels at the shove of another is all too often sufficient to generate punches and even gunshots between them, and these actions seem unmediated by any judgments of what a terrible idea it is to retaliate or how doing so might or might not satisfy their overall aims. Indeed, cases of revenge generally illustrate this point, but so also do familiar cases of our being impelled by the evaluations of fear to run away from a perceived threat, and our being impelled to laugh at something funny, even during a funeral or sermon.

[28] This is much more than a mere terminological difference, however. See D'Arms and Jacobson 2003, 135–6.

There is a third psychological phenomenon I want to introduce that reflects a *deliberative* aspect of the encapsulation of our sentiments from our judgments, and it will be especially salient for cases of responsibility. Sometimes when we are unsure about what to do, and where the counsel of judgment is indeterminate or simply runs out, we projectively imagine ourselves into alternative scenarios as robustly as we can in order to discover how we will *feel* about them. When I am unsure if a joke I am considering telling is funny, I may imagine myself as a bystander to see whether I would be amused. When I am unsure if I should tell a particularly salacious anecdote at my friend's wedding, I may imagine how I would feel if my friend's parents were horrified by it. Or perhaps I am considering attending a party and I know that a guy who owes me a lot of money will attend. I may imagine running into him there to gauge my own reaction, in order to determine whether I ought to attend.

So why is it important to emphasize this encapsulating feature of sentiments for our theorizing about responsibility? It is for the very simple reason that sometimes our responsibility responses exhibit one or more of these three psychological phenomena. My lingering response to my daughter's boyfriend wearing his cap backwards at the dinner table still counts as disdain, even in the face of my judgment that he is a good kid after all. This is a recalcitrant responsibility response, one that is simply inappropriate. Alternatively, my anger at your dissing me may lead to immediate and unthinking punching, contrary to all judgments of the disvalue of doing so. Finally, I may deliberatively test my regret-response when judgment runs out. In the above scenario, were I to imagine my friend's parents being disgusted by my naughty wedding toast and my subsequently feeling regret, I will view my counterfactual decision to tell the joke as *regrettable*, and thus as something for which I would have been responsible (and blameworthy), independently of any judgment constituting my emotional responsibility response.

What I have just given is an argument for not overlooking the sentiments in our theorizing about responsibility, but I have not yet given an argument for *featuring* them over other responses, which is what I will be doing. Won't we be failing to account for some of these other responses by doing so? We will not, but the arguments for this point vary, as it turns out, with each type of responsibility, so I will present them individually in each chapter of Part I.

For now, though, I just wanted to make clear why I am at least including the language of our responsibility sentiments in the book. Doing so fleshes out Strawson's discursive wish, it generates the possibility of a theory of universal human responsibility, and it provides a crucial source of data any complete theory needs to account for. These deeply familiar pan-cultural emotions evaluate some features of agency independently of judgment. In speaking of their appropriateness, I will most often use the language of "fittingness." To explain, sentiments represent their objects as having certain properties. Fear, for example, represents its object as a threat. Sentiments are *fitting* when these representations are accurate, that is, when the properties they represent their objects to have actually inhere in those objects. But this way of talking is still neutral between the B- and H-traditions, as these properties may be either antecedent responsibility-constituting properties or responsibility properties in virtue of being the target of a range of human attitudes, so again no questions should be begged by my engaging in it.

The Master Argument

> What I have to say consists largely of commonplaces. So my language, like that of commonplaces generally, will be quite unscientific and imprecise. The central commonplace that I want to insist on is the very great importance that we attach to the attitudes and intentions towards us of other human beings, and the great extent to which our personal feelings and reactions depend upon, or involve, our beliefs about these attitudes and intentions. I can give no simple description of the field of phenomena at the centre of which stands this commonplace truth; for the field is too complex.... There are simplifying ways of handling it in a general way.... These simplifications are of use to me only if they help to emphasize how much we actually mind, how much it matters to us, whether the actions of other people—and particularly of *some* other people—reflect attitudes towards us of goodwill, affection, or esteem on the one hand or contempt, indifference, or malevolence on the other. (Strawson 2003, 75–6)

Here is a sketch of the master argument. It is obvious, and often stated, that we tend to care about our fellow agents. But equally obvious, if less often stated, is the fundamental Strawsonian point the argument starts with: we agents tend to care about the *agency* of our fellow agents. My more fine-grained observation is this: we care about three agential features, namely, what *kinds* of agents people are, the *judgments* they make, and the *regard* they have for us. That is to say, we care about their general character, about how and what they judge worthy in particular cases, and about how they view us. These are the three different targets of our three different *Pure Quality of Will* theorists, of course. What I want to emphasize, though, is that we clearly care about *all three*.

Caring is emotionally dispositive: to care about X is to be disposed to respond emotionally to, and in sync with, the up-or-down fortunes of X.[29] If I care about you, I am disposed to be pleased in construing your fortunes as good and upset in construing them as bad.[30] So when I care about a specific feature of your agency, I am disposed to respond emotionally to, and in sync with, its changing fortunes.

Now at one end—the neurotypical end—of the spectrum, those with whom we interact are susceptible to the entire gamut of our emotional responsibility responses. And at the opposite end of the spectrum, those with whom we interact are susceptible to *none* of our responsibility responses. Examples here are bears and babies, fish and fowl. But the marginal cases provide something in-between for our investigative fodder, namely, agents seemingly susceptible to *some* responsibility responses but not others. It is in surveying our mixed responses in these marginal cases that we can actually start to get a feel for the full range of our responsibility responses themselves and then start to see distinct categories of them emerge. Once we have identified the relevant categories, we can try to construct an account of their fittingness conditions, and so by extension an account of the conditions of responsible agency generally.

Here, then, is a preview of how I will proceed from here. Thinking about our ambivalent responses to the marginal cases reveals that there are three distinctively characteristic, pan-cultural emotional syndromes (along with their paired opposites) responding primarily to the three different cared-about agential features. Such responses are more or less captured by some familiar folk psychological emotion terms, although our relevant data points will be the recognizably universal *syndromes*, not the emotion terms themselves (which typically refer to something much messier). These syndromes will constitute the responsibility sentiments on which I will focus. The rest of our responsibility responses are organized around one or more of these sentiments, I will suggest, although some such (nonsentimental) responses may be "cognitively sharpened," culturally bound, or vary cross-culturally in some aspect of their syndromes. The responsibility sentiments evaluate their objects—agential wills—as good or bad (they put the "quality" in quality of will), but the sentiments in the three different categories have three different objects (differentiating the "will" in quality of will), and insofar as each sentiment also has different fittingness conditions from the

[29] To the extent that one perceives the relevant fortunes, of course. See Shoemaker 2003, esp. 91, as well as Frankfurt 1999, 159–62, and Jaworska 2007.

[30] That's not to rule out these responses occasionally being masked or otherwise blocked from expression.

sentiments in the other categories, the distinct types of responsibility that arise out of them all implicate different agential capacities.

So what are these three characteristic sentimental pairs?[31] I will put these in third-person terms here, but as we will see, they have first-person analogs, and in one case (e.g., responses to judgment), I will mostly make use of the first-person version in discussion (for reasons I will explain in Chapter 2). At any rate, the sentiments characteristically evaluating quality of character are more or less captured by our emotion terms *disdain* and *admiration*. The negative syndrome includes feelings of superiority, thoughts about failures to live up to certain aretaic standards, and a motivation to be better than the object (or at least a motivation to non-imitation). The relevant positive syndrome includes feelings of uplift and attraction, thoughts about excellence, and motivational impulses to emulation and self-improvement (Algoe and Haidt 2009). The sentimental pair characteristically evaluating quality of judgment is somewhat captured by our emotion terms *disapproval* and *approval*. I think the relevant responses are actually more resonant in their first-person form, though, and these are roughly captured by the emotion terms *regret* and *pride*. The relevant negative syndrome includes feelings of letdown, thoughts about mistakes, and motivations to change judgmental policies (Zeelenberg et al. 1998; Lopez-Perez and Vorsatz 2010; D'Arms and Jacobson 2006b). The relevant positive syndrome includes feelings of self-satisfaction, thoughts about successful judgment, and motivations to persist in or reinforce one's judgmental policies. The sentimental pair characteristically evaluating quality of regard is more or less captured by our emotion terms *anger* and *gratitude*. The relevant negative syndrome includes feelings of intense heat and aggression (Eatough and Smith 2006), thoughts about slights, and motivational impulses to revenge or retribution (communicated as such). The relevant positive syndrome includes feelings of warmth, thoughts about beneficence, and motivational readiness to show appreciation, or return kindness, to the benefactor(s).

These distinct sentimental syndromes respond to distinct qualities of will, and so they reveal or determine the contours of the three types of responsibility I will articulate and defend in Part I of the book. This tripartite theory is thus

[31] There is one responsibility sentiment I will occasionally discuss that cuts across all categories, namely, agential shame. When targeting agents for their attitudes and actions, it may take as its object qualities of character, judgment, and regard on different occasions. This is what makes it complex (but also interesting). (Shame also, of course, takes as its object oneself in light of various non-agential features, such as one's ugliness, height, or even parents and upbringing. Thanks to Justin D'Arms and Dan Jacobson for discussion on this point.) For simplicity, though, I am focusing on the sentiments I think primarily target distinct types of "will" in their characteristic deployments.

motivated by the *fact* of our ambivalence in the marginal cases. But what is the precise *nature* of our ambivalence in each specific marginal case, and how well does the tripartite theory do in predicting and accounting for these specific ambivalences (in combination with the relevant empirical information)? These will be the questions I address in Part II.[32] In the next section, I will explain just how each chapter of the book will fit into this overall discussion.

The Map of the Book

In Chapter 1, I will develop an account of the first type of responsibility, *attributability*, which, I will argue, consists in a structural expression relation between one's character and one's attitudes. In making my case, I will start by examining the subcategory of responsibility responses organized around the sentimental syndromes characteristically thought of as admiration and disdain, emotional responses targeting quality of character. I will focus mostly on "admiration." Exploring this sentiment's fittingness conditions will enable us to identify the privileged subset of psychic elements we take to be truly representative of agents, a subset many have labeled the *deep self*. There have been two general competing theories of the deep self, identifying the self in either its noncognitive caring strand or its cognitive evaluative strand. I will argue that there are actually good reasons to be ecumenical here and include *both* strands as representing the deep self. I will then articulate the nature of attributability in a way that incorporates both strands. Finally, I will defend this as a stand-alone type of responsibility from objections by Susan Wolf, who thinks it is not genuine responsibility.

In Chapter 2, I will develop an account of *answerability*. While attributability is about volitional structures—how our motivational attitudes express our deep selves—answerability is something agents have in virtue of their ability (in principle) to "answer for" their actions, to respond to others' demands for justification by citing their judgments about the worth of some reasons over

[32] Just to be clear, the argument does not move in any kind of circular way, wherein the tripartite theory is constructed from our reactions in the marginal cases in a way that it becomes able to magically (and cheatingly) predict just what reactions it presupposed. Instead, I will be moving from the fact that we are ambivalent in marginal cases *generally* to the fact that there are three distinct categories of responsibility sentiments revealed thereby, and in constructing the fittingness conditions of those responsibility sentiments independently from any of our specific intuitions about the marginal cases, I will construct the tripartite theory, which we can *then* test in Part II by seeing how well it does in predicting our intuitive reactions in specific marginal cases. My thanks to Eddy Nahmias for discussion of this point.

others. Several theorists, including Smith, Scanlon, Duff, and Oshana, agree with me that answerability is a type of responsibility.[33] Where I differ with them is in their view that answerability is the *only* type of responsibility. In this chapter, I will discuss the nature of answerability and then offer my own argument in favor of answerability as a distinct type of responsibility—drawn primarily from exploration of a characteristic first-personal sentiment (regret) evaluating the quality of agential judgments—but in doing so I will also argue against the monistic presumptions of the aforementioned theorists. In particular, I will show a number of ways in which attributability and answerability are importantly distinct, covering different agential terrain and implicating different agential capacities.

In Chapter 3, I will develop an account of *accountability*. This is perhaps the most widely discussed type of responsibility, as it is often thought to implicate the kinds of sanctions or rewards that are taken to fall most obviously under the rubric of "holding responsible." However, I no longer think that holding to account necessarily involves sanctions or rewards. While it does implicate *confrontation* (or at least the motivation for such), such confrontation, in and of itself, implicates neither harms nor benefits to its targets. What it does do is communicate, in the negative case, anger over slights. I thus will be following Aristotle's basic presentation of anger here, but there will be a lot to develop and get clear on, including why a focus on the anger syndrome is better than a focus on resentment or indignation (contrary to the line taken by most contemporary theorists), what the nature of slights is, and what anger's communicative aim is. It is this discussion that will reveal why and how accountability is crucially distinct from both attributability and answerability.

At the end of Part I, I will have presented and defended attributability, answerability, and accountability as three distinct (noncompeting) types of responsibility, each carved out (or revealed by) three distinct subcategories of our responsibility responses. Attributability implicates quality of character, answerability implicates quality of judgment, and accountability implicates quality of regard. The fact of our ambivalence to marginal agents reveals these three subcategories of our responses, some of which apply to marginal agents and some of which do not, implying that they are responsible on some type(s) of responsibility but not others. To the extent that all of our responsibility responses are captured by one of these three interpretations of "quality of will," as I believe they are, we will have the possibility before us of a Pure *Qualities* of Will theory of

[33] Although Oshana calls it "accountability" (Oshana 1997).

responsibility, one whose multiple types of responsibility fall out of the three types of "quality of will."[34]

Part I is motivated by the general fact of our ambivalence in marginal cases. Part II is motivated by a desire to test the plausibility of the tripartite theory's predictions about the nature of our ambivalence in specific marginal cases. In what respects and why, precisely, do we have various kinds of mixed responses to various kinds of marginal agents, and does the tripartite theory offer the right explanation in each case? Only by delving into several specific cases can we know whether our Qualities of Will theory is *pure*, that is, whether qualities of will alone could also serve plausibly to explain the wide range of exemptions from responsibility, and so provide a complete story about the nature of paradigm responsible agency. Further, a plausible pure theory would not only issue in verdicts about the responsibility of our various marginal agents; it could also issue in recommendations for the *treatment* of marginal agents, recommendations to both caregivers and the marginal agents themselves. I intend to note such practical normative payoffs when relevant.

In Chapter 4, then, I will begin by exploring two marginal cases that raise difficult issues about *attributability*: clinical depression and a version of Obsessive Compulsive Disorder (OCD) known as scrupulosity. First, many clinically depressed people report that their motivational attitudes (or lack thereof)—the sadness, apathy, and judgments of their own low worth—are nevertheless fully representative of them, even on their darkest days, whereas third-person assessments of those in the throes of depression typically exempt or mitigate them. "She's just not herself," we say, "so don't attribute those despairing attitudes you see to her." Second, there is a subpopulation of those with OCD who are obsessed with morality, with doing the right thing, and these scrupulous agents differ from others with OCD by *embracing* their desires. Are these desires attributable to them, then? We would tend, after all, to let them off the hook for acting on those desires where their actions set back the interests of others (their spouses, for example).

These are actually very complicated, difficult cases. I will not have any definitive answers about them, but they at least provide a number of important lessons

[34] As I say, I believe there are three and *only* three types of responsibility, but I will not argue for the "only" part in this book. Instead, I leave it as a challenge: show me a distinct fourth (or fifth . . .) subcategory of responsibility responses carving out the contours of additional types of responsibility, and I will consider them. But it is very hard for me to envision anything in addition to character, judgment, and regard that could be the object of our responsibility responses, and I cannot envision any responses that do not fit into one of the three subcategories, so I remain fairly confident that these constitute the limit.

for our general investigation. First, they reveal the importance of getting as clear as possible on the object of our various responses. Doing so, with empirical help, enables us to see that there are several possible volitional and attitudinal objects, some of which are attributable while some are not. Second, getting the psychological details right for each type of case illuminates very different reasons for why each agent may succeed or fail in being attributability-responsible. Finally, investigation into these cases through the lens of the tripartite theory reveals some important insights into the nature of character generally.

The next two cases I will discuss, in Chapter 5, will be those of psychopaths and people with high-functioning autism, especially as they pertain to exemptions or mitigation from *accountability*. Psychopathy has become widely discussed in the philosophical literature on responsibility within the last 20 years, and my contention is that nearly all such discussions have been either mistaken or seriously misleading. The primary problem is that they lean too heavily on the results of the general moral/conventional task as deployed on a few incarcerated psychopaths by James Blair in the mid-1990s. Here I will argue for a robust skepticism about the so-called distinction as it has been understood, which speaks against certain sorts of such appeals. I will then show how one might nevertheless try to rescue some remnants of the Blair experiments to support the positing of a crucial difference between psychopaths and the rest of us that *is* relevant to membership in the community of morally responsible agents, namely, their inability to recognize authorizing permissions we may offer to one another, an inability whose source is in their seeming lack of empathy. But there will be some reason to worry about this result, given that those with high-functioning autism—who many have thought *are* accountable—also seem to lack empathy. I will thus explore in greater detail the nature of empathy and how its different types are relevant to accountability. The surprising, albeit quite tentative, verdict of the tripartite theory is that both psychopaths and those with high-functioning autism may indeed not be accountable, albeit in virtue of different empathic impairments, and I think this result will be intuitively plausible once we have laid bare the relevant empirical details.

In Chapter 6, I will turn primarily to exploring *answerability* and its relation to attributability by focusing on some different features of psychopaths, namely, their alleged prudential impairments and how these might undermine their capacity for character. I contrast psychopaths here with cases of adults with mild intellectual disability (MID), who, as far as I know, have not been discussed elsewhere in the philosophical literature (except in my own papers, Shoemaker 2007 and Shoemaker 2009). These are agents who have, it seems, a kind of *restricted* membership in the moral community, restricted in two respects:

(a) the range of things they are responsible for, and (b) the range of people to whom they are responsible. Nevertheless, with their caregivers, friends, and family, adults with MID are quite often treated as full-fledged moral agents (at least with respect to a subset of moral demands), susceptible to full-throated reactive emotions and other responsibility-responses. Why is this? Here I will suggest that the tripartite theory plausibly implies that while they may be accountable and attributability-responsible for their actions or attitudes, they may not be answerable, and this is in accord with our intuitive ambivalence toward them. I will also offer methods by which the range of those to whom these agents may be accountable might be expanded.

In Chapters 4–6, I will have shown how the tripartite theory is boosted in plausibility by how it handles several marginal cases. But there will remain one type of marginal case Strawson discussed that looks like it will have difficulty fitting into our scheme, namely, the person from poor formative circumstances. The reason this case poses a challenge is that the qualities of will approach is a time-slice, ahistorical view of responsibility: what matter to the fittingness of various responses are just the current qualities of the target's will. But the case of someone from poor formative circumstances seems to suggest that some additional history-related component is needed to render any theory of responsibility viable, for otherwise we would have no nonarbitrary way of differentiating between what would sometimes be differentially responsible agents with identical current qualities of will.

To put these worries to rest, in Chapter 7 I will explore this purported exempting plea. I allow that, while history does matter, it matters only epistemically, and so my qualities of will approach can preserve its ahistoricity against this worry. In doing so, I show why poor formative circumstances in fact do not exempt from responsibility; rather, at most, they *mitigate* responsibility (of some types), and when they do, it is in virtue of impairments to the agent's current qualities of will. I will then take a look at a different epistemic function of agential history by investigating one last severely underexplored marginal case: moderate-stage dementia in Alzheimer's patients. As it turns out, this is a very tricky sort of case, but it is one that the tripartite theory handles quite well. What the theory interestingly and plausibly predicts is that our ambivalence toward demented agents is a function of their being exempted (or significantly mitigated) from both accountability and answerability responses but being eligible for some attributability responses. And here we will see a new, distinctive, epistemic role for agential history: it can sometimes reveal, not what one's quality of character is, but *that one still has the capacity for* quality of character.

In the concluding chapter of the book, I will do three things. First, I will summarize the book by weaving together the discussions of Part I and Part II. Second, I will discuss some possible limitations or gaps in my account. In particular, I will explore whether my *Pure Qualities of Will* theory can really account for *all* we mean with respect to concepts I do not say much about in the book until then, namely, desert, blame, and free will. Finally, I will explore some additional virtues of the tripartite theory. For one thing, it looks well-positioned to dissolve the dispute between deep self theorists and reasons-responsive theorists over the best way to characterize and theorize about responsibility. For another, its (universalistic) pluralism might undercut the motivation of some theorists to push a relativistic or skeptical line about responsibility. And for another, the tripartite theory could actually go a ways toward explaining some persisting disagreements in normative ethics, as each of its three targeted agential features (character, judgment, and regard) are spotlighted in different theories (virtue ethics, consequentialism, and deontology). At the end of the day, therefore, I believe the theory will be able to explain a large amount of data, not only with respect to how we theorize about responsibility and morality, but also with respect to the ways in which we actually live our lives with one another.

PART I

The Tripartite Theory of Responsibility

> There is not, and there never could be, . . . just one correct conception of responsibility. . . . [W]e ourselves, in various circumstances, need different conceptions of it.
>
> Bernard Williams (1993, 55)

In Part I of this book, I attempt to account for the fact of our ambivalence in the marginal cases, the fact that some of our emotional responsibility responses to marginal agents seem fitting whereas others do not. *Pure Quality of Will* theorists cannot explain this fact. But rather than abandon the quality of will approach in light of their failure, I will advance a *qualities* of will approach that explains the data. On this view, there are three distinct "wills" our different responses construe as good or bad—character, judgment, and regard—each implicating different agential capacities and so generating different types of responsibility, namely, attributability, answerability, and accountability. To argue for this tripartite theory, in each of the following three chapters I will begin by identifying a distinctive subcategory of our responsibility responses and its characteristic sentiment, provide an account of that sentiment's fittingness conditions, and then give a detailed explanation of the type of responsibility thereby implicated. I will also show how each type of responsibility may obtain independently of the others, and so by the end of Part I these arguments together will constitute a defense of the pluralism of the overall theory.

The Tripartite Profile: A Chart

The chart below lays out the three types of responsibility to be developed in Part I, labels for each type of "will" whose quality is being assessed in each case, the characteristic sentimental syndrome pairs assessing them, and the numerous other related emotional responses.

Type of Responsibility	Evaluated "Will"	Characteristic Sentimental Syndrome Pair	Emotion Family
Attributability	Character	Agential Disdain/ Admiration	*Negative*: Disdain, disesteem, contempt, abhorrence, hatred, revulsion, shame *Positive*: esteem, awe, elevation, pride, veneration
Answerability	Judgment	Agential Regret/ Pride	*Negative*: Disapproval, disappointment, irritation, frustration, shame *Positive*: approval, appreciation, approbation
Accountability	Regard	Agential Anger/ Gratitude	*Negative*: Resentment, indignation, guilt, hurt feelings, shame *Positive*: gratification, warm feelings

1

Attributability

Consider once more Skip, the psychopath from the Introduction. Once we come to know the details about him, it would just seem *pointless* (as a form of communication) to be angry with him for treating people as poorly as he does, even though he still seems in doing so to be a complete jerk who remains worthy of a variety of *other* negative emotional responses. He is a cheater, a manipulator, a downright cruel person, after all, and so seems worthy of contempt. Recall the weary plea of his mother, after learning of his wedding plans, wondering why he had to marry the poor girl and ruin her life. In her plea there is both recognition of, and resignation at, just what kind of awful person he is.

Consider also a moderately demented parent or grandparent. One can imagine that she has become incapacitated in certain key respects, so that a wide range of responsibility responses—anger, gratitude, moral disapproval, or criticism—would be inappropriate. Yet we can also easily imagine that she occasionally acts in a generous or kind way. This behavior would seem to render admiring responses to her generosity or kindness perfectly appropriate, as these attitudes seem to express who she is in certain fundamental respects. She is *still* generous and kind, we may think.

Consider finally someone who is moderately autistic, someone essentially incapable of reading faces or social cues, and so who makes all sorts of social faux pas and delivers deeply uncomfortable or hurtful truths to people's faces. Again, once his incapacities are known, anger at these remarks, and perhaps anger at him generally, will tend to be suspended. Nevertheless, he may be deeply concerned about the truth, or about following various social norms, and so in that respect would be, we might think, appropriately venerated.

In this chapter, I will attempt to articulate the relevant subcategory of responsibility responses to which these sorts of marginal agents are still susceptible, explain precisely what they are responses to, and then show how they can help us identify or carve out the boundaries of a distinct type of responsibility—attributability—one which may apply to each of the above agents despite their not being responsible on some other types. In the heart of the chapter, I will motivate and develop a new, pluralistic, understanding of the attributable *self* that resolves a long-standing stalemate in the literature, is buttressed by the response-driven account of responsibility, and accounts for all the relevant data. I will conclude by defending this theory of attributability as a theory of *responsibility* against two objections.

Agential Admiration

In the above marginal cases (and in many others), the sorts of responsibility responses we persist in having, despite the suspension of many anger-associated responses, are *aretaic*, that is, they are responses to the faults or excellences of others.[1] This makes them responses in the zone of what Gary Watson first labeled "responsibility-as-attributability," something he took to be a distinct "face" of responsibility (Watson 2004, 260–88). Watson put his basic point in terms of blaming and praising responses to agents. "In one way," he wrote,

> to blame (morally) is to attribute something to a (moral) fault in the agent.... [Such] blaming and praising judgments... invoke only the attributability conditions, on which certain appraisals of the individual as an agent are grounded. Because many of these appraisals concern the agent's excellences and faults—or virtues and vices—as manifested in thought and action, I shall say that such judgments are made from the *aretaic perspective*. (Watson 2004, 266; emphasis in original)

What this subset of responsibility responses takes as its object is what many have termed the agent's *deep self* (see, e.g., Wolf 1987; Sripada 2010; Faraci and Shoemaker 2010), which, according to Watson, is the source of and expresses "what activities and ways of life are most choiceworthy." Importantly, the "choiceworthy" is not limited to the world of the "moral," where that is construed narrowly to refer to the requirements of interpersonal relationships. One may, for example, betray one's own ideals in a cowardly fashion or be lazy in their pursuit—warranting negative aretaic appraisals in both cases—without violating any moral requirements (Watson 2004, 266–7).

While I will discuss later Watson's own account of the conditions of attributability (suggested by his talk of what is "choiceworthy"), for now I just want to draw from this discussion the point that attributability, whatever it is, at least grounds aretaic responses. Now Watson is careful to note just that *many* of these responses to attributability concern agential virtue and vice, so we have to allow

[1] Some of the material that follows is drawn from Shoemaker Forthcoming-a.

for the possibility of non-aretaic attributability.[2] But to the extent that most such appraisals *are* aretaic, we can best get a handle on this type of responsibility generally by focusing on them, and in particular on what their precise objects are and what makes them appropriate. Once we have done this, we may find the resources within the version of attributability these appraisals carve out to explain the nature of non-aretaic attributability.

We begin, then, with our aretaic responses, of which there are many, of both the moral and non-moral variety. On the positive side, they include esteem, veneration, and awe; on the negative side, they include contempt, abhorrence, hatred, and revulsion. All of these are forms or close relatives of what seems to be the characteristic emotional pair of *admiration* and *disdain*. While there has not been much empirical work done on either of these emotions, there has recently at least been a little work on admiration, so I will draw mostly from that literature to construct the relevant sentimental *syndrome* here, although much of what I say should resonate phenomenologically regardless. In this section, I intend to bring clarity to what the syndrome is (including why it is a sentiment), what the precise nature of its object is, and what its fittingness conditions seem to be. From this discussion we will then be prepared to survey our fitting aretaic responses to articulate the contours of attributability, at least after we have fought through the quagmire in which contemporary attributability theory finds itself.

So what is admiration generally? In what psychological literature there is, it has been offered as the label for a response to displays of *non*-moral excellence, whereas "elevation" is the more artificial label for what we tend to feel in response to displays of *moral* excellence (Haidt 2003a; Algoe and Haidt 2009). I do not see how such a distinction will stand, though. For one thing, the borderline between the moral and the non-moral is stubbornly gray. Is what I feel in response to the excellent development of someone's talents, or how good someone is as a parent, moral or non-moral? For another thing, the phenomenology of my feelings with respect to the uncontroversially moral or non-moral can be remarkably similar: what I feel in response to excellent artists, say, may feel exactly like my response to the magnanimous or exceedingly kind. I think we are in less murky waters, then, just thinking of the relevant sort of response here as one to *excellence*.

But excellence of *what*? We tend to have "admirish" responses to excellent objects, deeds, and doers. I may, for instance, "admire" the Grand Canyon, or "admire" what the Tiananmen Square protester did when standing up to the tanks. But only doers—*agents*—could be responsible. Indeed, all of our responsibility

[2] Thanks to Michael McKenna for reminding me of this point.

responses have only agents as their objects, that is, we praise or blame only agents *for* their actions or attitudes (and *in virtue of* some quality of will, I am contending). So what we must do is restrict the range of whatever positive aretaic responsibility response we want to explore to its agential manifestation. And this is actually how admiration is usually treated in the psychological literature, where only admiration for the excellence of other agents is the relevant object of study. It is then taken to have the following syndrome: feelings of uplift, thoughts about agential excellence, and action tendencies for emulation and/or self-improvement.

Even so, "admiration" as a folk psychological term does not quite fit this syndrome, for there are some agents about whom we speak in the language of admiration where a significant feature of the syndrome is distinctly absent. I may, for example, "admire" Michael Jordan *qua* athlete without being inclined in any way to "Be like Mike," despite the ad campaign to the contrary. Now one might be an emotion-term chauvinist and insist that, in virtue of my lacking the motivation described by admiration's syndrome, I am better described as experiencing "awe." Or one might be an emotion-term Unitarian, welcoming a multitude of action tendencies under admiration's tent. This is a debate that does not interest me, for mine is not a project about identifying the right emotion terms. Rather, I just want to identify the right emotional *syndrome*, and I think the above-articulated syndrome for admiration captures just what is going on in the subcategory of positive aretaic responsibility responses. And in fact, this is just what seems to be captured by the *central range* of folk psychological "admiration" responses anyway: they take as their object agential excellence, involve feelings of uplift, and motivate emulation and/or self-improvement. To have a label that accurately picks out just this central range of the folk psychological concept, I will use the term "agential admiration," and I want to make it absolutely clear that I just have in mind this *syndrome* as its referent, the central, most familiar, version of the wider emotion.[3]

So is agential admiration a sentiment? For my purposes, recall (from the Introduction), this requires two features: (a) it must be a pan-cultural emotion, and (b) it must be encapsulated from judgment, which itself involves recalcitrance, unthinking action, and playing a certain sort of deliberative role. Again, it

[3] Hoi Yee Chan pointed out to me that, in Chinese, while there are three words that translate roughly to the English "admiration," there are actually important differences between them. The term 欣賞 primarily refers to the response one has to natural wonders, and so is more like "appreciation" or "aesthetic awe." The term 崇拜 primarily refers to the worshipful feelings one has to great artistry. The term 敬佩 primarily refers to the response one has toward agents in recognition of their virtues or good general character. It is this last emotional response I am urging as the relevant responsibility sentiment, calling it "agential admiration."

is understudied, but from the available evidence agential admiration looks to be pan-cultural (Fessler 1999; Haidt 2003b). It also displays the relevant encapsulation from judgment. First, it is recalcitrant. Imagine meeting your hero in a bar, where you see him berating people and he treats you terribly. Your long-standing admiration may not dissipate immediately in the face of your sincere new judgment that he is a nasty person after all. As an example of the second feature, extraordinarily kind or brave actions, when witnessed and represented as admirable, often spur admirers to do something similar, independently of their "better" judgment. Courage can be contagious, and it is spurred by "the feelings of moral elevation in the members who witness the acts" (Kilmann et al. 2010, 16; see also Algoe and Haidt 2009). As an example of the third feature, consider familiar cases in which one might deliberate about what kind of person to strive to become, in the face of indeterminate judgments about it, by projecting oneself into the shoes of others to see what their emotional responses might be to one's revealed character traits. The expected admiration of others tends to inform one's character construction in cases where judgment runs out.

For these reasons, I take agential admiration to be a sentiment. To admire marginal agents is to evaluate them as *admirable*, independently of one's judgment. But such evaluations can be unfitting. So what does their admirableness consist in? We have already discussed the feeling of agential admiration's syndrome (uplift) as well as its characteristic action tendency (emulation/self-improvement). What then, finally, are its associated thoughts?[4] Earlier I mentioned the generic "thoughts about agential excellence." But excellence of what? If we think about the paradigm cases of agential admiration (where the whole syndrome is in place), we tend to admire agents insofar as they reveal something excellent about who they really are. This goes for artists successfully expressing their vision, for misanthropic drunks who turn their lives around, for those who sacrifice their time in the service of others, for those who uncompromisingly demand justice, and so on. These excellent features are enduring (not fly-by-night), and they are most often captured by aretaic predicates describing their qualities with respect to practical agency. It should be clear, then, that these are all features of *character*, which admiration evaluates as excellent—as virtuous—relative to some ideal.

[4] And by "associated thoughts" I certainly do not mean that they are *constitutive judgments*. Instead, these are thoughts that prototypically *accompany* (fitting) agential admiration's emotional evaluation.

Agential disdain (the emotion term I am using as a gloss for the opposite range of our negative aretaic responses to agents[5]) has an analogous syndrome, including feelings of superiority, thoughts about aretaic failure, and a motivation to be better than the disdained agent, or at least not to emulate him or her (see, e.g., Rozin, Lowery, Imada, and Haidt 1999, 575 on contempt). When I disdain someone in light of his revealed pattern of psychological spousal abuse, I am, again as Watson (2004, 266) notes, tracing these attitudes and actions to a fault, a *vice*, of his. It is an expression of his poor character. By contrast, when an otherwise placid, loving person who has become involuntarily subject to hallucinogens snaps and yells at her spouse, we tend *not* to disdain her (or admire her, for that matter). Why? Because we view her outburst as having been genuinely *out* of character. It just did not express anything about who she really is.

I will thus take our fitting aretaic emotional responses to target agents in light of their expressions of character. But what does any of this have to do with *responsibility*? I am going to draw on this treatment of agential admiration and disdain (and their cohort) as a way of plugging a significant gap in previous theories of responsibility-as-attributability. In the next section, I provide some history of, and motivation for, viewing attributability as a type of responsibility. I will then be in a position to expose the flaws in previous theorizing about the object of attributability, the deep self, and so to develop a new version of attributability-as-responsibility that takes seriously the relevant aretaic sentimental responses.

Motivating Attributability

There were two motivations for introducing talk of attributability into the contemporary literature on responsibility. First, compatibilists about free will needed a way to blunt counterexamples to the crude accounts offered by their ancestors that built a conception of free agency out of mere intentional agency. Hobbes, for instance, located the self in the will—effective desire—and claimed that, as long as no external impediments prevented the execution of one's will, one's action was free. The counterexamples came from the thought that one's actions might also be impeded from the "inside" by certain psychological forces and states such as manias, compulsions, and addictions. When these forces and states "replace" or "install" one's will, then even if a produced action is causally

[5] One might think instead that "contempt" is the better negative term, but it seems an over-the-top description of our reaction to minor character flaws. Nevertheless, I am borrowing some of my description of the disdaining syndrome from psychological work on contempt.

dependent on a desire within one's psychic domain, it cannot be thought to reflect one's agency. If one's actions are produced in this way, one is *alienated* from one's will, that is, one's will does not reflect the subset of one's psychic domain constituting one's deep self.[6] So even if one's motivating attitudes derive from the "inside," if they lack a proper connection to one's deep self—whatever that is—they are not genuinely *attributable* to one. One familiar way this point has been put in the literature is that the agents do not *identify* with their motivating psychic elements.

The second motivation was to capture features distinctive to us as free and morally responsible agents. Sometimes in this capacity we are referred to as *persons*, as creatures (in contrast to other animals) who have the special ability for reflection, for stepping back and critically examining our wills, for having attitudes about these wills, and, presumably, for replacing them with alternative wills (Frankfurt 1988, 11–25). When we take up this reflective stance toward various attitudes and actions and then go on to adopt a certain sort of attitude or position with respect to them, we *render them our own*, attributable to us for purposes of freedom and responsibility. This reflective procedure is distinctive to us (Frankfurt 1988, 12, 23; Watson 2004, 13–32; Taylor 1976).

Of course, some view talk of attributability as unmotivated insofar as all the relevant distinctions here can ostensibly be made in terms of *volitional control*. On this view, all of the elements making up our psychic domain are, well, *ours*. Freedom or responsibility with respect to some attitudes or actions, then, is (at least partially) a function of whether we have control over their expression or performance. Manias, compulsions, and addiction may thus be viewed as producing attitudes and actions outside the scope of our volitional control, and what distinguishes us from other animals with respect to freedom and responsibility is precisely our capacity for controlling various of our actions and attitudes *via* the relevant sort of sophisticated reflective cognitive machinery. Talk of deep selves and attributability, therefore, at least with respect to agency and responsibility, seems unnecessary (see, e.g., Mele 1992 and 1995). Further, and more fundamentally, one might think that talk of the deep self is just ontologically mysterious: What *is* it, after all? Many explications have been offered, all of which face powerful counterexamples. Even friends of the deep self approach to

[6] The "deep" in "deep self" simply refers to the psychic element's place in an agential structure as the ultimate psychological *source* of various "surface" attitudes subject to its governance. Some prefer the term "true self" instead (see, e.g., Newman, Bloom, and Knobe 2013), but its contrast—"false self"—misleadingly describes the attitudes it governs. Thanks to Chandra Sripada, Jeanette Kennett, and Randy Clarke for discussion on this point.

responsibility have expressed serious worries about the deep self's elusive nature (Watson 2004, 169). So given both worries, why bother with it?

In what follows, I directly aim only to answer the latter, more fundamental, question about the nature of the deep self. I will respond to the former worry, about the superfluity of talk of the deep self, more indirectly, insofar as it will simply become obvious how some of the constituents of the deep self—constituents producing attitudes that are attributable to us for purposes of responsibility—are not, it turns out, subject to our volitional control.

The Competing Strands of the Deep Self

In using the term "deep self," I am referring to a privileged subset of our psyche that includes some elements but excludes many others. Among the excluded elements, we tend to think, are the following: (a) pains, itches, and reflexes; (b) what I call *psychic junk*, for example, the obsessional, compulsive, and addictive urges and cravings of many psychologically disordered people, as well as the random thoughts, impulses, and images that cross the consciousness of everyone from time to time; and (c) some attitudes formed on whims or as the result of altered states of consciousness. To discover the boundaries between the included and the excluded, I suggest, we can lean on our fitting aretaic sentimental responses. We tend to admire excellent quality of character and disdain poor quality of character. But what precise features are we responding to in these ways? My aim here is to develop a new theory of the contours of the privileged subset, one which builds on a story about why some psychic elements are (agentially) *admirable* or *disdainable* and some are not. Before telling this story, however, I need to show why the current theories of the deep self are inadequate.

There have been two strands of thinking about the nature of the deep self as it pertains to attributability. The first is roughly Humean, articulated by Harry Frankfurt in a justly famous series of papers. Frankfurt's original answer was to say that one's will—what he called, with Hobbes, the desire causally effective in action—could be genuinely attributed to one (attributable to one's deep self) via active endorsement of that first-order desire, endorsement consisting in one's forming a second-order desire that it be one's will (what he called a second-order *volition*). One identifies with one's will just in case one forms a (second-order) volition about it, that is, when one *wants to want* to do the thing in question (Frankfurt 1988, 11–25). One's deep self is thus a higher-order desirer, expressing itself in such volitions.

But what actually makes those *volitions* one's own? Watson's famous critique of Frankfurt's early story pressed this question: "Since second-order volitions are themselves simply desires, to add them to the context of conflict is just to increase the number of contenders; it is not to give a special place to any of those in contention" (Watson 2004, 28). Nothing about its higher-order status gives any desire the special authority for self-determination that is presumably provided by identification, for all that that higher-order status amounts to is that there is a different object of the desire: rather than targeting actions (as first-order desires do), second-order desires target other desires. But a difference in target does not provide it any special authority in representing the self.

Watson's alternative understanding of identification advances a second, Platonic, strand in this debate. Instead of locating the agent's deep self in (higher-order) desires, it locates it in Reason, more specifically, in the agent's evaluative stance. Desires may move us to action, but to the extent that they operate independently of our values, we are not free, for it is not *we*—agents *qua* valuers—who authoritatively determine our action in such cases.[7] When confronted with various desires to do this or that, I decide what to do about those desires in accordance with my judgments of what it is best for me to do, and in so doing I render them and their dependent actions truly mine (Watson 2004, e.g., 29).

As Watson later conceded, this proposal was too rationalistic (Watson 2004, 167–9). Not only did it conflate judging valuable with valuing (I may judge some things good—like going to an avant-garde jazz concert—that do not move me in the least), but it also did not account well for what he called "perverse cases," in which some action could be fully embraced as one's own (identified with) even though one did not judge it to be best (or even though one judged it not to be best), where this did not consist in compulsion or weakness of will either. For example, I might judge it best to do some writing today but go play golf instead because it is just more fun. If (or when) I do so, this action is not weak-willed and its motivation will be, surely, attributable to me, even though it does not seem to express some general evaluative standpoint to which "I" am inexorably attached. Consequently, as Watson says, "We are left with a rather elusive notion of identification and thereby an elusive notion of self-determination" (Watson 2004, 169).

Still, many have continued to take up the challenge to provide the account of identification that will lead us out of the wilderness. Each typically attempts to

[7] This way of putting it should make clear that Watson's original theory was about *free agency*, not responsibility. The same could be said of Frankfurt's original theory. They were first transmogrified into deep self theories of *responsibility* by Wolf 1987.

locate the deep self exclusively in one strand or the other.[8] There are going to be powerful problems, though, for every such attempt. We have no need to go through them individually, however, because the problems just extrapolate from the above discussion. Very generally, if one locates the deep self exclusively in the Humean strand (in noncognitive desires or cares, say), one will have no place for agential *authority* in one's story of the deep self, where this is a matter of our authorizing various pursuits insofar as they track the good (cf., Bratman 2007, 231–2). The advocate of the pure Humean strand must deny the relevance for attributability of the fact that one's judgments of what it is best for one to pursue occasionally determine various volitions, where these run contrary to or independent of one's cares or desires. But denying the relevance of one's stance as an evaluator and authorizer robs one's deep self of a huge chunk of its presumed practical role, and so a huge chunk of what we ourselves deem to reflect who we genuinely are. We have to plan all sorts of courses of action, moral and non-moral, and we often do so solely with an eye on what is worth doing, sometimes regardless of what we care about or desire (think in particular of moral pursuits). These plans often give birth to our commitments, those things we *stand* for solely because we judge them good. If this wide-ranging source of volitions is not incorporated into the deep self, then the theory will be wildly and absurdly revisionary, as we surely attribute such attitudes to agents (ourselves first and foremost) all the time.

On the other hand, locating the deep self exclusively in the Platonic strand would have us occasionally denying *authentic* volitions as one's own: sometimes one's passions, even when they run contrary to, or independently of, one's judgments of the worthlessness of their objects, nevertheless seem to reveal who one really is. Think here of the teenager raised in a deeply religious family who finds himself with powerful homosexual desires. These seem much more revelatory of who he really is than do his conscious judgments that such desires have no worth (as such evaluative judgments generally may be the product of false consciousness).[9] Consequently, neither strand can adequately capture

[8] For defense of the Humean strand, see various of the essays in Frankfurt 1999. See also Bratman 1999, 197–206, as well as related pieces in Bratman 2007 for what looks ultimately like a defense of the Platonic strand (although he leaves room for an important role to be played by noncognitive cares). Velleman 1992 seems to locate the deep self ultimately (and exclusively) in a desire, albeit a desire to act in accordance with evaluative judgments. In Shoemaker 2003, I located the deep self exclusively in the Humean strand, in the agent's nexus of cares. Sripada 2010 and 2012 seems to do the same, although he has a wider notion of cares than I had. Lippert-Rasmussen 2003 critically discusses various of these attempts. See also Arpaly and Schroeder 1999 for critical discussion.

[9] Although see Newman, Bloom, and Knobe 2013, and Newman, De Freitas, and Knobe 2014, for very intriguing studies suggesting that assessments of authenticity in such cases may vary based on assessors' own normative outlooks.

both the authenticity and authority elements of the deep self, the source of attribution.

In addition, neither strand typically accounts for the entire range of attitudes we tend to attribute to deep selves. Most attributability theorists, after all, focus on explaining identification just with respect to the attitudes structuring agents' *volitions*, that is, their motivational states. But these are not all of the attitudes we attribute to agents under the responsibility rubric. As Angela Smith has insightfully shown, we also attribute to agents—and blame them for—forgettings, noticings, and some impulses and spontaneous emotional reactions (Smith 2005, esp. 240–50). Someone might really hate members of races other than his own, but he may be prudent and never let his hatred structure his will. Nevertheless, were we to come to know this about him (perhaps it is revealed when he accidentally lets slip a "Woo hoo!" when he sees a KKK cross-burning one day), we would certainly attribute this hatred to him: *he* is a racist, we would want to say, even though he never does (or perhaps never even desires to do) anything racist. And this seems quite right: we are entitled to think less of him as a person, solely in virtue of his (nonvolitional) attitudes.

The object of our investigation, then, is wide, for we are looking for an account of the deep self to which both volitional and nonvolitional attitudes are attributed and that can also capture both authenticity and authority. Now one option, given the problems with previous theorizing about the deep self, is just to abandon the attempt to find a unified object of attribution. Perhaps some attitudes are attributable (if they are) to one kind of thing, whereas other sorts of attitudes are attributable (if they are) to something else. Abandoning the quest would be too quick, however, for there remains a very plausible, albeit unexplored, alternative, namely, perhaps the deep self consists in *both* strands, in both Reason and Passion. In what follows, I will attempt to develop and defend just such a theory, leaning once more on our aretaic sentiments in so doing.

Ecumenical Deep Self Theory

Recall the general formulation of responsible agency from the Introduction:

To be a responsible agent is to be worthy of X for Y in virtue of Z.

To this point, we have seen how I would like to fill in the variables for attributability:

To be an ***attributable*** *agent is to be worthy of* ***agential admiration/disdain*** *for* ***attitudes (volitional and nonvolitional)*** *in virtue of* ***their expressing one's deep self.***[10]

My aim in this section is to give an account of the deep self, one that can avoid the problems of previous theories. I call the view I construct the *Ecumenical Deep Self* theory, and the basic idea is that the deep self consists in elements from *either* the Humean or the Platonic psychic strands. Another way to put it is that my deep self may be expressed in either authenticating *or* authorizing ways.

Before presenting my argument for the Ecumenical Deep Self theory, I need to say what I take the *expression* relation to be. Many deep self theorists assume this relation is (all and only) *causal*: one's attitudes must causally depend on one's deep self (whatever that is) in order to be attributable to one for purposes of agential admiration or disdain. The fundamental motivation for requiring this condition stems from worries about manipulation cases, taken by some to be paradigms of non-attributability: were an external manipulator to implant some attitude in me, it could not be mine, it is often thought, for purposes of responsibility, precisely in virtue of its not being causally dependent on any features of my deep self. While I have some hesitations about this requirement, I will let them pass and incorporate it here.[11]

What I want to add to the causation requirement is a variation of a relation proposed and discussed at length by Chandra Sripada, namely, a *content harmony* relation (or a reasons-based congruence relation).[12] Sripada focuses just on actions as the relevantly expressed attributable items, but I think the question of attributability most fundamentally applies to attitudes (as I have stated in the formulation above). Bodily movements, for example, must depend on intentions in order to count as actions, so actions are derivative from attitudes. To the extent that an action is attributable to me, therefore, it will really be in virtue of its intention being attributable to me, so it will be more efficient to focus just on

[10] The restriction just to attitudes is new, and I defend it shortly in the text.

[11] My basic worry is that manipulation cases generate the intuitions they do in virtue of being cases in which the agent's attitudes or values are made to be very *different* from her original attitudes or values. So there are actually two alterations being lumped together, namely, the causal source of the attitude and the content of the attitude. I am inclined to think that altering the causal source alone, without any change in the content of the attitude, might preserve attributability, but as I say, I will not argue for that point here. See my initial discussion of this idea on Flickers of Freedom, URL: <http://agencyandresponsibility.typepad.com/flickers-of-freedom/2012/06/survey-attributability-and-manipulation.html> and PEA Soup, URL:<http://peasoup.typepad.com/peasoup/2012/06/survey-says.html>.

[12] See his "Self-Expression: A Deep Self Theory of Moral Responsibility," unpublished manuscript, University of Michigan. Importantly, Sripada also requires causal sensitivity in his account of self-expression.

attitudes as the more fundamentally attributable objects.[13] Nevertheless, I think we can alter Sripada's stated view without too much difficulty: as long as one's *attitudes* display content that is congruent with one's deep self, they express it.

The basic idea, then, is that there is a subset of attitudes that one might be characteristically disposed to have given the content of some element of one's deep self. So, for example, if an evaluative judgmental stance were part of my deep self, then were I to judge my work on this book to be valuable, the content of this judgment would be captured by my being disposed to have certain specific attitudes, namely, the intention to work on it, a desire for quiet as I work, the aim of getting the exposition of others' work right, and so forth. Attitudes would thus express my deep self to the extent that they would be congruent with its content, that is, reliably expected to be within the set of attitudes characteristically associated with components of the deep self.

More needs to be said, of course, about the nature of the content harmony condition, but I think the basic idea is clear enough. The motivating idea stems from the worry that it might be possible for an attitude wildly at variance with one's deep self somehow nevertheless to be causally cranked out by it. In such a case, we would be inclined to think the causally dependent attitude not to be attributable to one. The content harmony relation stifles this worry.

Onward, then, to the positive presumptive argument for the Ecumenical Deep Self theory. What I need to show is that there are two distinct psychic sources of attribution. When we evaluate others' quality of character by agentially admiring or disdaining them, we do so by way of attributing attitudes to a privileged subset of their psyche, their deep self. To the extent that these attitudes have two distinct psychic sources, so too does the deep self.

Both sources actually play a role in many, if not most, of our attitudes. I will argue for the Ecumenical Deep Self view, then, by prizing them apart, offering some resonant illustrations of attitudes we take to express the deep self (as revealed by our aretaic responses) that seem to have distinct, exclusive, psychic sources. It will be particularly important to illustrate attitudes drawing exclusively from the non-evaluative Humean strand, and I will offer seven such cases. I will then say more about the nature of character *traits*, a discussion which will buttress the case for the Ecumenical Deep Self theory by revealing how these traits also have the distinctive sources it identifies. That will be the extent of what is really just a burden-shifting argument for the Ecumenical Deep Self theory in

[13] What about omissions? To the extent that these are attributable to me, I think they would be still in virtue of their having some relation to my attitudes, where these could be my intentions but may also be things like my insufficient caring about the matter.

this chapter: The prima facie best explanation for the variety of cases I give will be that there are two distinct strands of the deep self, and the burden will now be on monists to explain away this appearance.[14]

Cares, Commitments, and Character

We are trying to capture that privileged subset of psychic elements representative of who the agent really is, and to do so we will lean on our aretaic responsibility responses. So what are the fitting triggers of such responses? Let us first consider two nonstarters. That some attitude or action is a product of a mere desire is not sufficient to trigger fitting aretaic responses, and this is because many desires are fleeting and/or unrepresentative of agential character. That sudden desire of the otherwise upstanding citizen to steal something may seem to come out of nowhere and usually does not represent who she really is in the least, and neither does the sudden desire of the mother to drown her bawling infant in the bathtub (for the first sort of example, see Lippert-Rasmussen 2003, 371–3; for the second, see Watson 2004, 19).[15] Neither desire properly triggers disdain (or admiration!) for the agent. And of course unrepresentative desires do not just have to be fleeting; they may be persisting as well, as in Watson's example of someone who thinks his persistent sexual desires are of the devil, and so alien to him (without, let us suppose, his minding them or having any disdainful responses to himself for having them) (Watson 2004, 19).

The Platonic advocates are sometimes taken to locate the deep self in our *specific* evaluative judgments, but this cannot be right either, as these too may not express who we are in a way that grounds fitting agential admiration or disdain. The most familiar examples are evaluative judgments made when drunk or high. Some of these may express who one is, of course, but many will not, insofar as the drink or drug may cause one to take seriously funky evaluative standards one would ordinarily reject out of hand, or cause one blurrily to see worth where there is none. But one might also make *whimsical* evaluative judgments, where one's judgment is spur-of-the-moment, uninformed, and completely out of character. These examples are perhaps what motivated Watson to locate his equivalent of the deep self in the agent's valuational *system*, "that set of considerations which, when combined with his factual beliefs (and probability estimates), yields" an

[14] Those who are interested in the complete argument, wherein I engage in some scholarly exchanges in defending the pluralism of the Ecumenical Deep Self theory against competing explanations of the data, may consult Shoemaker Forthcoming-a.

[15] *Acting* on such attitudes would be a very different story, however.

agent's specific all-things-considered judgments (Watson 2004, 25). And the values constituting this system are "those principles and ends which [the agent]—in a cool and non-self-deceptive moment—articulates as definitive of the good, fulfilling, and defensible life" (Watson 2004, 25). These are one's evaluative *commitments*, then, and together they make up one's evaluative *stance*, which may not necessarily be expressed in every concrete evaluative judgment.

Many attitudes do have their source in our commitments, and when they do, they seem the fitting triggers of aretaic responses. After all, they reveal, as I have already noted, what one *stands for* (cf., Watson 2004, 271), and if what one stands for does not generate fitting admiration or disdain, what could? But it also seems that many representative attitudes have their ultimate source in our *cares*, where these, recall, are dispositions to respond emotionally in sync with the fortunes of the cared-for object. Where one is disposed in this way, agential admiration and disdain also seem fitting in light of the attitudes expressed by it. We often admire and disdain people on the basis of their emotional investments. What you care about reveals something of who you are. Think also here of the many character traits Aristotle discussed whose virtuous means consist in feeling appropriate degrees of emotions such as fear, anger, and shame (Aristotle/Irwin 1985, 71–115 [1115a20-1128b35]). Roaring anger, say, is inappropriate in response to an accidental bump on a busy sidewalk, and people who are disposed to respond in this way are disdainable, expressing the vice of "a kind of irascibility" (Aristotle/Irwin 1985, 105 [1126a1]).

So cares and commitments both seem to express character. These are both forms of *mattering*.[16] And they look to be the fitting targets of the aretaic sentiments. But do they capture the authenticity and authority features we need to account for in a deep self theory of attributability? In other words, are cares and commitments the *ultimate* sources of attributable attitudes? Further, are they *distinctive* forms of mattering, or do they together still fall under a monistic rubric? In the remainder of this section, I attempt to answer both questions through a series of what I hope will be resonant illustrations.

I have already noted how the requisite authority is located within the Platonic strand. When my intention to Φ depends on my general evaluative stance about the worth of Φ-ing (or about the worth of Φ-like things), that intention surely has

[16] Susan Wolf uses similar language. In talking about Watson's view, she agrees with him that values carve out the realm of the deep self, but she amends his view to say that values may also include some of what I am calling cares. The deep self, for her, thus includes "all and only those things which *matter* to a person in some positive way" (Wolf 1990, 31; emphasis in original). Because I think "hates" belong under this rubric as well, however, what I think of as cares is not restricted to the positive.

the imprimatur of my deep self; it has been officially *authorized*—given my worthiness stamp of approval—by my general evaluative stance. But even in Watsonian "perverse cases," self-expressing authorization may be in place. When I decide to play golf rather than work, even after having judged work to be all-things-considered best, it could be that I have nevertheless judged golfing to have some value—it's fun!—even though it does not have the *most* value. This could even be true when the evaluative commitment on which my will and specific judgment depends is that the targeted action has very *little* positive worth in comparison to relevant alternatives. As long as my will or other attitudes depend on any of my evaluative commitments, period (where my stance toward the object is that it has at least some worth), it clearly seems attributable to *me*, representative of who I really am. I am, after all, an *evaluator*, and those attitudes expressing my genuine evaluative commitments are mine. This point should be fairly uncontroversial.[17]

But is my deep self, who I really am, anything *more* or *different* than an evaluator? Those from the Platonic strand of attributability-theorizing think not. But we have already seen one case—the homosexual desires case—wherein the attitudes expressing the agent's authentic self seem to be distinctively different from, even contrary to, the attitudes dependent on the agent's evaluative stance. These are *authentic* desires, something evaluational theories of the deep self have a very difficult time with. But are there any other examples wherein one's attributable attitude expresses something other than, or contrary to, one's evaluative stance? What follows are several such examples, intended to garner their plausibility from our aretaic intuitions. These are cases where only cares are the source of the attitude in question. My strategy is to get us to ask ourselves in each case, "Would the agent in question be the appropriate object of some form of admiration or disdain for the attitudes in question?" To the extent that the answer is "yes," then the response will be one to the agent in virtue of the attitude's being perceived as an expression of the agent's character—what I am construing as his or her deep self—and so an attitude thought to be attributable to the agent thereby. And if the distinctive and ultimate source of the attitude is the agent's cares but *not* commitments, we will have in place a strong presumptive

[17] It also, plausibly, makes some nonperverse akratic actions—acting against one's better judgment in perhaps a regretful way—attributable to one, just as long as the action did express some aspect of one's evaluative stance, i.e., one at least judged it to have *some* worth, even if it didn't have as much worth as the alternative. In cases where one judged there to be *no* worth to the akratically performed action, its intention could still be attributable to one, however, where one at least cared about its related object. In other words, the Ecumenical Deep Self theory will have the resources to explain attributable akrasia of both sorts, whereas monistic theories of either strand will have difficulty doing so.

case in favor of ecumenical pluralism about the deep self, one that at least shifts the burden onto the deep self monists.

Start with a filled-in version of the mother case above. Suppose as she bathes her child and the desire to drown him arises, she lingers over it, entertaining the image of her doing so again and again, and subsequently she becomes ashamed for having the desire. She may well judge that this desire was for something of absolutely no worth, but it might have revealed that there is nevertheless a part of her that hates her child, *against all reason*. Such a desire might then say something about her insofar as it expresses that hatred (which is a care), and so in virtue of that expression her shame, her self-disdain, might well be appropriate, as might our disdain for her.

Second, consider a case Frankfurt briefly mentions: revenge (Frankfurt 2002, 89; this is a response to Bratman 2002, 74–8). When I am moved by a vengeful attitude to harm you after you have harmed me, justification or evaluation of either that desire or the hate that stokes it may, and often is, moot. Typically, of course, revenge is unthinking, motivated directly by an anger that is insensitive to evaluative judgment. But its desire may also be nursed and dished out cold. I may thus have plenty of time as I am plotting my revenge to judge that my appetite for it is very bad, that it will lead to terrible consequences for everyone involved, especially me. Indeed, this may give me some pause. Nevertheless, I may still care deeply about producing your destruction, values be damned. I may know full well that it is a terrible idea but still want more than anything to do it just because I hate you so much. If so, I would seem to be a disdainful person in virtue of this destructive attitude's (and dependent action's) being attributable to me.

A third case in which evaluation-independent cares seem to generate fitting aretaic responses is volitional necessity (Frankfurt 1988, 86). These are cases in which one cannot *bring oneself* to do other than what one does, as it would betray a fundamental (and involuntarily generated and maintained) care. When I lived in a rather shoddy apartment after graduate school, I discovered a mouse behind the refrigerator. I first tried shooing it out the back door, but it was limping horribly; a leg had obviously been broken. I realized then that I should put it out of its misery. But as I held a baseball bat over my head, ready to swing down, I discovered that I couldn't bring myself to finish it off. I felt foolish and cowardly to some extent, but I also realized that going ahead with it would be deeply upsetting, as it would betray some essential part of me: I would not be able to live with myself were I to kill the mouse, as its being alive *mattered* to me in a way I didn't expect or couldn't have predicted. Of course, my eventually nudging it out to the backyard just prolonged its misery, surely, and I continued to judge that sparing its life was the wrong thing to do, indeed, the noncompassionate thing to do (so I regretted doing it). Still, this was not akrasia, I think, or Watsonian "perversity;" it was volitional necessity, involving a will structured by an involuntarily generated and maintained care, a care operative independently of my evaluative stance. In telling this story to others, some people have responded with admiration to my expressed attitude, and others have responded with disdain. In either case, though, there seems to be no question that some aretaic response or other would be fitting, as the attitude in question expressed some feature of my character, and so seems attributable to *me* thereby.

Fourth, consider cases of so-called "moral dumbfounding" (see Haidt 2001). Entertain for a moment, if possible, the image of your eating a human corpse, or having sex with a dead chicken you then fry up and eat. You may well be utterly convinced that there is nothing immoral, imprudent, or generally disvaluable about doing so. Nevertheless, I strongly suspect that such evaluative judgments will be quite irrelevant to the structuring of your will or your attitudes about doing so. In considering these cases myself, it does not feel as if my aversion shapes my will by providing me with a *reason* to act either (or is something I decide to treat as a reason). It is simply the direct source of my motivation. Our overwhelming aversion to such activities speaks directly and loudly for us![18] When it does, we may be the appropriate object of agential admiration or disdain, but in either case such aretaic responses attribute the attitudes in question to our characters.

Fifth, consider an artist and philosopher who straightforwardly cares nothing for justification. He is not a wanton, someone who does not think or care about who he is or what he does; it is rather the opposite: he has discovered that he cares about being the type of person who lives beyond the realm of justification (and not because he judges this to be a good way to live!). Call him Friedrich Gauguin. Perhaps, even, when he judges one alternative to be the best for him, he finds himself with a perverse desire to do the very opposite, a desire whose satisfaction genuinely *matters* to him. We may disdain him or admire him, but in either case this perverse desire is surely attributable to him (as are its dependent actions), for it reflects the very type of person he most deeply cares about being, namely, a kind of morally transcendent gadfly (or so he thinks).

Sixth, consider what it is sometimes like to become and remain a fan of a sports team. Suppose that I move to New Orleans, and while I enjoy watching football,

[18] Jacobson 2012 argues that people in the dumbfounding cases may well have reasons for their reactions that they just can't articulate. I agree, but as Jacobson also notes, this possibility is compatible with people not having any reasons for their reactions at all. My point here is that the absence of such reasons wouldn't at all imply the absence of attributability for subsequently formed volitional structures.

I do not have any particular team loyalties. As I walk around the town on game days, though, I feel the excitement in the air when the New Orleans Saints play, and after watching a few games with true fans, I start to feel the excitement on game day myself. I find myself rooting harder and harder for them. I start to follow their trades and injury reports. I become elated at their victories and dejected by their defeats. I have become a true fan, and various attitudes expressing my fandom will be attributable to me, without my at any point judging that the Saints were good or that these attitudes of mine were worth having; indeed, they often distract me from other things I ought to be doing. Of course, now that I care, my caring may generate prima facie reasons about whose worth I need to make judgments: When invited by some know-nothing to go to the opera with him on a Saints game day, I will judge that it would be a terrible idea to miss the game, and so I will refuse the invitation, or when I move to a different football-crazed city, I may judge it best to put reminders of the Saints all around my house and pay to subscribe to their TV game feeds in order to preserve the care I have for them. True enough, all of these later attitudes may have their source in my evaluative stance. But these evaluations themselves are all *ultimately* grounded in my judgment-independent care about the Saints, the care that set my touchstone for (football) value in the first place. Fandom is, for the most part, just nonrational (some might say *ir*rational).

Seventh, consider cases of love, in particular, parental love. Were my child to become a serial killer, for instance, I may settle on the evaluative assessment that he is a worthless human being. And yet when I read of his upcoming execution, I may well up with tears, or fall into a depression. "It turns out I still care about him," I may say. "There are no reasons to do so—he's worthless—but it still matters to me what happens to him." This sort of comment is also heard sometimes about people's exes: "Yes, I know he treated me in a horrible fashion and wrecked my life, but I still care about him (against all reason!)." Again, we may admire these agents ("What a devoted mother!") or disdain them ("She's so weak in still loving her ex!"), but in either case our aretaic responses are to the character traits of the targeted agents that these attitudes are taken to express, attitudes that nevertheless have an evaluation-independent source.

There are thus many attitudes to which we would tend to respond with agential admiration or disdain that certainly look as if they have no source in any evaluative commitments. These attitudes seem to be just as attributable to agential characters as those flowing from evaluative commitments, though. While the attitudes produced may not be actively *authorized* by these agents' evaluative stances, they are nevertheless *authentic* expressions of who these agents are, insofar as they clearly express what they care about. Cares are thus distinct from commitments. To the extent that the deep self is about who these agents really are and what we admire or disdain them for, and these things may be a function of *either* psychic source, an ecumenical pluralism about the deep self should start to seem quite plausible.

The Argument from Character Traits

Leaning on our sentimental aretaic responses has given us strong prima facie reason to carve out the boundaries of the deep self at the boundaries of our cares and commitments. Together, these strands make up our character. But we are now in a position to see how attributability might generate *non*-aretaic responses as well, or even no responses at all, for the character traits we deem virtuous or vicious are only a subset of the larger set of our cares and commitments. Some of my attitudes, after all, will express cares or commitments that are simply neither excellences nor faults; rather, they may be either neutral or not among the kinds of agential features we think of in excellence/fault terms. Nevertheless, these attitudes will still be attributable to me.[19]

Agential admiration has as its fitting object character traits, evaluating them as excellent relative to some ideal.[20] But what precisely are character traits? Are they just cares and/or commitments? As it turns out, not usually. In this section, I will explain what I mean by introducing some ideas about the nature of character traits that will (a) be significant for several of our discussions about specific marginal cases in Part II, and (b) provide a last bit of additional support for the Ecumenical Deep Self theory.[21]

If there are multiple constituent parts of our deep selves, then there are obviously going to be conflicts and tensions between them (see Shoemaker Forthcoming-a for discussion). What I care about will sometimes be in tension with what I deem good. I take such tension to bolster the psychological plausibility of the Ecumenical Deep Self theory, though, for it makes a lot of sense to say in these kinds of cases that the agent is *torn*, as both sides of the tension reflect parts of who he or she really is. We have no reason to believe, in other words, that agents must be wholehearted.

[19] This point will thus illuminate Watson's claim (quoted earlier) that only "*many* of these [attributability] appraisals concern the agent's excellences and faults—or virtues and vices—as manifested in thought and action ..." (Watson 2004, 266; emphasis mine).

[20] So the *full* story of their fittingness requires a story about the correct ideals. I do not have such a story to tell here.

[21] Some of the material that follows draws from Shoemaker 2014a.

Here, though, I want to acknowledge and investigate what is much more often the case, namely that, due to the psychological pressure for integrity and the elimination of cognitive dissonance, there are typically *harmonious* relations among our cares and commitments. More importantly, cares and commitments often function to temper or bolster each other. In other words, caring for or being committed to something may manifest itself in a wide variety of attitudes and behaviors, but which ones are manifested is typically delimited by *other* cares and commitments in one's psychological network. To take an example, if the only thing I cared about were my wife, and there were no other psychological elements on which my volitional structure depended, then my behavior to protect her or advance her interests would know no bounds: I would constantly attend to her, fend off threats with spectacular violence if need be, do whatever was necessary (and I mean *whatever* was necessary) to advance her interests, and so forth. But as it happens, I am committed to many normative principles (both moral and nonmoral), I care about my own needs and desires, and I value other people. These other cares and commitments serve to restrict the wide variety of ways in which my caring for my wife is manifested. Losing these other cares, however, would correspondingly loosen those restrictions.

Call these tempering and bolstering groupings of cares and commitments our "care-commitment *clusters*." What I want to suggest is that, insofar as agential admiration and disdain typically target character traits, they are targeting such clusters. So courage might be thought of as (at least) a strong commitment to the worth of some cause, bolstered by a deep fear (care) for its loss or betrayal, but tempered by a care or commitment to preserving one's own life (so that one is not foolhardy) that is nevertheless somewhat weaker than it is in other agents. Alternatively, kindness might be thought of as caring about the well-being of a wide range of needy others, bolstered by a commitment to the worth of helping them, but tempered by a judgmental stance discriminating the worth of various levels of need (so that one is not responding in exactly the same way to broken nails as one does to broken legs). And it is not much of a stretch, I think, to see many of the rest of the psychological features we admire or disdain *qua* character traits as consisting in such clusters. On this way of talking, a person is admir*able* (fitting to admire) when her attitudes express certain care-commitment clusters in a way that approximates some characterological ideal.[22]

[22] I should at this point more directly address the issue of control: Is the formation of these care-commitment clusters under one's *control*, or *up to one*, in any relevant sense? Neither cares nor commitments, I think, are subject to direct, immediate voluntary control. To the extent that commitments are a function of one's assessments of various evaluative standards, though, they may be "up to one" in terms of one's having *rational* control over them, i.e., they are sensitive to judgment (at least in the ideally rational). But what about cares? Many of these are involuntarily

Returning to the Ecumenical Deep Self theory, then, the question is whether agential admiration evaluates only one or the other strands of a cluster—cares or commitments—as relevant. It does not. To see why, note first that occasionally we fittingly admire someone not for a particular care-commitment cluster, but for just one of her expressed psychic strands. But, importantly, these may be *either* her caring *or* her evaluative strands. We admire those who exhibit excellent evaluative stances, of course, but we certainly also admire those whose cares alone exceed certain standards, for example, those with exquisite emotional attunement. And just as we disdain those who consistently exhibit a nasty evaluative stance, so too we may disdain those with vicious cares, for example, those moved to joy at the suffering of others, even if they never act on it. But as I have suggested, most of our character traits—good and bad—are actually clusters of cares and commitments. Were the tempering or bolstering relation between the individual components of the cluster not in place or lost, the trait itself would not exist in these cases, often regardless of which strand it comes from. I may not count as kind, for example, if I am not emotionally moved by the plight of others, or if I lack any commitment to improving their well-being. It would make no sense, then, to say that when the trait does exist, only one of these components—cares or commitments—gets full credit, to say that one component alone is the fitting target of agential admiration (or disdain). The pluralism of the Ecumenical Deep Self theory, therefore, is buttressed by thinking about how both cares and commitments typically operate *together* in clusters—they *co*operate—in forming the character traits targeted by our aretaic responses.

Attributability as Responsibility

The positive, presumptive case for the Ecumenical Deep Self theory is now complete.[23] We can now include it, along with the other refinements made over the last several sections, in the final, official formulation of attributability:

formed, so to what extent could one have *any* type of control over them? Consider, though, the motivational impulse of agential admiration, which is to emulate the admired agent. How does one go about such things generally? Compare: how does one, as Pascal would require, come to believe God exists when one's passions resist? It is a matter of behavioral therapy. So one method is to start behaving *as if* the admired agent's cares were one's own, such that eventually one comes to care as that agent does. Sometimes more radical measures are needed. But we seem able to make such care-transformations occasionally, and so even if they are not subject to our immediate, direct voluntary control, there may be other respects in which they are "governable" or "up to us." I say more about control and its relevance to this project both in Chapter 3 and in the Conclusion.

[23] Again, the full argument depends on showing that this theory *better* accounts for the available data than rival theories, and that is what I attempt to do in Shoemaker Forthcoming-a.

Attributability: *One is an attributable agent just in case one is liable for being a fitting target of a subset of responsibility responses to one—organized around the paradigm sentimental syndrome pair of agential admiration/disdain—in virtue of one's quality of character. To have quality of character, an agent must have cares, commitments, or care-commitments clusters (a deep self) that are expressed in the agent's attitudes. An agent is attributability-responsible for any specific attitude (volitional or non-volitional) just in case it expresses the agent's deep self, that is, just in case it is causally dependent on, and its content is harmonious with, at least one of the agent's cares, commitments, or care-commitment clusters.*

This pluralistic approach has great explanatory power, accounting for all of the phenomena and puzzles of attributability that motivated us. Specially, it explains (a) why some attitudes of the compulsive and obsessive are not attributable to them (given that they do not express their actual cares or commitments), (b) the way in which we persons are distinctive practical agents (insofar as we *have* cares and commitments, which require some sophisticated psychological machinery), (c) how there can be nonpathological, non-attributable out-of-character attitudes and actions (e.g., whims),[24] (d) the variety of cases in which attitudes are attributable to agents without having any source in evaluation, and (e) the source of the stalemate between exclusively Humean and Platonic theories of attributability, along with its dissolution. If we take *both* the Humean and Platonic strands as constituting our deep selves, we can sift out the psychic junk while also accounting for the variety of attitudes—sometimes in significant tension with one another—expressing our agential voices in the world.

I am putting forward attributability as a type of *responsibility*. Our assessments of the attributability of various attitudes have been a function of our tendency to respond to their agents with variations on agential admiration or disdain, the characteristic aretaic responses. These are the types of emotional responses that persist toward many marginal agents, even when other types of emotional responsibility responses no longer seem fitting (and so they are a major source of our ambivalence). Focusing on agential admiration, I argued that it is a sentiment, and so is a pan-cultural form of evaluating quality of agential character as excellent, independently of judgment. To the extent that it is a paradigm type of *responsibility* response, as it clearly seems to be, then what its fitting deployment carves out—attributability—is indeed a type of responsibility. Attributable agents are then those *capable* of having cares or commitments, and of having those cares or commitments expressed in attitudes and actions, so that

[24] Very importantly, these attitudes and actions may still ground negative responses on other types of responsibility, as we will see that they in fact do.

aretaic responses may be fitting to them and aretaic predications may be true of them. To have cares or commitments, one must be capable of having a wide range of emotions (and the ability to recognize up-or-down fortunes in cared-for objects) or be capable of taking an evaluative stand, that is, adopting "principles and ends... which [one]... articulates as definitive of the good, fulfilling, and defensible life" (Watson 2004, 25).

Now typically our fitting aretaic responses to manifestations of this type of responsibility are triggered in light of a *pattern* of attributable attitudes. In other words, when I fittingly admire you I am typically evaluating as good some care-commitment cluster—a character trait—I perceive to be regularly expressed in your attitudes (and dependent actions). Of course, I may not need a pattern to evaluate your character as such: one extraordinarily kind act or attitudinal display may be sufficient for fitting admiration, just as one extraordinarily stingy, cowardly, or cruel act may be sufficient for fitting disdain. But in these cases my response is really just a shorthand reference to a presumed pattern: someone who is extraordinarily cruel in one instance, say, can be expected to display cruel attitudes in many such instances.[25] And interestingly, there are many aretaic characteristics that are a function *only* of a certain pattern. Think, for instance, of someone who is a ditherer, or flighty, or undependable. No single attributable attitude will be sufficient to reveal such qualities of character at any given time; these are revealed only diachronically.[26] Nevertheless, what *makes* an attitude attributable to an agent is just that it expresses the agent's deep self, whether or not we recognize it as such.

[25] Couldn't one behave shoddily just *in the moment*, such that the shoddy conduct is attributable to one even though it is out of character? Here is one place in which my view of attributability comes apart from Watson's, who seems to allow something like this possibility (Watson 2004, 265, and Michael McKenna affirms this possibility as well in private correspondence). I deny that such conduct is attributable, at least in the robust stand-alone sense I defend. If the conduct reflects neither the cares nor commitments of the agent, then it simply does not generate fitting agential admiration or disdain. But never fear! This sort of conduct will certainly be captured by either/both of answerability and accountability, so there will be plenty of blame that will fittingly attach to it. In addition, there is a thin sense of attributability that surely applies here as well: in order for us to be responsible on any of the three types, the action or attitude for which we are responsible must at least be ours in the sense of its depending on *some* element of our psychic system (e.g., an intention), as opposed to someone else's (see Shoemaker 2009). So I can at least say that the conduct of the person who performs a shoddy action out of character is still something *he* performed (as opposed to someone else), as it at least depended on an intention to do so from within his psychic system.

[26] I am aware of the Situationist challenge to the existence of global character traits, but my arguments and position are unaffected by it. I am merely trying to give an account of the fittingness conditions of various character-based attributions, not an account of whether any individual responses *are* actually fitting, i.e., of whether there are in fact any global traits which these responses fit.

There remain two objections we need to consider against the proposal that attributability is a type of responsibility, both of which come from Susan Wolf.[27] First, people may lack responsibility for the deep selves they happen to have. This would be true of the insane, those subject to thoroughgoing psychological conditioning, and those from severely deprived or traumatic childhoods (Wolf 1990, 37). Attributability is simply about one's attitudinal *structure*, though, asking simply, "Do one's attitudes express one's deep self?" This does not seem enough for responsibility, then. What we need in addition to attributability, Wolf argued, is that deep selves have the proper *orientation* to the normative world, that is, they must have normative competence. The psychotic, for example, cannot correct himself in light of the values there are, and so he cannot yet be responsible, even if his attitudes meet the conditions for attributability (Wolf 1987).

I allow for now that normative competence might be necessary for being *accountable* for one's actions (although this discussion will have to wait until Chapter 3). But what I think has been made clear throughout the Introduction and this first chapter is that there is at least one responsibility sentiment, as well as a host of associated responsibility emotions, that responds simply to attributability as given, a type of responsibility which does not require normative competence. The trigger for these (fitting) responses *just is* the agent's expressed attitudinal structure, which is solely about the internal relation between the agent's attitudes and her deep self: "Does this attitude speak for her," we ask, "and what does it say about her?" True enough, some character assessments—courage, for one—may require more robust agential capacities like normative competence: one might have to be able to distinguish good causes from bad in order to count as courageous. But the fittingness of agential admiration and disdain does not require it for most others: one may be a disdainable mafia enforcer even if that is the only life one has known; one may be an admirable charity worker even if one has no understanding as such about the nature of kindness or generosity.

But this sort of response leads directly to Wolf's second objection, which is that attributing an action to a deep self seems to involve nothing more than attributing a bad (or good) act to a bad (or good) act-maker. This is primarily just to hold the agent *causally* responsible for an event that, depending on our

[27] A bit of the material that follows is drawn from Shoemaker 2011a, 504–11. I should point out that it is not so clear that Wolf any longer holds these views. See her "Responsibility, Moral and Otherwise," unpublished manuscript, for what looks to be a new view about the depth and importance of attributability for responsibility of all kinds.

interests, has positive or negative value. "But," according to Wolf, "when we hold an individual morally responsible for some event, we are doing more than identifying her particularly crucial role in the causal series that brings about the event in question" (Wolf 1990, 40–1). Instead, we are holding *her* responsible, "judging the moral quality of the individual herself in some more focused, noninstrumental, and seemingly more serious way" (Wolf 1990, 41). This is *deep responsibility*, and insofar as it is what genuine *moral* responsibility must be about, attributability alone is alleged to be an insufficient account of it.

I take Gary Watson's response to this worry to be on the right track. On his view of attributability, to make the relevant assessment of someone is to attribute an action, say, to some character trait—good or bad—in the agent. So if I risk my life in saving someone, that action is traceable to my character: *I* am admirable. My action was expressive of my ends and values, and insofar as *that* is the target of others' attributive evaluations, it is surely sufficiently deep: "To adopt an end, to commit oneself to a conception of value in this way, is a way of taking responsibility," for it is an expression of one's *practical* identity, and as such it has "ethical depth in an obvious sense" (Watson 2004, 271).

I have presented a more inclusive construal of attributability than this, though, one that identifies the deep self not only with one's evaluative stance, as Watson would have it, but also with one's purely emotional dispositions (cares). Obviously, I think these latter express one's practical identity too, for they may also structure one's attitudes via desires for the defense of what *matters* independently of one's evaluative stance. And when it comes to our caring about other agents' practical identities, we do not restrict our responses merely to the volitional structures whose source is in their evaluative commitments; it also matters to us when others have aspects of their character shaped exclusively by their cares. In both sorts of case, then, we view agents' practical identities as being expressed, and here Watson's point remains sharp: attributability alone has ethical depth in an obvious sense.

Of course, one might agree that attributability has ethical depth insofar as it involves a form of deep moral *appraisal* without yet agreeing that it is a type of *responsibility*.[28] Whether the dispute here is merely terminological or substantive depends, of course, on the nature of responsibility. I have adopted a very wide construal of it, one according to which "praise" and "blame" are its worthy responses. So what are "praise" and "blame"? Without giving a definition,

[28] Thanks to Randy Clarke and Jeanette Kennett for pressing this line. Julia Driver also takes a position like this in her unpublished paper "Appraisability and Moral Agency in Hume's Account of Virtue."

which may not be possible, it at least seems clear to me that the sorts of responses we have discussed in this chapter—agential admiration and disdain, contempt, esteem, and so forth—count as examples (see also Watson 2004, 266). There is, then, more than mere aretaic *predication* or *grading* going on here; there is also genuine praise or blame in the world of attributability, and that seems sufficient to render it a type of responsibility. In addition, these are the sorts of engaged emotional responses that deeply affect our interpersonal relations with the praised or blamed agent, and this fact also seems to indicate that we are in a responsibility zone.

Attributability is thus a type of responsibility. Is it a *distinctive*, stand-alone type of responsibility, however? It is, but in order to see why, we first have to get the other two types of responsibility laid out on the table. That is the task of the next two chapters.

2

Answerability

Recall from the Introduction the words of Naoki Higashida, an autistic teenager: "When I see I've made a mistake, my mind shuts down. I cry, I scream, I make a huge fuss, and I just can't think straight about anything anymore...." He is clearly holding himself responsible in some sense. Specifically, he is responding negatively, in however overwrought a manner, to a mistake pertaining in some way to his judgment: perhaps he judged something worth doing that in fact was not worth doing, or perhaps he did something impulsively without waiting for what would have been the different verdicts of his judgment. I think we would allow for the appropriateness of *some* degree of negative reaction to his poor exercises of judgment (even if it is clear that his own reaction is way over the top). In other words, as long as he can generally recognize and judge the worth of various pursuits, it does seem appropriate to respond negatively when he fails to do so properly.

But now consider the self-report of another person with autism, Wendy Lawson:

> There are days when just trying to make sense of the rules for social interaction is too difficult. It is especially so when we take into account that individuals often write their own rules! For example, it's fine to take your clothes off to have a bath, but only a model takes her clothes off for the photographer; or you can laugh at that story, even though it's about a fat lady, because it's a joke. (Lawson 2001, 98; quoted in de Vignemont and Frith 2008, 280)

Now suppose you are at a party at which a tipsy person is telling a very cruel story about an overweight party guest who is standing nearby, cringing and distraught. You become distraught as well, and then immediately become angry at the storyteller. Suppose, however, that the person next to you laughs loudly at the story. Presumably the scope of your anger will now widen to include the laugher as well. But now suppose you turn to see that it is Wendy Lawson laughing, and you know her back story. Your anger at her, it seems, will dissipate, or at least will be recognized as unfitting. She cannot recognize, you may presume, that this is not a joke, that instead of being funny, the story is wounding the overweight party guest, and that her own laughter is hurting that person too. Of course, once told this, Wendy is very likely to stop laughing and start regretting what she has done. Perhaps, for instance, she overlooked something important in the delivery of the story or the look on the party guest's face that could have revealed the relevant social cues. And to the extent that she had been able to avoid overlooking these things (given much practice with her mental rolodex), her regret may actually be quite appropriate.

Finally, consider again Skip, the successful psychopath, and recall his mother's plea to him: Why did he have to marry his unsuspecting fiancée, why did he have to do that to her? His chilling response—"We both know she'll never know what hit her"—tells us we are dealing with someone who seems almost alien. His mother's resignation in the face of his monstrosities, however, side-by-side with this last-ditch appeal to his reason, suggests her own ambivalence toward him, an ambivalence I suggest that many of us would share once we were fully familiar with him and his condition: there is no point to a certain range of responses to him, no point, for example, in railing at him with anger, indignation, or resentment, yet he is nevertheless capable of a kind of justificatory exchange that does seem as if certain of his normative failures warrant disappointment, disapproval, and even criticism.

In this chapter, I want to articulate the range of responses we tend to think still apply to Naoki, Wendy, and Skip (and other sorts of marginal agents), and then show how these responses enable us to identify or carve out the central range of a second type of responsibility, *answerability*. As suggested in the Introduction, answerability implicates quality of judgment, and its characteristic sentimental syndrome pair is something like regret and pride, although the wider emotional family here includes disapproval, disappointment, irritation, frustration, and shame, in negative cases, and approval, appreciation, and approbation, in positive cases. In getting clear about the nature of answerability, I will argue for why it calls on the same capacities and responses across both nonmoral and moral domains, as well as why it is distinct from attributability.

Regret

Let us remind ourselves of the general argumentative strategy of Part I. Motivated by our ambivalence in marginal cases, I have proposed to develop a *qualities* of will theory of responsibility by exploring the sentimental syndromes that take different qualities as their objects, syndromes around which many other emotional responses are organized. In Chapter 1, I aimed to investigate quality of character (as giving birth to attributability), and to do so I explored the sentimental syndromes constituting familiar versions of admiration and disdain. And in Chapter 3, I aim to investigate quality of regard (as giving birth to accountability), and to do so I will explore the sentimental syndromes constituting familiar versions of anger and gratitude. Now both of these sentimental pairs are third-personal, the kinds of responses we tend to have to other agents. But there is not really a distinctive third-personal sentimental pair evaluating quality of judgment, and this fact might seem to undermine my Strawsonian strategy of leaning on different sentiments to reveal or carve out the boundaries of different types of responsibility. Of course, we often do criticize or compliment judgment in others, but these responses do not necessarily implicate any emotions, let alone sentiments; good or bad judgment tends not to hit us in the gut the way good and bad character and regard do.[1] While we are often *disappointed* in others' judgments, fitting disappointment is not at all restricted to agents (my disappointment that the weather has ruined my picnic seems quite appropriate). And while fitting *disapproval* does seem restricted to agents, there is not much agreement on just what it is, including whether it is even an emotion. It sometimes lacks a characteristic motivational profile, after all, and some psychologists view it as a kind of moral judgment that itself *builds on* some antecedent emotional response or other.[2] And even if it were a pan-cultural emotional response, the range of agential features to which we tend to respond with disapproval cuts across all three qualities of will: we may disapprove of poor characters, judgments, and regard. Consequently, it will not help us to get a bead on the contours of and capacities for quality of judgment alone (although I will occasionally appeal to it in fairly uncontroversial contexts to buttress my first-personal approach).

We should not give up, however. Instead, I think there is a familiar sentimental syndrome pair that, at least in its central cases, distinctively evaluates quality of judgment in a way that will help us carve out our second type of responsibility, answerability. In its negative manifestation, it is roughly the emotional response Naoki Higashida has (in a wildly overblown fashion) to his own mistakes, and it is very familiar in our lives. The relevant syndrome is most closely aligned with our folk psychological concept of *regret*, about which there is some relevant psychological literature. Its positive analogue is a version of pride (cf., Mauro,

[1] My thanks to Jeanette Kennett for this way of putting it.

[2] See, e.g., the different accounts of moral disapproval in Huebner, Dwyer, and Hauser 2009 (4) vs. Greene and Haidt 2002 (519).

Sato, and Tucker 1992).[3] So while I build the story of attributability and accountability out of third-personal sentimental syndromes, I build the story of answerability out of a first-personal syndrome. This is primarily so I can tell the most resonant sentimental Strawsonian story, however, so I hope the disanalogy will not prove distracting or worrisome.

So what is the relevant syndrome? In the psychological literature, regret is most often taken to target poor decisions (Zeelenberg et al. 1998; Zeelenberg, et al. 2000; and Pieters and Zeelenberg 2005). It often tends to be a feeling closest to embarrassment, but in stronger manifestations it can have something like a cringing, sickening, flagellating feel. A typically associated (but not constitutive) thought is "If only I had done or decided otherwise." Its action tendency is typically to change one's practical deliberative policies, including a motivational impulse to improve one's future judgments about the worth of various practical reasons in order to make better decisions (Zeelenberg et al. 2000; Jacobson 2013).

We are seeking the syndrome we tend to have in response to various qualities of judgment, but the folk psychological construal of regret may still include too many objects for our purposes. After all, decisions just tend to settle uncertainty and issue in intentions, and this settling and issuing need not be the product of evaluative judgment (Mele 2000). True enough. But quality of judgment does not have to be restricted to *actual* judgments; rather, it could merely be about missing judgments, where one's decisions were at least *governable* by judgment. This is evident when we consider what to do in light of a regrettable decision in which evaluation was simply not involved, as in stealing something on a whim. To the extent that one has the relevant action tendency of regret—a motivational impulse to change one's deliberative policies in the future—surely one thing at the forefront of one's mind will be to *heed* one's judgment next time, or at least to get one's judgmental oversight mechanism involved, perhaps by avoiding scenarios in which it tends to be silenced or ignored.

Nevertheless, we do occasionally regret decisions, actions, or states of affairs (Williams 1981, 27) where our judgment and its role in self-governance was unimpeachable. These most often tend to be cases in which we made the most reasonable decision or did the most reasonable thing given our information at the time, yet things still went horribly awry. For example, I may sign the parental consent form to let my child go on a school trip to the natural history museum,

[3] Like shame, pride (as a folk psychological emotion category) ranges across multiple qualities of will, as well as nonresponsibility features (e.g., my pride in my devastating beauty), so my leaning on the "pridish" syndrome to investigate quality of judgment might conjure up connotations that will just confuse matters. That is another reason I focus primarily on regret.

but on the way her bus is struck by lightning and she dies.[4] I will very likely obsessively return to that fateful decision with anguished regret, despite the fact that I could not possibly have foreseen any reason to do otherwise at the time.

As discussed in Chapter 1, I have no desire to be an emotion-term chauvinist. Rather, I am interested in the sentimental *syndromes* that will best enable us to identify or carve out the various types of responsibility there are. What we need to focus on, then, are those syndromes that are most clearly *responsibility* responses, and here I think we are best served by focusing on the central range, or paradigm instances, of regret as we know it. So yes, perhaps I can correctly be said to regret that certain things happened (even when I had nothing to do with them), or that I did or decided to do certain things that wound up horribly, independently of my exquisite judgment. But these are not really responsibility responses on my part, as they track no *fault* of mine, a point revealed by the fact that none of these cases sensibly includes the relevant action tendency of the syndrome in its paradigm manifestations, namely, the motivational impulse to *improve* my judgmental policies. After all, in none of the cases just discussed could there be any intelligible reason to be motivated to change such policies, given that there was nothing wrong with them in the first place.

The difference between paradigm and nonparadigm cases of regret is also revealed by our third-person reactions (when there are such reactions). For one thing, we tend to counsel people away from their regret in the exquisite judgment or judgment-independent cases, as, again, these agents made no mistake, and so there is nothing they should beat themselves up for and nothing about themselves they need to change. And we also tend to suspend our disapproval of people in these circumstances, as any badness that occurred was not their fault, precisely given the judgment-independence of the results.

While the term "regret" may well properly apply to these other cases, then, I am simply announcing that I will be drawing from its most uncontroversial central range of cases—when it is clearly a responsibility response—as an emotional syndrome one tends to feel in response to poor (or ungoverning) judgment, and whose action tendency is judgmental policy change. This ought to be a deeply familiar syndrome. For clarity's sake, then, call it *agential regret*.[5]

[4] The example is Walter Sinnott-Armstrong's. Thanks also to Angela Smith for pressing a similar point.

[5] I do so fully aware of Bernard Williams' coinage of the term "agent-regret" to refer to a sentiment whose "constitutive thought" is "how much better it would have been had I done otherwise" (Williams 1981, 43). There are a few differences between Williams' sentiment and the one I am interested in. First, it is unclear if Williams intends to articulate a heretofore unrecognized but distinctive *emotion* or intends just to introduce a new emotion *term* to describe a familiar distinctive emotion. It often seems as if he is after the former. I have in mind only something like the

So is agential regret a sentiment? It is certainly pan-cultural (Landman 1987; Roberts 2003, 185). It also seems encapsulated from judgment, evincing stable recalcitrance, unthinking action, and the relevant deliberative role. We were just in the zone of recalcitrance above. As a specific example, consider the lorry (truck) driver in Bernard Williams' famous paper "Moral Luck" who regrets hitting a child through no fault of his (Williams 1981, 28).[6] The driver represents what he did as *mistaken*, as involving some sort of judgmental error: "Oh, I should have braked much sooner," he may moan, or "What a terrible idea it was to go down that street!" What we will do is counsel the driver not to feel that way: "It's not your fault," we will say, or "There is nothing you should have done differently." He may nevertheless continue to feel agential regret, *even after he has convinced himself of its irrationality.* "I'm really not at fault after all," he may come to judge, without his regret budging in the least. On the sentimentalist story I am telling, his evaluative judgment is now in conflict with his sentimental evaluation: he still *feels* he made a mistake, despite *judging* that he did not, and despite such regret being unfitting by his own lights (cf., Jacobson 2013).

Second, agential regret regularly motivates unthinking action. One can easily imagine the lorry driver running to the child's parents and apologizing profusely, despite his lack of fault. Or one might, in cases of *fitting* agential regret, act unthinkingly, and against one's evaluative judgments. Suppose after one terrible financial decision, I hand over all household financial decisions from then on to my spouse, who is much worse than I have ever been at such things. Terrible decisions often follow upon terrible decisions, precisely because one's evaluative judgments cannot gain a toehold in the face of the motivational power of agential regret.

Third, consider the nonjudgmental deliberative role of agential regret. Often when we are stumped about what we ought to do, where evaluative judgment yields indeterminate verdicts, we opt to project ourselves into alternative futures, post-decision, to test whether we can anticipate our future selves—unmolested by

latter, where I am just labeling a familiar sentimental *syndrome*. Second, a key difference is that Williams identifies his (new?) emotion by a constitutive thought. I, however, have in mind a sentimental syndrome independent of any constitutive judgment, identified primarily by its action tendency (to change one's judgmental policies). This allows for the possibility of recalcitrance of what I am calling agential regret, where the emotion lingers in the face of one's evaluation that one did everything right, whereas such recalcitrance is, implausibly, just conceptually impossible for Williams: if one does not have the constitutive judgment, for him, then what one feels cannot be agent-regret.

[6] It is a nice example, despite Williams' somewhat implausible discussion of it, given his problematically cognitivist readings of regret and agent-regret (see footnote 5). See Jacobson 2013 for insightful discussion.

the fever pitch of the current deliberation—regretting what we have decided. Indeed, this method of decision-making—testing for anticipatory regret—is well recognized and has come to be the subject of psychological and economic investigation (see, e.g., Zeelenberg 1998 and 2000). "Don't do something you'll regret," as the saying goes. We certainly view the quality of our judgment as, at least in part, a function of whether its generated decisions would be *regrettable*, the appropriate target of a sober sense of agential regret.

Agential regret, then, represents one's governing judgment for some decision or action as poor, and so to the extent that this representation is correct, agential regret is fitting; that is, the judgment is *regrettable*.[7] But of course we evaluate the quality of others' judgmental governance in these terms as well, where the response is also a responsibility assessment, so I think we can definitely learn something valuable about our second quality of will and its associated type of responsibility from thinking about regret and its object(s).

Purported Answerability

The syndrome of agential regret that we take to be a clear-cut responsibility response evaluates one's own quality of judgment as poor. But what precisely does quality of judgment have to do with responsibility? As discussed in the Introduction, many theorists take judgment to be the key to a type of responsibility labeled *answerability*. This is because they take responsibility to be about what is "up to us" as practical agents, and what is most fundamentally up to us, it is thought, is our practical judgment. In addition, they take it that holding others responsible implicates their judgment too, insofar as it assumes their ability to *answer* for, to defend, what they have done. What I will do in this section is construct the view of answerability on which these theorists generally agree. I will then test its adequacy in light of the sentimental syndrome I have articulated as our response to its poor exemplars. In the remainder of the chapter I will clarify and refine it in several ways and then show how it is distinct from attributability.

[7] Some may think that a fitting response to bad judgment is *anger*, even when it does not implicate disregard of any kind for others. Perhaps, for example, someone tends to respond with anger when she sees people reasoning poorly about how to advance their own prudential ends. (Thanks to Doug Portmore and Eddy Nahmias for presenting this sort of case.) For my own part, I think this response may be better termed "frustration," as we would tend to counsel people like this away from their anger with lines like "What is that to you?" Nevertheless, as I have said repeatedly, I do not want to be an emotion-term chauvinist, so I can allow that this might well be a form of anger. But I think most would agree that it is not the typical or central response to poor judgment in and of itself, nor is this its most central or paradigm object (which, I will argue in Chapter 3, is poor regard), so it is not the right sort of sentimental syndrome to focus on.

Antony Duff gives us the first pass: "To say that a person is responsible for some action or result is to say that he is answerable for the action or result, which is to say that he can properly be called to answer or to account for it" (Duff 2009a, 298).[8] Elsewhere, he writes that answerability is a two-stage process: "[W]e attribute an action or event to the person as its author, and request (or demand) that she answer for it . . . " (Duff 2009b, 980). Note here the very close connection between attribution and answerability. Duff also claims that answerability is necessary, but not sufficient, for *liability* (which for him amounts to being on the hook for sanctions or punishment), given that among one's answers might be legitimate justifications or excuses.

Although T. M. Scanlon uses the confusing (for our purposes) terminology of "responsibility as attributability" (Scanlon 1998, 248), what he really has in mind is answerability as well. In expanding on the nature of our responsibility for all and only our judgment-sensitive attitudes,[9] he says, "[W]e can in principle be called on to defend these attitudes with reasons and to modify them if an appropriate defense cannot be provided" (Scanlon 1998, 272). He refers to this sort of responsibility as *attributability* because it is in virtue of an agent's being answerable for them that attitudes are *the agent's* in the sense required for us to take them "as a basis of moral appraisal of that person" (Scanlon 1998, 248).

Angela Smith, in expanding on and defending a Scanlonian view of responsibility, is quite explicit about this connection between attributability and answerability:

> In order for something to be attributable to an agent for purposes of moral appraisal . . . , we must show that the agent is connected to that thing in a way that makes . . . answerability demands intelligible. . . . To say that I am "morally responsible for Φ" is just to say that I am "answerable" for Φ and therefore open to legitimate moral criticism if it should turn out that Φ violates any moral norms or expectations. (Smith 2012, 578)

In the final analysis, then, to say that an agent is answerable for something "is to say that that agent is open, in principle, to demands for justification regarding that thing" (Smith 2012, 577–8).

Gary Watson's account is in accord with those thus far stated.[10] He too draws a close connection between answerability and attributability: "Attributability . . . is

[8] Duff points to other statements of this view in Duff 2007, Ch. 1; Lucas 1993; and various works by Gary Watson, which I will detail shortly.

[9] Actions are a function of attitudes (e.g., intentions), and so the ultimate object of appropriate criticism for actions, according to Scanlon, is actually the attitudes motivating them.

[10] Interestingly, despite the fact that his collection of essays is entitled *Agency and Answerability*, Watson actually talks about answerability very little inside it, aside from a few mentions in the Introduction.

a kind of responsibility. In virtue of the capacities in question [those making the individual open to appraisal], the individual is an agent in a strong sense, an author of her conduct, and is in an important sense answerable for what she does" (Watson 2004, 263). He later suggests that this kind of responsibility requires adopting ends and committing oneself to values, so that one is thereby "ready to stand up for, to defend, to affirm, to *answer* for" (Watson 2004, 271, emphasis mine).

I take these theorists to be advancing some version of the following view, which I have put together both from their remarks quoted above and their additional statements elsewhere:

Purported Answerability: An agent is answerable for Φ just in case Φ is attributable to her in virtue of its reflecting her evaluative judgments in such a way that she may intelligibly be called on to defend or explain Φ by citing the reasons in favor of Φ she judged sufficient, where having no available successful defense would make her liable to criticism generally and, when the content of violated norms is moral, blame.

There are three features of *Purported Answerability* worth exploring in some detail, and they are features that all of the aforementioned answerability theorists incorporate to some extent. First, they take answerability to be the (only) proper account of attributability-as-responsibility. In other words, to the extent that something is attributable to an agent *for purposes of responsibility*, they think, the agent must be answerable for it. There may be other, wider, notions of attributability. Perhaps all of one's physiological and psychological features are "attributable" to one in this wider sense. But when it comes to practical or normative attributability, the type of attributability relevant to responsibility, an element is attributable to an agent only if she is answerable for it, and she is answerable for all and only those features reflective of her evaluative judgment. What this means is that answerability is really what most fundamentally matters with respect to responsibility.[11]

Second, it looks like the ultimate aim of establishing answerability is to establish the crucial necessary condition for *holding* people responsible in some

[11] Two points are worth noting about Watson. First, he explicitly advocates two faces (types, senses) of responsibility, so I just want to make clear that he does not think, as the other theorists cited do, that answerability is the *only* face of responsibility. But he nevertheless does think that answerability is really what's at issue when it comes to the attributability face, and so my second point is that, while this may seem a surprising interpretation of Watson, I don't see how to read him otherwise. He seems clearly to be saying that attributability is only a face of responsibility *in virtue of* its rendering one answerable, which thus makes answerability, by my lights, fundamental. Indeed, in the introduction to the collection he seems to agree: While in the article just cited he contrasts attributability with accountability, he now says (instead?) that "Responsibility is . . . bound up with the ideas of *answerability* and accountability" (Watson 2004, 8; emphasis mine).

way or other, what it is that crucially contributes to their being "liable to moral blame" (Duff 2009a, 298). In the nonmoral practical domain, if one is answerable for some norm violation and one's answer is somehow unsuccessful (non-exculpatory), one is then the appropriate object of criticism or disapproval. In the moral domain, if one is answerable for a moral violation and one's defense or explanation is unsuccessful, one is then ostensibly *blameworthy*. In other words, one's answers (explicit or implicit) may reveal something about one that licenses various sorts of distinctive negative responses and treatments, including moral blame.[12]

Finally, and relatedly, *Purported Answerability* implicates one's reasons, and reasons of a specific sort. The answerability demand may come in many forms: "Why did you do that?" or "What were you thinking?" or "How could you find that funny?" or "Why do you believe that?" and so forth. But in every case this demand is fishing for the reasons one took (or takes) to *justify* Φ, where Φ is what one did, thought, was amused by, believed, etc. For one to be ready to stand up for or defend oneself, one must be ready to relay the considerations that one took to make Φ *worthy* of doing, having, or believing, and so these theorists ultimately attach answerability explicitly and exclusively to agents' evaluative judgments. To relate this point to the first, then, insofar as these theorists advance answerability as the only proper account of attributability, they locate the deep self squarely and exclusively on the Platonic side of the map, identifying it solely within the evaluative strand. Consequently, all that it means to say that Φ is properly attributable to one for purposes of responsibility is just that Φ is connected in the right way to one's evaluative stance, itself allegedly a matter of which reasons one takes seriously (or which ones one does not), reasons which in principle could serve as one's answers to the answerability demand(s).[13]

In what follows, I will discuss all three of these features in detail, in reverse order. There are either unclarities, gaps, or other problems with each one. In addressing these problems, we will be developing a richer, more adequate account of answerability that is also quite distinct from attributability, and we will do so in part by paying close attention to the role and aim of our characteristic sentimental syndrome, agential regret.

[12] For Watson, this may merely consist in a judgment of blameworthiness (of an aretaic sort), but as he puts it, "judging blameworthy is virtually blaming" (Watson 2004, 278). In other words, to judge that someone's conduct was faulty is just to deploy "aretaic blame" (Watson 2004, 278). I think it must involve more than this, but I won't pursue that disagreement here.

[13] I am grateful to Angela Smith for discussion of both the general formulation of *Purported Answerability* and my remarks about it here.

Answerability Reasons

Answerability demands are very familiar to us, part and parcel of interactions between everyone from close friends to complete strangers. They are indeed demands for reasons, but what kind of reasons do they demand?[14]

There are two possibilities we can eliminate immediately. Suppose you demand to know why I kicked your sister last night, and my truthful response is, "I didn't do it." This is an answer to your demand, but it is obviously not of the right sort, for it reveals a complete lack of connection between me *qua* practical agent and the action, and so reveals no *thing* I could sensibly regret. Second, suppose I did kick your sister, but my response to your answerability demand is "Because various of my neurons fired in such a way that my leg swung out in an arc that made forceful contact with her." This sort of answer may give some kind of *explanation* of my action—explain what caused it, what physically moved my limbs—but it is also not an answer of the right sort to your demand, as it also lacks anything to which regret might sensibly latch on. What is missing is any reference to *justification*. You want to know what considerations in favor of kicking your sister I thought were worth acting on.

We are obviously, then, in the realm of Scanlonian judgment-sensitive attitudes.[15] These are the "class of attitudes for which reasons... can sensibly be asked for or offered," attitudes that would obtain or extinguish in the ideally rational in coordination with their judgments about the sufficiency of reasons in their support (Scanlon 1998, 20). These are also, as we saw in the previous section, the sorts of things we tend to regret, in virtue of their actually being a function of poor—or absent—judgment about the worth of various reasons. Let us then grant this way of talking about the reference to reasons in *Purported Answerability*: our answerability demands ("Why did you do that?" etc.) are addressed to agents with respect to their judgment-sensitive attitudes, and these demands request justifications for the relevant attitude(s). Nevertheless, I think we need to say more about the nature of these justifying reasons than has previously been said.

Is the mere fact that one had justifying reasons for some attitude sufficient for one to be answerable in a responsibility sense? It might well seem so, and it has to

[14] While sometimes the demand "Why did you do that?!" is really an accusation that the agent actually *didn't* have any (good) reasons for what she did, I am speaking in generalities about what is literally conveyed by this question, not what may be conversationally implied by it in certain contexts. Thanks to Matt Talbert and Michael McKenna for discussion.

[15] We are still in this realm even if the "answers" are "I felt like it," or "No reason," as one's intention was still, presumably, govern*able* by judgment, even if one didn't so govern it.

these previous answerability theorists. Were Johannes to seduce young and naïve Cordelia and then abandon her, the reasons he cites for his intentions—"She seemed ripe for the picking, I was bored, and I wanted to see if I could pull it off"—seem quite sufficient for him to count as answerable—and criticizable—for doing so. Nevertheless, I think more than this is needed for genuine answerability, given our fitting sentimental responses to quality of judgment.

To see what it is, suppose Johannes is actually a Seducetronix-3X, a humanoid built to seduce the young and naïve by a billionaire bent on corruption of the youth. Johannes-S3X is capable of recognizing and responding only to a very limited number of reasons, namely, facts about women's youth and naïveté, facts about his own boredom, facts about whether some possible seducing scenario would be a challenge to his skill set, and of course facts about what seducing technique would work best in various circumstances. When such facts are not present, he is simply unmoved to do anything. When they are present, he recognizes and responds to them. Is he an answerable agent? I cannot see that he is, even though he can cite the reasons that moved him. This is much like the case in which I cite the firing of my neurons in response to the answerability demand: while it is an explanation of sorts, it is still missing anything for agential regret (or its third-person analogues) to sensibly latch onto.

What may seem to be missing is any *judgment* on his part, so let us add it to the mix. Suppose that all and only the facts he judges worth acting on are the aforementioned facts about naïveté etc., and that whenever he becomes aware of such facts he also judges them reasons worth acting on. These are the *only* "reasonish" facts (facts appearing to be putative reasons) he sees, and so they become, by default, the only reasons worth acting on. One might say that his evaluative stance has been set exclusively to "seduce." Is he an answerable agent? Again, I do not think so, even though he now has the capacity to judge that the only reasons available to him are also valuable. Even were he capable of experiencing the emotion of agential regret, there could as of yet be no intelligible target for it. Why not? Agential regret views longingly the road not taken—"Arrgghhh, I should have done *that* instead of *this*!"—but there just are no untaken roads for Johannes-S3X.

What is really missing, then, is not judgment in and of itself, but any *quality* of judgment, which requires access to, and judgment among, a contrast class of reasons relative to which one's judgment may be better or worse. Johannes-S3X can answer the "Why did you Φ?" demand in a way that goes beyond mere explanation to justification. What he is incapable of answering, though, is the question, "Why did you Φ *instead of not-Φ*?" that is, why seduce instead of refrain, *given the range of countervailing reasons*? The reason he cannot answer this question is because he is incapable of *seeing* any countervailing "reasonish" facts. He is incapable of seeing facts about Cordelia's own interests and well-being as being even putative reasons against seducing her, and so they cannot operate for him as the sort of countervailing reasons that they would for us.[16] In responding to a demand for what I will call this "instead of" reason, one's answer will need to specify why one judged the reasons in favor of Φ *more* worthy than those in favor of not-Φ. But if one is genuinely incapable of seeing the reasons in favor of anything other than Φ, one is obviously incapable of including them in one's deliberations or judging as to their *relative* worth, and so, it would seem, one could not give a sufficiently robust answer to the answerability demand about one's doing Φ, even if one took oneself to have justifying reasons in favor of Φ.[17]

For Johannes-S3X, agential regret cannot gain a toehold, for there is nothing—no untaken road—for him to regret. To the extent that we take agential regret as our characteristic, guiding sentiment in this responsibility-zone, therefore, its fitting deployment seems to require a more robust capacity than has previously been recognized by the answerability theorists, namely, the capacity to recognize "instead of" reasons and make judgments about their relative worth, as our answerability demands go to why agents Φ *instead of not-Φ*.[18] As we shall see in Chapter 6, this capacity bears directly on the answerability of psychopaths, for they are perhaps real-life examples of Johannes-S3X.

We could thus explain children's burgeoning answerability by pointing to their burgeoning ability to recognize an increasing variety of "reasonish" facts. At a certain point in their development, for instance, they come to recognize that the

[16] Dale Dorsey articulates a somewhat similar account of what he calls *contrastive* reasons, which are reasons "to Φ *rather than* any other action Ψ one might perform" (Dorsey 2013, 192; emphasis in original). I am interested only in the class of *relevant* contrastive reasons, not the multitude of other possible courses of action. Relevance here is determined by context, relationship with the demander, and many other factors. We want to know of Johannes, why did he seduce her instead of just leaving her alone, rather than why he seduced her instead of driving to Walla Walla, or eating couscous, or rescuing a Shih Tzu.

[17] I explain why this implicit demand for "instead of" reasons as part of moral answerability preserves a crucial distinction between institutional (e.g., criminal) and non-institutional responsibility, given the law's inclusion of strict liability, in Shoemaker 2013b, 164–5.

[18] Some free-will theorists may balk at all my talk of "capacity" here without any further explication. The reader may simply assume her favorite understanding of "capacity." I take no stand on whether such a thing requires free will, however. Recall from the Introduction, Strawson's two aims in constructing a *Pure Quality of Will* theory: (1) to see if it could account for all we mean by "free will," "desert," "responsibility," etc., and (2) to use it to show that none of our responses and practices are thereby threatened by the theoretical truth of determinism. In this book, I am only attempting to develop and defend the first aim, not the second, and so I take no stand here on whether the answerability capacity (or either the attributability or accountability capacities) requires free will or what its status is if determinism is true.

fact that it will leave stains on the wall is actually a reason *against* drawing on it with a permanent marker. But then this suggests that we ourselves could be less than answerable to certain others. Imagine some superhumans (or aliens) who claim to recognize all sorts of "reasonish" facts we cannot. Perhaps the fact that it has an icon of a blue ribbon in addition to having a pop top is (yet another) reason not to consume cans of Pabst Blue Ribbon beer, but for a reason we simply cannot fathom (facts are "reasonish," when they are, for a reason, after all). When asked by these superhumans to defend why we drank some, and we respond, "Why, for its velvety taste and because Dennis Hopper demanded it in *Blue Velvet*," we are not answerable *to them* for drinking it if we are unable to recognize the relevant (to them) "instead of" reasons for not drinking it.[19]

Now of course incapacitation is quite different from capacitated failure. Many people respond single-mindedly only to the reasons in favor of Φ, without ever considering reasons for not-Φ, but that cannot mean they are not answerable when they do so. As long as they were *capable* of recognizing the purported "instead of" reasons, they may be answerable for failing to do so.[20] I may fittingly regret judgments about the relative worth of some reason over another *and* judgments about the worth of some reason where I failed even to consider the alternative(s). In the latter case, my answer to the answerability demand—"I didn't even think about that!"—is neither justification nor excuse. It is instead a concession that I had no *good* answer. It is regrettable nonetheless.

And this point provides a segue to our next section. Answerability is, at the end of the day, about agents' liability for evaluation of a certain sort. We do not make our answerability demands just to hear others' "instead of" reasons full stop, as in, "Oh, I see, so you killed him because you thought it would be more fun than helping him? Great, thanks for your quick reply!" Instead, hearing the reasons sets the stage for a response, one that evaluates the agent's level of "self-governance," in Scanlonian parlance (Scanlon 1998, 268–9). Our question now, therefore, is whether our fitting responses are the same across all answerability domains, or whether there is some subset of responses fitting only for *moral* answerability.

[19] Thanks to Mike Valdman for discussion and to Kenny McMichael for inspiration.

[20] This way of putting it may also reveal how to deal with answerability for negligence, as this would consist in one's having been capable of recognizing and judging as to the worth of some "instead of" reason, even if one didn't consider it at the time of action. But these are complicated cases, and I will not take them up here, both for lack of space and lack of understanding.

Moral and Nonmoral Answerability

Answerability obviously obtains across a wide variety of practical domains, including the athletic, the aesthetic, the epistemic, and the prudential.[21] Our sentimental syndrome clearly fits across all of them: We may (fittingly) regret a poor chess move, a terrible aesthetic choice, a hastily formed belief, or an imprudent decision. We also tend to have analogous third-person responses to others' poor judgments across all of these domains. I may disapprove of your poor chess move, your recent aesthetic choices in your artwork, your beliefs about climate change, or your decision to spend all your money on a Harley-Davidson. Such disapproval sometimes issues in criticism. Now most other answerability theorists would likely agree with these points. But where they draw a clear line is between other practical domains and *morality*, for moral answerability (at least in negative cases), they claim, implicates an additional range of responses, what many think of as *blaming* responses. When one has violated moral standards, in other words, and one is answerable for doing so, then one may *thereby* be the fitting target of emotions like resentment and indignation. But these are what I (and many others) take to be the *accountability* emotions. If the answerability theorists can explain why such responses are rightly included as well under their rubric, then accountability may not be a distinct type of responsibility after all.

In this section, I intend to advance a partial rejection of this view that I will complete in Chapter 3. I will begin by explaining why I think moral answerability *as such* does not render fitting any additional or different responses from non-moral answerability. Importantly, this will mean that, insofar as the so-called blaming emotions of resentment and indignation are not fitting for nonmoral answerability, they are also not fitting for moral answerability *as such*. This will lay the groundwork for a full defense of the distinction between answerability and accountability that I will develop in Chapter 3, once the nature of accountability has been laid bare.

To see why I think moral answerability as such is no different from nonmoral answerability, let us start with a very familiar nonmoral case:

American Idol (AI): Young, undiscovered singers are brought together to compete against one another, with the winner receiving a million dollars and a recording contract. A panel of judges, the most famous and trusted of which is Simon Cowell, evaluates the performances. On today's show, all the contestants have been given the assignment of singing the same song, Wilson Pickett's "Midnight Hour." Carrie sings a haunting rendition in a

[21] A tiny bit of the material in this section is drawn from Shoemaker 2013c.

minor key. Asked why she decided to do that, she responds, "I thought I would bring out a threatening side of the song, as from the perspective of a stalker who is going to wait till the midnight hour for his 'love' to come tumbling down." The judges are impressed, complimenting her thoughtful and aesthetically rich decision. Clay sings the song as a polka in a monotone while doing the chicken dance. Asked why he decided to do that, Clay responds, "The chicken dance is fun, and I didn't want any melody to distract from the catchy polka beat." Simon sharply criticizes Clay's decision: "You completely ignored the song's melody, which is its power, for a ridiculous reason, and your dancing is nothing anyone would ever want to pay to see. What a terrible decision!" Clay immediately regrets his decision, and only Carrie makes it to the next round.

Consider both the tenor and content of the judges' responses in this familiar scenario, as well as what they are responses to, precisely. Now consider the same issues in the following, less-familiar, scenario:

American Moral Idol (AMI): Contestants from around the country vie to participate in this reality show, in which the winner will be given a million dollars and a certificate as a new moral paragon (many bracelets will be sold once the season is over, asking, "What Would [the winner] Do?") Each week on the competition, contestants are presented with various moral scenarios, and then they must deliberate and announce what they have decided they ought to do. They are then assessed by three famous judges, the most curmudgeonly (but most trusted) of whom is Simon Blackburn. In this week's episode, contestants are given the following scenario:

At the park suppose you find a pair of crutches behind some bushes. There is a pawnshop across the street with a sign that reads, "Big money for used crutches!" You see a young woman whose leg is in a cast hobbling around the park. She occasionally shouts out "Has anyone seen my crutches?" followed by a description clearly identifying them as the very same ones that you see behind the bushes. What should you do?

The contestants are then asked to deliberate and answer, while suspenseful music plays in the background. The first contestant, Carrie, announces that she should give the found crutches to the young woman, and she is asked "Why?" She answers, "They are her crutches! Yes, I recognize that I could get 'big money' for selling them, but that would in essence be thievery, taking money that is not mine, and it would violate her rights to her property." The judges approve of, and compliment her for, her thoughtful judgment. Clay reveals, by contrast, that he thinks he should sell the crutches at the pawn shop. When asked "Why?" he answers, "I recognize that the crutches are not mine, but this woman needs to learn a life lesson, that she should keep a better eye on her belongings! That and the sweet money I would get together serve to outweigh her so-called property rights." The judges disapprove of Clay's judgment and Simon sharply criticizes him: "You gave way too much weight to the 'life lessons' and personal gain considerations. The fact that the crutches were the woman's property and that selling them violated her genuine rights, or at least expressed serious disrespect for her, should have been sufficient for you to return them to her. Indeed, don't you think she would have a serious complaint against you for selling them? Did you even take that into account? What a terrible decision!" Clay immediately regrets his decision, and only Carrie makes it to the next round.

Across this pair of cases—the first nonmoral, the second moral—the critics' positive and negative responses to the contestants' quality of judgment strike me as essentially identical in tenor and content. In *AMI*, Simon's moral criticism of Clay is a good one. But there is nothing distinctive about it *qua* criticism, that is, it seems not at all different from Simon's criticism of Clay's poor *artistic* judgment in *AI*. In both cases poor judgment is the target, relative to some judgmental ideal, and in both cases disapproval and criticism are the expected and, it seems to me, *fitting* third-person responses (to the extent that disapproval is an emotion), while agential regret is the expected and fitting first-person response. Clay's fitting agential regret in each version would also likely have the same feel and force. Finally—crucially—no further negative responses like resentment or indignation seem called for in *AMI*, even though it is clearly a case of poor moral judgment.[22]

In opposition, Scanlon insists that "moral criticism is a special case of . . . more general rational criticism," insofar as "[m]oral criticism claims that an agent has governed him- or herself in a manner that cannot be justified in the way morality requires, and it supports demands for acknowledgment of this fact, and for apology, or for justification or explanation" (Scanlon 1998, 272).[23] His view (one to which some of the other answerability-only theorists would sign on) is that quality of judgment *about moral reasons* is essentially no different from what I am calling quality of regard. On Scanlon's contractualist story, for example, to be in the realm of justification to others is just to be in the realm of regard for others, specifically, regard for their standing as rational co-deliberators in the scheme of selecting principles no one could reasonably reject. The relevant values giving rise to reasons in this realm are allegedly quite distinctive: they are moral values, which have their source in other people, in contrast with other values—artistic, athletic, epistemic, and (perhaps) prudential. Indeed, the fundamental moral value is said to be *mutual recognition*, and ignoring or discounting this value in one's practical judgments is just to ignore or discount other people, that is, to *disregard* them (Scanlon 1998, 162).

Until I have laid out my view of the nature of regard, I cannot fully defend my claim that answerability across all normative domains is roughly identical and

[22] I also doubt that moral disapproval and criticism in and of themselves are *blame*. Note, for instance, that the judges in *AMI* may sort of chuckle at the amazingly poor quality of Clay's moral judgment, while still of course evaluating him as *having had* poor judgment. But a critical response alone—even when expressed to the criticized agent—seems neither to presuppose nor to ground what we may think of as blame or blaming emotions, even if it stings. Many truths hurt too, after all, regardless of the domain in which they are uttered, but truth-telling (as such) just is not blame.

[23] For my more extended engagement with Scanlon's views on this matter, see Shoemaker 2013c, 110–11.

fittingly grounds just agential regret and its emotional family. This will be a central task of Chapter 3, but without going into any of the details just yet, I can at least offer a couple of teasers here. First, it is important to make explicit just how narrow the range of regard-based "moral" judgments is for Scanlon: the relevant sort of "moral" judgments are restricted just to *what we owe to each other*. But it is worth noting that there are plenty of examples where we tend to respond negatively to what seem to be poor judgments about moral reasons where the targeted agents do not in fact violate what we owe to each other. First, many people treat sexual perversity or other forms of impurity as moral violations (Haidt, Graham, and Joseph 2009).[24] Second, in many societies, violations of the demands of honor are treated as distinctly moral failures (Finkel, Harre, and Rodriguez Lopez 2001; Sommers 2012, esp. Ch. 2). Third, failures to do as well as one might at work, or failures to develop one's talents, also often count as morally criticizable. And finally, being a bad friend, or an uncaring parent, may not violate demands of what we owe to each other, but may still be morally criticizable (for these last two illustrations, see Scanlon 1998, 171–7). The range of judgment about "moral" reasons—and so the range of the "morally" criticizable—tends to range much more widely for many of us than the range of regard, which (for the Scanlonians) exclusively tracks what we owe to each other.

Nevertheless, let us focus on quality of judgment just in the cases of what we owe to each other and how it relates to quality of regard. Now criticizable judgment of this sort is taken to be a matter, for Scanlon, of poor *self-governance* (see, e.g., Scanlon 1998, 268–9, 272, 274). But one might plausibly think that what appropriately rouses my resentment of you for some injury is not a matter of how you governed yourself but, more fundamentally, how you viewed *me*. This suggests at least a possible conceptual wedge between moral judgment and regard. This wedge may be bolstered a bit, second, by thinking about the natural way we would have for putting the matter, namely, that our poor judgments about moral reasons *express* our disregard for one another. Third, one might plausibly wonder whether there could be some disregarding attitudes we have that are not judgment-sensitive. These might come, for example, from various of our nonrational cares, to draw from our discussion in Chapter 1. I will not here say what those might be. I merely want to plant some suggestive seeds for what will follow in Chapter 3.

[24] Indeed, some studies have found that emotions like disgust *moralize* sexual impurity. See, e.g., Horberg et al. 2009.

For now, though, I think at least a presumptive case has been made via *AMI* that there is a distinct family of responsibility responses—including resentment and indignation—that does not necessarily fit with poor quality of moral judgment as such. As it is, the only kinds of responses uncontroversially called for by answerability—members of the agential regret family—seem no different in tenor or content in the moral domain than they do in our many other nonmoral practical domains.

Given the refinements suggested by the past two sections, we can now replace *Purported Answerability* with a richer, more adequate formulation:

Answerability: One is an answerable agent just in case one is liable for being a fitting target of a subset of responsibility responses to one—organized around the paradigm sentimental syndrome pair of agential regret/pride—in virtue of one's quality of judgment. To have quality of judgment, an agent's attitudes must be generally governable by the agent's judgments about why they are more worthy than (some relevant) others, i.e., judgments about "instead of" reasons. An agent is answerable for some specific attitude or action just in case the agent could in principle cite his or her "instead of" reasons for having the attitude or performing the action.

Someone is an answerable agent generally, then—a member of the answerability community—to the extent that she is capable of having, not just judgment, but *quality* of judgment, which requires not just the capacity for self-governance but also the capacity for it in light of the relevant "instead of" reasons. One could, therefore, have various local blindnesses, that is, be able to recognize the "instead of" reasons only in some normative domains but not others. This would render one an answerable agent only within those former domains.

Answerability vs. Attributability

While I have offered some teasers about why answerability is distinct from accountability, I have yet to give a full characterization of accountability, so I cannot yet complete their distinctive stories. But I *have* given a full characterization of both answerability and attributability, so in this section I will show why these two types of responsibility are distinct. Recall that all of the advocates of answerability I discussed earlier view it as the complete and correct account of attributability. I disagree, of course. In this final section I will offer three reasons why.

The first simply repeats an argument presented in Chapter 1: answerability implicates only evaluative judgment, whereas there are many aretaically attributable attitudes that nevertheless express non-evaluatively grounded cares. That argument established the first important difference between attributability and answerability, namely, the former ranges more widely. Attributability is therefore not sufficient for answerability.

The second difference I mentioned only in passing in Chapter 1: There is an important difference between one's evaluative judgments and one's evaluative *commitments* (that is, one's evaluative stance) that is typically glossed by answerability theorists. That I may be called on to defend some specific judgment is quite different from whether I am committed to the defense of some general evaluative take on the world. This should be most obvious in out-of-character cases of poor judgment. Suppose that I go to a concert and afterwards, fired up by the music and the communal vibe, I hand over all my money to a stranger who I simply overhear talking about how broke he is. I soon realize that I am stuck there, unable to get a cab or even pay for public transportation. When I sheepishly call my wife to pick me up, she demands to know, "Why did you do that?" "I thought it was a good idea at the time," I say, "but I quickly realized how stupid it was." I am clearly answerable for my boneheaded decision, but it may not be attributable to me in the sense grounding fitting aretaic responses, as that latter sort of grand generosity is not a state to which I have *any* evaluative commitments and so my money-giving attitude on this day reflects nothing about who I really am. (Contrast me with the hippie who does these sorts of things regularly.) Now one might nevertheless want to insist that the bad decision was at least *governable* by my evaluative stance, and so still might reflect a kind of "flightiness" or "easily influenced by hippiedom" trait that is attributable to me, but this too may be inaccurate. Perhaps normally when I am in such circumstances I am unfazed by them, but today I was. At any rate, I think it makes perfect sense to talk about individual evaluative judgments for which I am answerable but that are nevertheless out of character and so not attributable to me. Attributability is therefore not necessary for answerability.

The third argument for distinguishing these two types of responsibility is drawn from considerations about ways in which we might be responsible for irrationality.[25] To see what I have in mind, consider Angela Smith's version of answerability, according to which one is answerable for Φ just in case Φ bears a rational connection to one's evaluative judgments (Smith 2005, 251). For her, irrationality with respect to one's attitudes involves "a direct inconsistency between the judgments I explicitly make and the judgments entailed by the attitude I in fact hold" (Smith 2005, 253). For example, when I aver that spiders are not dangerous yet I nonetheless fear them, Smith claims that my fear actually

[25] In the next three paragraphs, I borrow some argumentation and language from Shoemaker 2011b, 607–12.

implies that I do judge them to be dangerous, so my irrationality really consists in my simultaneously holding two contradictory judgments about the danger of spiders.[26] Consequently, "What makes the charge of 'irrationality' rather than 'nonrationality' appropriate in such cases . . . is precisely the fact that both of these conflicting evaluations seem to be correctly attributable to [me]" (Smith 2005, 255). I am, on this analysis, and in virtue of such an attribution, answerable for each.

Let us suppose for the moment that there are two conflicting evaluative judgments here and that I am indeed answerable for each. A question that immediately arises is whether I could be answerable *for my irrationality* on Smith's view. In other words, if my irrationality consists in the simultaneous presence within my psychology of the two conflicting attitudes, it is unclear how I could be answerable for this state of affairs, given that I make no judgment about the worth of *having such a conflict*; indeed, I judge to the contrary that such a conflict would be bad, that is, irrational. But now my irrationality itself looks like a psychic condition that bears no rational connection whatsoever to my evaluative judgments. Consequently, even if I am answerable for both conflicting judgments, I could not be answerable for my being irrational. But surely irrationality is criticizable, that is, I do seem to be answerable for my irrationality. So which is it?

Smith does want to hold that people are responsible—answerable—for their irrationality, and she also agrees that her view would have a hard time explaining how this could be true if answerability demands asked people to justify the *conflict* between their attitudes. But in responding to my worry she draws a distinction between two senses of "responsibility for irrationality." The first is the one I have suggested: responsibility for "a certain configuration" of the agent's psychic system (Smith 2012, 579). This is a sense she finds quite implausible, however, claiming that what we usually mean instead "is that an agent is responsible for holding each of two attitudes that, together, *make it the case that* she is guilty of irrationality. Her responsibility for her irrationality is, in effect, simply a consequence of her responsibility for the attitudes that together constitute her irrationality" (Smith 2005, 579–80; emphasis mine). By way of analogy, she discusses someone who is responsible for being a racist or for being selfish. This person's particular attitudes ground these descriptions, and there is

[26] When I originally discussed this example in Shoemaker 2011b (607), I mistakenly attributed to Smith the view that the case was of a phobia, so I also attributed to her a serious vagueness in exposition, given that phobics shouldn't be viewed as answerable. Smith has since pointed out that she had in mind simply an "ordinary case of irrationality" (Smith 2012, 579, fn. 7), and not a phobia.

not "some additional thing, over and above the attitudes that constitute her racism or her selfishness, that is potentially morally attributable to her and for which we can raise questions about moral responsibility" (Smith 2005, 580).

I completely agree that this is the right treatment of the racist and selfish person cases. But these examples are disanalogous with that of the irrational person as such, given that there may be nothing objectionable at all about any of his individual attitudes; indeed, it may *only* be the conflict between them that grounds negative appraisal. Suppose I explicitly aver the value of an uncluttered, minimalist home, but I continually go out and buy intricate and extravagant objets d'art that I use for decoration all over the home. On Smith's view, my actions entail my judgment of the worth of showy objets, and insofar as this judgment is in conflict with my explicitly averred judgment about the worth of minimalism, I am irrational. But unlike with the racist or the selfish person, there is nothing criticizable about *either* of my judgments in and of themselves; there is nothing wrong, other things equal, with minimally *or* intricately decorated homes.[27] Negative appraisal can only be grounded, then, by the *conflict*, a response to an overall psychic condition in which both judgments are affirmed. But again, this is a conflict about which (as Smith 2012 [579] admits) the irrational person will have no favorable evaluative judgments and so is a conflict for which the agent could not, in fact, be answerable.

I actually agree that such agents are not answerable for their irrationality: The fact of evaluative conflict within one's psychic system will (typically) not itself be governed (or governable) by one's judgment about the relative worth of the reasons in favor of being rational. But this way of formulating the condition of irrationality reveals how it can easily be accounted for on my pluralistic view, for even if such an agent is not answerable for her irrationality, it may still be *attributable* to her. Indeed, "being irrational" is an aretaic assessment, describing the character of the targeted agent, and as we are seeking patterns of actions and attitudes to provide evidence of the quality of such character, many diachronically conflicting judgments would fit right into the investigative mix. That such individual judgments are each attributable to the agent as well (perhaps reflecting tensions within the agent's evaluative stance), and that they conflict within some relevant time span (as conflicts between one's childhood judgments and one's contemporary judgments may not), together would reveal that the agent is

[27] Smith mentions this sort of response in a footnote (Smith 2012, 580, fn. 9), but she doesn't really respond to it, other than to suggest that perhaps there is still something criticizable about one or the other attitudes, even though we don't know which one. I think that is an implausible reply in a case like the one just given.

irrational, and the irrationality is precisely in virtue of the attributability of the *conflict* to her. But insofar as she has no favorable evaluative judgments *about this conflict*, the irrationality is attributable to her without her being answerable for it. What it simply expresses instead is the overall *state* of her commitment clusters, relative to each other.

Nevertheless, this treatment depends on the assumption I initially granted, that irrationality in such cases is a function of the agent's simultaneously holding two conflicting attitudes which entail two conflicting evaluative judgments. But of course I do not accept this assumption for all cases of irrationality. Instead, some cases are actually a matter of having *unfitting emotions*. Consider Williams' lorry driver case once more. I suggested earlier that his regret for hitting the child was unfitting: agential regret represents one's own judgmental governance as poor, but there was in fact nothing poor about the agent's governance in this case. As there is no reason to feel agential regret, yet he does, he is irrational. Nevertheless, suppose we attempted to counsel him away from his agential regret by pointing to his lack of fault, and he then immediately perked up and said, "Hey, you're right! I don't know why I was being so maudlin! Who's up for a beer?" We would think very poorly of him. He is quite *callous*, and this is expressed by his cheery attitude in the face of his playing a key role in a tragic causal chain. For most normal people, the agential regret would linger, and its recalcitrance would, by contrast with the sort of person just mentioned, be (agentially) *admirable*.[28] Such a person's irrationality (his unfitting regret) is attributable to him, then, in virtue of its expressing his caring about the life that was lost and his role in it (cf., Jacobson 2013, 114–15, who talks in terms of recalcitrant *guilt*, which would also make my point). Nevertheless, he is not answerable for his agential regret, as its sentimental nature is encapsulated from judgment.

For these reasons, answerability is a distinct type of responsibility from attributability. Attributability is about the volitional structures implicating quality of character. Answerability is about the justificatory source of specific attitudes and actions implicating quality of judgment with respect to the kinds of reasons relevant to and sufficient for those specific attitudes and actions. How both of these are distinct from our third type of responsibility, accountability, is one of the many tasks I take up in Chapter 3.

[28] Again, because Williams insists that his "agent-regret" has as its constitutive thought "how much better it would have been had I done otherwise," recalcitrance of this sort is just impossible.

3

Accountability

Love implies anger. The man who is angered by nothing cares about nothing.

—attributed to Edward Abbey

Neither set of emotional responses to attributability and answerability implicates *confrontation*. For example, while my agential admiration evaluates your quality of character as excellent, there is nothing about its fitting deployment per se that cries out for expression *to you*, just as my appropriate disapproval of the poor quality of your judgment does not cry out for expression to you. Of course, I *may* express these responses, but there is nothing about the having of the emotional responses in and of themselves that contains such a motivational impetus; rather, my being moved to say something critical about your judgment, say, depends on a host of additional factors, such as our relationship, my standing with respect to you, your own attitude toward what you have done, and so forth (see Smith 2007).

What I will argue, though, is that to be accountable for something is to be liable to being appropriately *held* to account for it, which is to be eligible for a range of fitting responsibility responses with a built-in confrontational element. To do so, I need to identify the relevant subset of responsibility responses and their fittingness conditions, reveal what they tend to respond to, discuss what their confrontational aim consists in, and show how this subset of responses helps us see the contours of a type of responsibility distinct from both attributability and answerability. Indeed, these are the tasks, in order, of the four sections of this chapter.

Freedom from Resentment

Our ambivalence to the marginal agents consists in our suspending one subset of responsibility responses to them without suspending others. In most marginal cases we have seen, what we tend to suspend is the subset of *angry* responses like resentment and indignation. These emotions seem unfitting for some people with autism, for instance, or for those in the throes of Alzheimer's dementia. More controversially, perhaps, angry responses have seemed to many to be unfitting for psychopaths or for those raised in poor formative circumstances. But in such cases many other responses still seem perfectly fitting. Agential admiration and disdain, for example, may often still feel appropriate, as may agential regret, pride, and disapproval. I have argued that these last two emotion families evaluate agents' quality of, respectively, character and judgment. The suspended—"angry"—family of responsibility emotions evaluates a distinct agential "will," namely, *regard*, and the type of responsibility built out of it is accountability.

We begin our investigation, then, with this final subset. But what shall be our characteristic sentiment? Many theorists, as we have seen, take our paradigm negative responsibility emotions to be *resentment* or *indignation*. They often start this way because that is what Strawson did. Now according to Strawson, these two emotions differ solely in terms of the respondent's relation to the offender: what I tend to feel toward you in response to your poor treatment of me is resentment, whereas what I tend to feel toward you in response to your poor treatment of someone else is indignation. Indignation is just "resentment on behalf of another, where one's own interest and dignity are not involved..." (Strawson 2003, 84). Consequently, in the discussion that follows, I will just talk in terms of resentment, for ease of expression, but I should be understood really to be talking about both.

I will not rely on resentment to reveal the contours of accountability, however, despite Strawson's own reliance on it. This is because the term, since Strawson's usage, has effectively been hijacked (or, in less inflammatory language, it has transmogrified). Most responsibility theorists nowadays take resentment to incorporate a constitutive *judgment* that what the offender did wronged the resenter and/or that the offender deserves blame or is responsible for having wronged the resenter.[1] As John Deigh notes, for leading theorists like "Wallace

[1] For just five examples, see, first, Wallace 1994, 245: "[R]esentment requires the belief that someone else has violated a demand to which I hold them." See, second, Darwall 2006, 67: "[R]esentment is felt as from the perspective of a wronged or injured individual.... To feel indignation toward someone is to feel that he is to blame for wrongful conduct and therefore appropriately held accountable for what he has done...." (I can read the second "feel" only as "judge," given all the high-powered content it imports.) And further, "We resent what we take to be violations against ourselves or those with whom we identify. If you resent someone's treading on your foot..., you feel as if he has violated a valid claim or demand...." See, third, McKenna 2012, 66: "As far as the narrow class of resentment, indignation, disapprobation, and guilt are concerned, I shall assume that they are at least partially demarcated from the wider class of both nonreactive and

and Darwall, the reactive attitudes have cognitive content that takes the form of a proposition, which necessarily makes them attitudes only rational beings can have" (Deigh 2011, 208). But this is just not what Strawson had in mind. Deigh puts it correctly: "On Strawson's account of resentment, the attitude is a natural response to the manifestation, in an action that harms one, of the actor's ill will or indifference toward one" (Deigh 2011, 212). Resentment, for Strawson, is merely an emotional response to one's discernment of ill will, but such a response requires no cognitive propositional content (e.g., "*that* he wronged me," or "*that* he is responsible") just as my aesthetic awe in response to perceiving a sunset requires no cognitive propositional content (e.g., "*that* it is beautiful"). Moreover, building in a constitutive judgment for resentment prevents it from being a *sentiment*, which, recall, is a pan-cultural emotion encapsulated from judgment. Strawson's aim, and so ours, was to build a story of *human* responsibility out of what he deemed the "moral sentiments," but requiring a judgment about the other agent's wrongdoing in the characteristic emotion unduly excludes the much wider range of what are surely human accountability responses too, from a (nonrational) child's sulking silent treatment to the flash of rage one may have in response to a blatant diss. And as I will detail below, it turns out we cannot construe the relevant natural response as necessarily being to a wronging, or even to a wrong, *even if* we do not judge it as such.

Nevertheless, because the term "resentment" has been successfully hijacked to refer to a reactive attitude requiring a constitutive judgment (about wronging, wrongness, desert, or responsibility), and in order to preserve our genuinely sentimentalist approach to responsibility while avoiding any terminological confusion, I will not refer to resentment in constructing the terms of accountability. Instead, I will lean on the emotion of which resentment and indignation are cognitively sharpened types, namely, *anger* (see, e.g., Morreall 1983; Russell and Fehr 1994; Hughes 1995; D'Arms and Jacobson 2003). Indeed, the sentimental syndrome I will construct is just what I think Strawson had in mind with his own talk of resentment.

reactive emotions by reference to the relevant propositional objects on which they depend.... In a case of moral indignation, for instance, as I see it, the relevant propositional object involves roughly the belief that an agent freely and knowingly performed a morally wrong act, and did so from a morally objectionable quality of will." See, fourth, Sommers 2012, 176: "We feel resentment when we believe that people have wronged us and deserve blame for doing so.... According to P.F. Strawson, the closely related feeling of indignation arises when we vicariously experience another's wrong and, again, believe that the perpetrator is morally responsible for the wrongdoing." Finally, see D'Arms and Jacobson 2003 (143), who call resentment a "cognitively sharpened" emotion, whose constitutive thought is that "one has... been... wronged."

Of course, anger might immediately be thought to capture too much, as we get angry at all sorts of things that are not responsible, let alone agents, including infants, computers, and the weather. And coming from the other direction, some creatures, such as babies and bears, clearly get angry too, even though their anger is not plausibly construed as a responsibility response. Here the object of the anger in all such cases may merely be goal-frustration. This aligns with some leading psychological treatments of anger. As Frijda (1986) puts it, the "action tendency of anger is interpreted as a tendency to regain control or freedom of action—generally to remove obstruction." I can grant all of this. As I have said all along, I am uninterested in emotion-term chauvinism. Instead, I merely want to identify the relevant sentimental *syndrome*, a triad of feeling, associated thought, and action tendency, that is our characteristic response to poor quality of regard. I will refer to this syndrome, then, as *agential* anger, and this kind of anger is a very familiar, even ancient, phenomenon:

> Anger may be defined as an impulse, accompanied by pain, to a conspicuous revenge for a conspicuous slight directed without justification towards what concerns oneself or towards what concerns one's friends. If this is a proper definition of anger, it must always be felt towards some particular individual.... [S]lighting is the actively entertained opinion of something as obviously of no importance... (Aristotle/Roberts 1954, 92/1378a-b)

The syndrome essentially consists in (a) feelings of heat and aggression (Eatough and Smith 2006), (b) thoughts about slights,[2] and (c) action tendencies to revenge or retribution (communicated as such). So yes, while we do (fittingly?) get angry at non-agential objects, the syndrome of *agential* anger is distinctly different, a difference most notably manifested in its action tendencies. It is simply unintelligible, for example, to be motivated to take revenge on the bad weather for its ruining your party.[3]

Aristotle's description of (agential) anger still resonates powerfully. It matters when we are slighted, when we are viewed as "obviously of no importance," when we are, in language Aristotle also uses, *disregarded* (Aristotle/Roberts 1954, 94/1379a).[4] But there is much here to explain and refine. We need to begin with agential anger's eligibility for sentimental status.

Of the emotions I have thus far advanced as candidates for the sentimentalist treatment, agential anger should be the least controversial. It is clearly a basic,

[2] Importantly, these are not constitutive judgments. They are instead *typically* associated thoughts.

[3] Interestingly, Aristotle himself categorized *agential* goal-frustration under the more inclusive category of slights: "Spite is another kind [of slight]; it is a thwarting another man's wishes, not to get something yourself but to prevent his getting it" (Aristotle/Roberts 1954, 93/1378b).

[4] Importantly, slighting treatment can range from minor to murderous.

pan-cultural emotion, if anything is,[5] and it meets the three conditions of being encapsulated from judgment, namely, being stably recalcitrant (think here of Plato's talk of our unruly spirit in *The Republic*), producing unthinking action (see any tavern in the U.S. late on a Saturday night), and serving as a phenomenological touchstone in moral deliberation (we often consult our "sense of slight" in deciding what to do, when judgment runs out, by vividly imagining ourselves into various circumstances to test whether we would feel anger). As a sentiment, then, agential anger evaluates its object as "angersome," as meriting anger. Aristotle may thus be construed as characterizing anger as "fitting" slights. In more Strawsonian language, the angersome consists in poor quality of *regard*.

One final word on resentment and indignation. To the extent that they are clearly forms of agential anger, we ought to be able to capture some important features of all their instances by talking in the more general terms of agential anger. But more importantly, even if we grant that resentment and indignation have a special relation to the blameworthy, say, the type of responsibility they implicate—negative accountability—may actually range more *widely* than the blameworthy.[6] In other words, agential anger's wider scope may be a virtue, as it may reveal the contours of a type of responsibility for which the blameworthy is only a part. Of course, this is a fairly bold claim, so one of my primary aims in the next section is to vindicate it.

Quality of Regard

Michael McKenna is the only recent theorist to have offered a helpful discussion of quality of will in terms of regard. He distinguishes between good will, ill will, and indifference, and he explicates quality of will generally, one may recall from the Introduction, in terms of the worth of the agent's "regard or concern... toward others (or oneself), and toward the relevance of moral considerations, as manifested in one's conduct" (McKenna 2012, 59). My worry about this formulation is that requiring the conjunction of regard both to others (or oneself) *and* to moral considerations seems too strong. There may be some people who reject all of morality as such, who despise or laugh at moral considerations and we suckers who take them seriously, but who nevertheless have very high regard for others (and/or themselves).

[5] See its many treatments as a "basic" emotion in Eckman 2003, Frijda 1986, Griffiths 2004, and Mauro, Sato, and Tucker 1992.

[6] I am grateful to Michael McKenna for suggesting an approach like this.

What, then, if we weaken McKenna's conjunctive characterization by making it disjunctive, requiring regard toward others (or oneself) OR toward the relevance of moral considerations? I worry about this attempt as well. Suppose I hate people but am a moral fetishist: all I care about is doing the right thing, no matter what it is, solely because it is the right thing.[7] I thus spend lots of time ensuring that I can discover the correct moral verdicts (but not necessarily the relevant reasons for them) in any circumstance, and I always conform my behavior to them. I have the highest regard for the relevance of moral considerations. Nevertheless, I seem to lack an essential sort of regard.

What these ruminations reveal is that it matters far less to us that you highly regard moral considerations as such than it does that you highly regard the *source* of those considerations, namely, us! Our interests are surely what, at least in part, determine the moral considerations, but if you have regard directly or solely for those considerations without regard for the people whose interests (at least partially) give birth to them, then what regard you have is simply misplaced, at least for purposes of the quality of regard relevant to accountability. That is because you are accountable (when you are) *to us*, not to morality.

What, though, of our attitudes to *animals*? One might think that inclusion of regard toward moral considerations is needed to capture how someone could act from a poor quality of will in torturing animals, even though he may have nothing but the highest regard for all humans.[8] As any plausible set of moral norms would reject such treatment, it could render negative accountability responses appropriate, it would seem, only in virtue of its being an expression of disregard for those norms. This does not have to be the case, though. One alternative story comes from contractualists, who sometimes advance the possibility that animals could be assigned trustees who would reject on their behalf principles allowing them to be tortured (Scanlon 1998, 182–5[9]). Violating such a rejectable principle, then, would wrong—disregard—*the animal.* What we may

[7] See M. Smith 1994, 75–6. I explore a case like this in Shoemaker 2007, 85–92. This case is different from Kant's prudent grocer or Aristotle's (merely) continent man. The fetishist conforms to the demands of morality solely because he worships morality, and so does what he does for the exclusive reason *that morality demands it.* Neither the prudent grocer nor the continent man are moved by this reason. The grocer may not care at all about either moral considerations or other people, and the continent man is one whose regard for morality is a function of his taking *specific* moral reasons seriously. That is, he, but not the fetishist, may be moved (with some struggle) to help someone in need *because they are in need*, not because that is what morality demands. But the continent man's motivation reveals his regard for that person in need. Thanks to Bruce Brower and Oliver Sensen for discussion of this issue.

[8] Thanks to Michael McKenna for urging me to consider this worry.

[9] Although after laying out this strategy, Scanlon admits that he is not inclined to take it himself (Scanlon 1998, 184).

do, then, is expand the notion of who counts as a potential object of regard. To this point, I have used the neutral phrase "regard to others," but this is compatible with us including (some) nonhuman animals in the set of who those others are.

In fact, there are some powerful reasons for doing so, and I will note them once I have delved more deeply into the conditions of regard. For now, though, I simply mean to be arguing that we can best capture our understanding of regard by restricting its scope to other *agents*, where these may be humans or (some) nonhuman animals. Indeed, this makes sense insofar as we think of accountable agents as accountable *to* others. When I get angry at you, I am lodging some sort of complaint or demand (whose nature has yet to be explored), not on behalf of morality, but on behalf of *me* (or my friends, on Aristotle's view). In addition, being able to capture what we want from regard by restricting its target to other agents brings out what I think is an important distinction between accountability and answerability, as the latter *is* concerned exclusively with one's relation to reasons and one's judgments of their worth. From here on out, then, I will restrict talk of regard to one's orientation to other agents, not to moral considerations.

So what does it mean to regard other agents? I think we can best understand it by focusing on *disregard* and looking for the fittingness conditions of its targeting sentiment, agential anger, which is what evaluates regard as poor. To do so, we can return to Aristotle's view of disregard: "[S]lighting is the actively entertained opinion of something as obviously of no importance...."[10] While this account does capture many instances of disregard, it is nevertheless incomplete. When you loudly blather away to your seatmate on the plane while all those around you are trying to sleep or work, you slight them, despite not actively viewing them as unimportant. In addition, it seems plausible to count as disregard viewing others as having merely *low* importance, or as having lower importance than they may have.

Let us return, then, to my "bold" claim at the end of the previous section that (negative) accountability may include more than what many people take to be the standard targets of resentment or indignation. Some contemporary theorists take

[10] Hobbes is insightful here as well: "For every man looketh that his companion should value him, at the same rate he sets upon himself, and upon all signs of contempt, or undervaluing, naturally endeavours, as far as he dares ... to extort a greater value from his contemners, by damage, and from others, by the example." This aspect of human psychology yields one of the three "principle causes of quarrel," namely, glory. In the state of nature, this would make people invade for reputation, which makes them use violence "for trifles, as a word, a smile, a different opinion, and any other sign of undervalue, either direct in their persons, or by reflection in their kindred, their friends, their nation, their profession, or their name" (Hobbes 1994, 75–6 (Ch. 13)).

the exclusively fitting target of our negative accountability responses to be a *wronging* (one might interpret Darwall 2006 in this way, for instance). Wrongings violate legitimate claims or demands we have against one another. This way of thinking may be thought to capture Strawson's talk of our reactive attitudes being in response to violations of the "basic demand" we express for good—or at least not ill—will (Strawson 2003, e.g., 76; see also Watson 2004, e.g., 223–4). But it might be too restrictive, as some anger-worthy violations of moral obligations—wrongs—could conceivably range wider than the violations of our claims on one another. I think it is safer to say, then, that most theorists who rely on resentment as the paradigm accountability response would agree that it fittingly and exclusively targets violations of moral *obligations*. On such a view, I am resentment- or indignation-worthy just in case and because I have done what I ought not to have done (see, e.g., Wallace 1994, 35–7; Nelkin 2011, 104–7).[11]

But once we turn to think about the fitting targets of *agential anger*, we can see that this resentment/indignation treatment may be too narrow, for it leaves out a wide range of untoward behavior toward which we would surely tend to be angry (in the agential way). Consider first so-called "suberogatory" actions. Julia Driver offers the example of a neighbor mowing his lawn early on a Sunday morning (Driver 1992, 288; see also McKenna 2012, 184). It may not be morally obligatory of him that he refrain, and I do not seem to have a claim against him that he refrain, but nevertheless what he is doing is very uncool, falling far short of the expectations I have for neighborly behavior. Of course, this is a controversial case; we might think, for example, that I *do* have a claim against him not to violate certain of my property rights, which may include constraints against noise pollution. Or perhaps it is just morally wrong to be inconsiderate this egregiously. But there are other less controversial cases that make the same point. McKenna offers a case in which Jenny could very easily help out Maria, who needs some medicine urgently but cannot afford it, but Jenny ignores Maria and goes on with her day. Jenny's suberogatory action may seem worthy of agential anger, even if it does not wrong Maria, and even if it is not morally wrong, period (McKenna 2012, 182–3). For another case, suppose I have brought only one pencil to an examination, whereas you, sitting next to me, have brought many. In the midst of the exam, I break my only pencil and look to you with a plea in my eyes. You notice the plea, glance at all your extra pencils, shake your head at my lack of preparedness, and return to your exam without giving me a single one

[11] McKenna 2012 is not among these theorists, however, as he adds a quality of will condition to the formulation.

(cf., Thomson 1990, 117).[12] You have not wronged me—I have no claims whatsoever on any of your pencils—and it also may seem that you have done nothing morally wrong. Nevertheless, my anger at you may well be fitting.[13]

Or perhaps in each of these cases it is only *resentment* (and, derivatively, indignation) that is not fitting, given that no wrong or wronging occurred. Perhaps, in other words, resentment is truly fitting only for violations of obligations, given that it (now) conceptually requires a constitutive judgment of wrongdoing. And perhaps further the offending agents in each case are thus also not *blameworthy*, if blameworthiness requires fitting resentment (which itself requires a judgment about blameworthiness). I am frankly unsure what to make of such claims. But what matters for our purposes is that, regardless of whether resentment or indignation fit such offenses, *agential anger surely does.* "I know I should have brought more pencils," our student may think, "and I know I have no claim on any of his stack, but *still*, goddam it, he could at least have given me just one measly pencil!"

Even though fitting agential anger ranges more widely than resentment, though, I cannot see it as anything other than an *accountability* response, given that its feel and motivational force is, phenomenologically, precisely identical to the feel and force of clear-cut cases of resentment and indignation (holding fixed the degree to which one experiences the emotion in question). In the latter instances of "moralized" anger, we have seen that what most contemporary responsibility theorists think is ostensibly included in addition to the feel and motivational force are judgments about wrongdoing, desert, or blameworthiness. But in all of the agential anger cases—moralized and nonmoralized—it is the "outrage" one feels that generates the motivational impulse to *hold* the target accountable, not any of these judgmental associations. Consequently, while agential anger is more capacious than its moralized versions, that is a good thing, as it can reveal to us features of our accountability experience and practices that the moralized versions cannot.

What we have seen thus far is that agential anger may be fitting, not just to wrongs, but also to violations of "mere" expectations, at least where these set forth requests for fairly minimal levels of kindness or generosity. Nevertheless, violations of norms of either stripe are not yet sufficient for fitting agential anger. Regarding expectations, I may have exceedingly high expectations for a

[12] Assume as well that you don't suffer from anxiety if you don't have the proper number of pencils, and that it would involve an extremely minimal sacrifice on your part to kick one over to me.

[13] Notice, though, the long discussion of, and controversy about, this case and general issue when Dana Nelkin raised it on *Flickers of Freedom* in January 2013, URL: <http://agencyandresponsibility.typepad.com/flickers-of-freedom/2013/01/blameworthiness-and-wrongness.html>.

relationship, and when these are dashed, only disappointment or sadness may be appropriate. Regarding wrongs, I may wrong you without yet rendering agential anger fitting. To illustrate, suppose you have come to inherit lots of well-marked forested property right next to a public park, and you become obsessed about monitoring it. You decide, for instance, to have surveillance equipment installed on every border of your property to detect all trespassers. You watch these videos every waking moment, letting your hair grow long and not cutting your nails, and every time you see people take a shortcut over even the tiniest corner of your property from the park, you become outraged, and you identify and prosecute them. Suppose that I am your best friend, someone you still trust and love, and I hate what this obsession has done to you. I think you are otherwise a good person who somehow needs to realize just how pinched, sour, and miserly you have become. To most effectively make my point, one day I deliberately cross from the park onto your property and stand there staring directly into one of your cameras with a pleading face. I have violated your property rights, but I did so with the intention of getting you to see that your prosecutorial tactics have gone way overboard. Arguably, your anger toward me would be unfitting, despite my having wronged you. Why? I have not yet *slighted* you.

So obligational and expectational breaches, in and of themselves, may be neither necessary nor sufficient to render agential anger fitting, which means that none of them wholly captures the element of disregard—slights—we are trying to explicate. So what is a slight if not one of these sorts of breaches? Let us consider one such case, wherein someone exhibits what we think of as poor regard while nevertheless adhering to, and perhaps even exceeding, all of the relevant demands and expectations. Suppose I meet every one of your demands and expectations solely because it amuses me; I find it hilarious to see you demanding and expecting things of your betters, and so I find it doubly hilarious to do what you ask. I am insufferably *condescending*. Anger seems fitting for me—I have slighted you—despite my adhering to all of your demands and expectations.

Or maybe I am just violating your demand or expectation that I adhere to your *other* demands or expectations *without a condescending attitude*? This is plausible. But then note the puzzle that immediately arises, a puzzle that actually helps get us to a better understanding of regard. I condescend to you (and so slight you), even when I meet your first-order demands and expectations, when I do not take those demands and expectations seriously. You may demand or expect of me that I do so. But if I do not take any of your first-order demands or expectations seriously, why should I take your higher-order demand or expectation that I do so seriously? It could not get off the ground with me. This is because the ultimate problem is not my attitude toward your demands and expectations but rather my attitude toward you: I do not take *you* seriously. You are not a joke, yet I view you as one. And now we are getting to the heart of slights.

So what does it mean to take someone seriously? Somewhat obscurely (for now), my taking you seriously is a matter of the extent to which I take your specific normative perspective to bear a weight in my own deliberative perspective in the generally valenced way it does for you. Your normative perspective is your take on what things are good or bad, and so includes your attitudes toward your treatment by others. For me to take you seriously, your view of the goodness or badness of such treatment, for example, must count for me too *qua* practical agent, and in sync with how it counts for you.[14]

Let me fill in the details of this view. There are two distinct ways in which your normative perspective may bear sufficient weight for me. I will call the first *evaluational regard*, which obtains when facts about what you take to be good or bad are also taken by me to then count sufficiently in favor of, roughly, promoting or respecting what you take to be good, or avoiding or thwarting what you take to be bad. We can get an initial handle on the idea by considering Scanlon's treatment of what reasons we have. He delineates two "critical stages" in the move from consideration of facts that seem to be reasons to the formation of attitudes. The first critical stage is one in which the agent decides whether something that *seems* to be a reason really is one. The second critical stage is one in which the various facts one has decided are reasons are weighed against each other and the agent decides which of them is more worthy for actual attitude-formation (Scanlon 1998, 65–6). One might think that evaluative regard occurs only at one or the other stage, as long as the relevant reasons are those stemming from others' normative perspectives. But as it stands there is a significant elision in the account, namely, an explanation of where those mere *seemings* come from, that is, where facts about people and situations come to *appear* to be reasons to us in the first place (these are what I called in Chapter 2 "reasonish facts"). Note that

[14] There are some pretty awful people out there, e.g., sadists, racists, male chauvinists, narcissists, and so on. Should we take *their* normative perspectives seriously? Are we slighting them by not doing so? (I am grateful to an anonymous reader with Oxford University Press for raising this concern, one also shared by Bas Van der Vossen and Bruce Brower.) The question of whether we should take seriously the perspectives of (all) others is a moral one, however, not a sentimental one. That is, I am interested in explicating the fittingness conditions for anger, which evaluates quality of regard as poor. On my characterization in the text, then, I may of course slight sadists, racists, etc. by failing to take their normative perspectives seriously, and when I do, their anger at me would be fitting. But it may simultaneously be morally permissible (or obligatory!) for me to slight them, in which case, it would be morally permissible/obligatory for me to do something angersome. I will explain this point in terms of the language of "wrong kinds of reasons" shortly in the text.

for the blathering airplane talker, facts about my desire for peace and quiet do not even cross his radar. So in order to make sense of this behavior as the slight that it is, we have to include under the rubric of regard a *pre*-critical stage of attitude formation, in which various facts appear to one as putative reasons in the first place. This pre-critical stage is a stage of *perception*, not judgment.

I may thus evaluationally disregard you in one of three ways, corresponding to what I have deemed the pre-critical stage and the subsequent two critical stages of Scanlonian attitude-formation: (a) when I do not perceive relevant facts about your normative perspective as putative reasons; (b) when I judge that putative reasons about your normative perspective (the relevant facts about your normative perspective that have already come to seem to me to be reasons) are not in fact reasons; or (c) when I judge that relevant reasons about your normative perspective are worth less than they are (in accordance with some accepted rubric) relative to some other reasons for attitude-formation. Three versions of our blathering airplane talker may illustrate each. In an illustration of (a), he either fails to notice that others around him are sleeping or trying to work, or he notes these facts without their appearing to him to be reasons of any sort, in the same way that he notes facts about the temperature of the cabin or the number of windows it has without their appearing to him to be reasons of any sort. In an illustration of (b), he notices that others are sleeping or trying to work, and so his talking might seem to bother them, but then he judges that that is just not a reason at all to quit talking. In an illustration of (c), he notices that others are sleeping or trying to work, and he decides that his talking *does* bother them, and so constitutes a prima facie reason to stop talking, but he judges that such a reason loses out to what he takes to be the much weightier reason to tell his neighbor in a loud voice about his remarkable grandchildren. In each case, he gives insufficient weight to the normative perspectives of those around him, and his disregard ranges from the clueless to the active.

The astute reader will have noticed that (b) and (c) involve poor *judgments*, and so it may look as if quality of judgment and quality of regard would be identical when such mistakes occur. While they do seem to overlap in many cases, we must keep in mind that judgments take as their object reasons, whereas regard takes as its object agents. So when, for example, I see your interests as providing reasons against stealing your money but I decide to steal it anyway, my decision is poor *insofar as* it reflects my disregard for you, my failure to take you seriously enough. So you may both be angry at me *and* disapprove of (and criticize) my judgment. But there are distinct objects here, respectively, poor regard and poor judgment. The distinction is brought out in two directions. From one side, there are plenty of cases of poor judgment that involve no disregard, as when we make bad decisions in nonmoral normative domains. But from the other side, there are plenty of cases of what I will call *pure* disregard that do not involve judgments. Cases like (b) and (c) are built on a foundation of pre-critical, pre-judgmental regard (what fails to occur in case (a)), that is, they both presuppose that the relevant facts about your normative perspective *do at least seem to be reasons*. And this pre-critical stage (where one simply perceives relevant "reasonish" facts) is not a stage at which judgment plays any direct causal role. Indeed, whether some facts appear to one to be reasons is not directly sensitive to, or a function of, judgment: they either appear that way to one or they do not, and so they manifest a feature common to encapsulated sentiments, namely, *recalcitrance* (as Scanlon 1998, 65, agrees). Things may seem to one to be reasons long after one has judged that they are not. And so it is in this perception of various facts about other agents' normative perspectives—their seeming to one to be reasons—that we find the nonjudgmental core of evaluational regard. As a result, we may still, in Scanlon's own terms, distinguish quality of (evaluational) regard from quality of judgment, for the former, in its most basic, "purest" form, is not about judgment at all.[15]

The second general way in which your normative perspective may bear sufficient weight for me—and the way simply not discussed very much, if at all, in the literature on responsibility—is what I will call *emotional regard*. This occurs when I *care* about your normative perspective, such that I am disposed to respond emotionally to its fortunes. In other words, when the things you view as good are respected or promoted, I am disposed to respond emotionally in sync with you, feeling happy, proud, or gratified, say; and when the things you view as good are undermined, or the things you view as bad are respected or promoted,

[15] Why aren't these perceptions, these noticings, a function of our standing judgments about what is important, though? Indeed, how could it make sense to get angry at you for failing to notice something about me if I weren't assuming that this meant you *didn't* judge me to be important (or, worse, you judged me to be unimportant)? This is Angela Smith's position and the source of her resistance to my characterization of evaluative regard (Smith 2005 and in private correspondence). But the perception of "reasonish" facts is, I maintain, not a direct function of judgments (nor of cares). Instead, it is a direct function of the enabling empathic stance I detail shortly in the text. Being committed to (or caring about) the well-being of someone is expected to generate only certain attitudes, such as the intention to take up the empathic stance, but it is that *stance*, and not the commitment (or caring) itself, which then is expected to enable the generation of the relevant perception. When I am committed to you and your well-being, I will tend to *put myself in the position* to see the "reasonish" facts about you. But it is my subsequent failure to see these relevant facts in which my "pure" slight consists. Now of course that failure will very often reflect insufficient cares or commitments if I wasn't even moved to take up your normative perspective in the first place. That is why in most cases of immorality, all three types of responsibility are represented, as slighting others typically reflects on the agent's character, judgment, and regard. But again, I am trying to isolate "pure" cases of each type in order to reveal the different qualities of will in play.

I am disposed to feeling dismay, frustration, embarrassment, or shame, say, right alongside you. This is also a kind of attitude that runs independently of judgment, of either my judgments of your value or my judgments with respect to the reasons flowing from it. Illustrations will be familiar to those in close interpersonal relationships. Suppose my spouse has been terribly mistreated at work one day, and she comes home very upset. Once she tells me the story, if I am not upset as well—upset along the same dimensions as her, and with respect to what was done to her—this will likely occasion her anger, and it seems to do so fittingly; my lack of emotionally in-sync response is, in other words, a slight. (And woe to me if I actually maintain good cheer.) I am not sufficiently emotionally attuned to her normative perspective. Nevertheless, I may judge her to be quite valuable, and I would surely judge that various facts about her normative perspective count as reasons for comforting her and making sympathetic sounds, just as I may also judge that these reasons have significant worth. I may still slight her exclusively through my failure to be emotionally wrought in the way that she is (even if not to the same extent), for this seems to reveal an importantly absent caring element. To love someone is not only to take facts about her normative perspective to count as reasons, it is also to be disposed to respond emotionally in sync with her fortunes *regardless* of the relevant reasons, and without any mediating judgment about reasons.

Each type of (pure) regard is typically enabled by a distinct type of empathic stance.[16] In the first, *evaluational empathy*, we take up the normative perspective of others to perceive what facts about their normative perspectives, if any, both seem to be, and actually count as, reasons. In doing so, we often ask about the sorts of attitudes or treatments they would have good reason to object to, or about the sorts of things that could successfully be justified to them. Taking up the normative perspective of another in this way consists in coming to see the other's projects as worthwhile *from her perspective*. To the extent that I would have a reason to reject some sort of proposed treatment if I had her particular set of interests and normative take on the world, then, in returning to my own perspective this fact about her typically comes to seem to me to be a reason against such treatment of her as well, a seeming reason I will likely judge to be an *actual* reason of significant worth against such treatment. Here we may say that during this process I *identify* with her as a fellow evaluator with particular commitments.

[16] I am grateful to Mark Timmons for this way of putting it. Compare and contrast to Darwall 2006, 43–8, whose focus is primarily on what I call the evaluative form of empathy.

Emotional regard is typically enabled by *emotional empathy*, wherein we take up others' normative perspectives in opening ourselves up to *feeling* what they do or would feel in various circumstances. How, I may ask, would my treatment of or expressed attitude to someone make him feel? Here I come to experience empathic emotional responses only to the extent that I robustly imagine his affective normative take on the world, which includes, at the very least, "trying on" his relevant cares (but very often includes *sharing* his cares, that is, actually having those very same cares myself). What this means is that, in order to feel what the object of my perspective-taking feels, I must project my *feeling* self into his perspective, and to be emotionally affected in sync with him, I have to imagine caring about the things he does (relevant to the context of evaluation) in a way that is roughly akin to the way he cares about them. Here we may say that I identify with him as a fellow emotional creature with particular cares.[17] This form of empathy enables the corresponding type of regard.

Of course, both types of regard presuppose a more fundamental recognition or acknowledgment, namely, that the other agent *is* a fellow evaluator or fellow emotional creature.[18] I will not be moved to engage in the relevant form of empathy with you (for purposes of evaluational or emotional regard) if I do not recognize you to be a fellow in the relevant respect. Such recognition is of your status *qua* evaluator or emotional creature in the abstract, as being someone whose general perspective is among those eligible to be taken seriously (via the more particular forms of regard), and I recognize this status as a function of my cares or my commitments, that is, I may simply find myself emotionally disposed to respond negatively, say, to failures to include your perspective among those I ought to take seriously, or I may judge your perspective to be among those worth taking up. I hesitate to call this stance "regard," as it does not have a *quality* in the sense our other forms of "will" do; rather, the other agent's relevant regard-status is either acknowledged or it is not. Call this, then, status-recognition. What is being recognized is whether the target of my empathy *has* a normative perspective, and this point is what buttresses my earlier claims about nonhuman animals. Having a normative perspective, after all, may just include having interests whose advancement or thwarting is something to which the agent could plausibly be said to have some sort of recognizable "pro" or "con" attitude.

[17] Both forms of empathy thus fall under the rubric of identification. I elsewhere restricted what I called "identifying empathy" to what I have here called emotional empathy (Shoemaker 2007; 2011; and 2014a). I am changing terminology now because evaluative empathy is obviously a kind of identification as well. I say much more about the nature of identification and empathy in Chapter 5.

[18] I am grateful to Christian Coons for raising and discussing this point.

Indeed, we can and do acknowledge the perspective-status of, and engage in empathy with, many higher primates, dogs, dolphins, and other animals, while being unable do so with many other animals, such as insects, shrimp, and slugs. Consequently, given that we may directly take up the normative perspectives of some nonhuman agents, we can lay to rest the worry about how to include such agents in our range of regard without having to require regard for moral considerations as well.

Once status-recognition is established, the slights consisting in failures of each of evaluational and emotional regard are familiar. A failure of evaluational regard, very generally a failure sufficiently to take up as reasons relevant facts about others' normative perspectives, is what we label *inconsiderate*. Much of immorality is fundamentally a matter of inconsiderateness, ranging from the trivially annoying behavior of the typical loud talkers on airplanes, to racist or sexist attitudes and behaviors, to the gross violations of rape and murder. These are at their core failures to take seriously enough the normative perspectives of others.[19]

By contrast, a failure of emotional regard, a failure to be sensitive to how others may be emotionally affected by various attitudes and treatments, is what we typically label *insensitive*. This is considered a slight usually just under the norms of fairly intimate relationships. It may not matter that some stranger is not emotionally affected by the failures of the projects I care about, but it matters an enormous amount if my spouse or close friends are not so affected. This is because they are presumed to care about *me*, or to share my cares, in a way strangers are not expected to. Nevertheless, strangers may emotionally disregard us. Suppose that as I am crossing an icy street, I slip and fall hard to the pavement, banging my head and breaking my arm. While several people immediately come to my aid, a group of men standing on the other side laugh hysterically at what happened. I got more than enough help, so it is not their failure to aid that slights me; it is, quite simply, their *amusement* at my plight.[20] Nevertheless, I am not in any sort of interpersonal relationship with them. What I think this sort of case indicates is that, while we do not expect strangers to care about many of the particular things we do (as we expect of our friends and loved ones), we typically do expect a *minimal* level of shared cares with strangers, cares for the basics we all tend to have as humans, for example, cares about avoiding

[19] It may sound jarring to call sadists, or Hitler, "inconsiderate," but they do fail to take seriously enough the normative perspectives of others; it is just that they do so to a staggering degree.

[20] And not just their *expressed* amusement. Suppose they are trying hard to squelch their laughter, but I can tell they are nevertheless amused. I would still tend to be quite angry, as would I'm sure the strangers who are helping me.

pain, meeting basic nutritional needs, and so on.[21] There is a kind of emotional attunement we expect when the fortunes of these shared cares take a hit, and failures of fellow feeling in such cases can easily be viewed as slights.

Considerateness and sensitivity are thus the two strands of regard whose quality we evaluate with various responses, the paradigm example of which is agential anger. But how do we get from agential anger to accountability, a distinct type of responsibility? We must first explore agential anger's role and aim.

Confrontation and Communication

In the previous section I focused on explicating the nature of agential anger's fitting object, what Aristotle called *conspicuous slights*. In this section, I want to focus on the other feature of Aristotle's definition, that anger's motivational impulse is for *conspicuous revenge*. My thesis here is that the *conspicuousness* is more fundamental than the revenge, and it is this feature of agential anger from which accountability is constructed.

Suppose I have promised that I will help you move, but on moving day, I deliberately leave you in the lurch and laugh about it on Facebook. You have been slighted. It is quite fitting for you to be angry with me, to feel the flush of heat in your face, to think about your humiliation, and to want to make your anger heard.

But you will also likely want to get back at me.

This last is the Aristotelian impulse to revenge, and it is what many psychologists' and philosophers' take to be the fundamental action tendency of anger.[22] In what follows, I intend to argue against this widely held view. While the motivation to revenge is deep-seated and *very often* accompanies agential anger, it is not agential anger's fundamental action aim, but rather, when present, merely *serves* that aim.

We have already assumed that your response in the above case would be agential anger. What sorts of motivational impulses would it actually stir up in you? I think for many people this would depend on several factors, including your relationship to me, how deep your anger runs (perhaps I have done this sort

[21] Of course amusement at someone's plight may be compatible with caring about that person. To the extent that there is a slight in such cases, then, it will be directed, perhaps, at the amused agent's *insufficient* caring.

[22] See, e.g., Spielberger et al. 1983; and Russell and Mehrabian 1974. In Smith and Lazarus 1990, the action tendency is put as being to "remove the source of the harm" (p. 620), but the idea is clear enough. For a richly insightful discussion of anger, both in Aristotle's terms and our own, see Stocker with Hegeman 1996, esp. Ch. 10.

of thing before, and so you may feel more sheepish than angry because you fell for it again), and what your character is like generally. So some may just want to "unfriend" me on Facebook. Others may want to call me and yell at me. Others may want to start a Twitter campaign against me. Others may resolve never to speak to me again. And others may wait for me outside my house with a baseball bat by their side, patiently tap-tap-tapping their legs.

Some of these are more "revenge-y" than others, and some do not seem to involve any revenge at all. For the moment, however, I will set this issue aside. Instead, I will ask, what is supposed to be meant by the "conspicuousness" of the revenge? It cannot mean that your "revenge" response must be public, or at least made known to third parties who witnessed or were aware of the original slight, for you may just be motivated to get back at me in a sly, subtle, cold way. But does your "revenge" response at least need to be made conspicuous to me, the offender, in order for its emotional base to count as agential anger?

Here we enter important territory. The basic thought I will pursue is that agential anger incorporates the following action tendency: *communicate it to the slighter.*[23] That is to say, one simply does not count as being angry at someone without having some motivational impulse to communicate that feeling to the agent *qua* slighting party.[24] This impulse may be squashed, of course; if Mike Tyson is the one who slighted me, I will do my best to keep my face a smiling, polite mask, regardless of his stated resolutions to be gentle. But the point is that there still will be a motivational impulse to communicate what I am feeling in such a case that has to be squashed. And note that bottled up agential anger can be deeply corrosive, eating away at one's insides, creating obsessions, nightmares, ulcers, and ground-down teeth. It is also enormously difficult to repress for long. Indeed, release—expression—of that anger often yields relief, the removal of a burden, as the anger has finally been set loose to fulfill its function.[25]

[23] There are many who have taken "holding responsible" of some sort to be communicative. See, e.g., the work of Antony Duff, Coleen Macnamara, Michael McKenna, Angela Smith, Matt Talbert, and Gary Watson. I have many subtle disagreements with each that I won't go into here. My primary disagreement with them all, however, is over what the precise content of the communication is.

[24] Coleen Macnamara, in insightfully discussing what she takes to be the communicative function of all reactive attitudes, describes them as having a "non-intentional purposiveness" and having an "interpersonal function of evoking uptake of [their] representational content in a recipient" (Macnamara 2013b, 8, 17). It should be clear that I think what she says is true, albeit only of the *accountability* reactive attitudes.

[25] It could be interesting to explore agential anger's communicative aim from the other end, via forgiveness. In forgiving you, I (at least) foreswear my anger toward you. In many instances, it would seem, I do so in virtue of your having already come to fully appreciate what it is my anger aims to communicate (yet to be determined). For recent discussion of forgiveness, revenge, and responsibility, see Puka 2002; Warmke 2011 and 2013; and Zaibert 2012.

Now the motivation to get back at the slighter—retribution—is probably the most powerful and obvious form of communicating one's agential anger. But there are many other forms of communicating it having nothing to do with retribution: yelling, speaking in a low and tremulous voice, shooting a nasty look, throwing one's hands into the air and stomping to another room, going silent, and more. Even people who are motivated to the most extreme form of revenge—killing—feel the strong impulse to let their victims know why: "This is for what you did to me!"[26] And my stronger claim is this: the "revenge" actually *serves* the conspicuousness, the communicative element that is itself more fundamental. Agential anger with successful, but uncommunicated, revenge feels incomplete, whereas agential anger with successful, but non-vengeful, communication does not. In illustration, consider two cases of angry, retributive responses to your injuring me. In the first, I cause your downfall without your knowing I had anything to do with it. In the second, I cause your downfall but I make it known to you ("This is for what you did to me!"). In the first, some aspect of my anger feels frustrated, unsatisfied, whereas in the second, nothing is. Only in the second was anger's communicative aim met.

One might object to this communicative view of anger by adopting some elements of the "protest" account of blame, according to which the fundamental motivational impulse of blame is taken instead merely to be *standing up for oneself* (Hieronymi 2001; Smith 2013; Talbert 2012b and Forthcoming). This is why, for instance, advocates of such a view think it could make sense to blame psychopaths, even if there is no communicative point to blaming them. While this could be the right account of blame—although I have serious reservations—it could not be the right account of fitting agential anger. While anger at a slighter may indeed serve to regenerate one's own moral equilibrium, or perhaps express or reestablish one's self-respect in light of the slight, there is still something crucial missing when no communication of it to the slighter is secured (cf. Macnamara 2013b). Again, we can consider two pairwise cases, in one of which the communication of one's protest to the offender is achieved, and in the other of which it is not. If the target of protest fails to recognize and understand one's protest *as such*, agential anger feels frustrated; it "aspires" to be more than just public noise. Mere protest, where only the protestor or non-slighting third parties make up the entire listening audience, is second best. In its

[26] Recall the mantra of one of the characters in the movie *The Princess Bride*, who is constantly rehearsing his avenging message for his father's killer: "Hello. My name is Inigo Montoya. You killed my father. Prepare to die."

fullest expression, agential anger has a confrontational, communicative motivational component.

Of course, talk of confrontation or revenge is what raises, for many responsibility theorists, moral concerns (see, e.g., Wallace 1994; McKenna 2012, 134–41; Pereboom 2014). One might thus worry that agential anger can harm its targets—causing them physical or emotional pain via its involvement in censure, sanction, revenge, or outright punishment—and to the extent that harming others requires moral justification, then it looks like we need a moral defense of agential anger and its deployment.[27] Further, there is a long tradition, going back to the Stoics, urging that we rid ourselves of anger for additional moral or prudential reasons, e.g., it is alleged to be unhealthy for the experiencer, corrosive to relationships, generally unproductive, and so on. So what may be said for agential anger on the other side?

Let me start by saying that even if there were no moral or prudential justification for agential anger, it would not matter for my project. This is because moral or prudential reasons against agential anger are the *wrong kinds of reasons* against it, and someone who argues that we ought not be angry for such reasons commits what D'Arms and Jacobson label the "moralistic fallacy" (D'Arms and Jacobson 2000). While it may be immoral, for example, to envy one's rival, that does not mean one's rival is not enviable. While it may be immoral to laugh at a cruel joke, that does not mean the joke in and of itself is not amusing. And while agential anger may cause harm to self, others, and relationships generally, that in and of itself does not mean the object of the anger is not *angersome*, that is, fitting for anger. Insofar as agential anger represents its object as committing a slight, one has a reason of fit to feel anger just in case it represents its object correctly. Of course, this is only a prima facie reason, one that may be overridden by other (prudential or moral) prima facie reasons in a determination of one's all-things-considered reasons. But the fact that sentiments like envy, amusement, fear, shame, and, yes, anger may lack a moral justification is irrelevant to whether we may still have a reason (of fit) to feel them (see D'Arms and Jacobson 2003 and 2006b).

Perhaps, though, anger is actually *unfitting*, for other sorts of reasons? This seems to be the view of Derk Pereboom, who argues that the angry core of reactive attitudes like resentment and indignation is inappropriate for metaphysical reasons, namely, because the agential objects of this emotion could not *deserve* it unless they could exercise a type of agential, libertarian control about

[27] The moral route most often taken appeals to *fairness*, as in, "What are the conditions that make it morally fair for us to adopt the stance of holding people responsible?" (Wallace 1994, 5).

whose possibility we should be deeply skeptical (Pereboom 2014). Adapted to my way of talking, Pereboom's position would be that anger at people who slight us is unfitting because they lack the requisite form of control over their slights to deserve it. Pereboom then goes on to argue that, while it is thus irrational to feel agential anger, anger has some pretty bad effects anyway (so we should not be too worried about giving it up), and besides, we may be able to habituate ourselves out of it and substitute emotional responses for it—like shock, disappointment, sadness, and concern—that do not presuppose metaphysically implausible conditions and yet come close enough to playing anger's roles that we may peaceably live without it.

I will leave off my discussion of control mostly until the concluding chapter. As for Pereboom's metaphysical arguments, they are beyond the scope of the present work,[28] which is simply to see whether a suitably refined quality of will approach to responsibility might account for all we mean when speaking the language of responsibility, and *not* whether the various types of quality of will I have laid bare are compatible with determinism. And Pereboom does seem to agree that quality of regard more or less as I construe it is the target of our natural accountability sentiments (see, e.g., Pereboom 2014, 183). So I can agree with him that, once all the dust settles, the metaphysical requirements for angersome slights *might* be pitched too high for us to meet, and so we might come to agree that agential anger is always unfitting (irrational).

Nevertheless, I think the motivation for seeking moral justification of these sorts of responsibility responses may be undermined, or at least significantly softened, once we come to see what the aim of agential anger's communicative impulse actually is. It is not to sanction, as I used to believe.[29] While revenge is often on the minds of victims of slights, it is not necessarily built into their anger, as illustrated above (the angry victims may, without frustration, merely be motivated to shun, or shoot a dirty look at, the slighter). Instead, what anger motivates, most fundamentally, is *making the slighter fully aware of what he has done*. It is a demand to get him to appreciate, to acknowledge, the emotional havoc (and worse) that he has wreaked. All of the ostensible "sanctioning" aims given in the literature about accountability—scolding the offender, punishing him, or getting him to feel guilt, apologize, or ingratiate himself to the community—require first and foremost that the offender *acknowledge* what he did. Otherwise, there could be no point to punishment, no possibility of guilt, no

[28] For my worries about those metaphysical arguments, see Shoemaker 2014d.

[29] I maintained otherwise in several articles, including Shoemaker 2007, 75–6, and as recently as Shoemaker 2011b, 616. The remainder of this paragraph draws a bit from Shoemaker 2013c.

genuine apology, no successful reconciliation. I will expand on this point below. For now, note that, while an angry demand for acknowledgment may also sting, these stings are merely contingent side effects of the demand, as illustrated by the many other demands *qua* demands that may also sting (e.g., "You've got to rewrite this terrible paper," "Don't cook that again!," "You should practice your free throws a lot more," "Cut it out!"). Moral worries about the sting in these latter cases are obviously distinct from the appropriateness of such declarations, as the moral worries have more to do with considerations of tact, standing, or hypocrisy, say, than whether the demand itself hits the mark.

Nevertheless, it would be foolish to deny that agential anger sometimes—even predictably—does have nasty, if contingent, effects, so does it at least have any offsetting value? It should be clear that I do not believe there is any sort of value-based justification—or any external justification at all—for the having of our sentimental responses; indeed, to ask for one would be to request a justification for our being human.[30] Nevertheless, there are at least three valuable features of agential anger and its communicative component worth discussing.

The sort of value Strawson himself cites goes to the inexorable tie between the reactive emotions and interpersonal relationships: we could not have interpersonal relationships, he suggests, without being susceptible to these emotions, and the costs would just be too high to rationalize our giving these relationships up, even if we could (Strawson 2003, 82–3). I am not sure the former claim is true, however. It seems possible for there to be close interpersonal relationships in which agential anger is not an option for the various parties. Perhaps this just "isn't their scene, dude," and "if you can't handle the 'no anger thing,' man, then I guess you should just move on" (see, e.g., Wallace Forthcoming for less colloquial examples). Nevertheless, these relationships, even if possible, seem unhealthy, or worse, for they close off a certain kind of vulnerability important to equal, caring relationships (see Shabo 2012). If you and I have an intimate relationship, to get to the point where my wronging you does not make you angry, it looks as if you have only two psychologically realistic routes to take: either cease caring about how you are treated, or cease caring about me *as an equal*. The former is quite worrisome: not to care about how one is treated is really just not to care about oneself. This makes for a very unhealthy relationship partner. The latter seems worse. On this option, what I do to you does not cause you anger because you take yourself to be either above or below me. If you take yourself to count for more than I do, then I am like a child to you, an amusing

[30] I am grateful to Sean Foran for this felicitous phrase. See Strawson 2003; Russell 1992 and 2013; and D'Arms and Jacobson 2006b.

irritant at times, but nothing more. If you view yourself as below me, then you may see yourself as unworthy of getting angry; perhaps you deserve your poor treatment (Hieronymi 2001; Scanlon 2008, 168–9). This is debasing. At any rate, while a close relationship may be possible without susceptibility to agential anger, I find it hard to view such relationships as healthy or morally defensible. Vulnerability to agential anger in a healthy relationship is just what is risked by caring about others as equal partners: like love and marriage, or a horse and carriage, you can't get one without the other.[31] This is just what the epigraph from Edward Abbey at the beginning of this chapter is meant to convey.

The second general sort of value of agential anger is prudential. Anger has motivational power, not just for one to communicate its emotional demands to the offender, but also to pursue other attainable benefits (see Aarts et al. 2010; and Veling, Ruys, and Aarts 2012). When we see something as beneficial, we tend to want it more, and so pursue it harder, when angry. In addition—albeit strangely—angry people tend to be more optimistic, and more closely aligned with happy people on risk-assessment measurements than others (Lerner and Keltner 2001; Lerner et al. 2003). Anger also tends to promote psychological insights. When one reflects on when and why one gets angry at others, it can reveal facets about oneself one wishes to change, and so for many people motivates self-improvement (Kassinove et al. 1997). There is also plenty of evidence to suggest that anger is a very effective tool of negotiation, with those who are angry tending to get what they want in a deal (Van Kleef, De Dreu, and Manstead 2004; Van Kleef, et al. 2006). Finally, as recognized by those protest theorists earlier mentioned, anger can be empowering. Standing up for oneself by communicating one's anger can restore one's view of one's standing relative to others, give one the strength and voice needed to fight injustice, and increase one's self-esteem (Wowra and McCarter 1999; Thomas and Jefferson 1996; Watson and River 2005). These are not benefits to be dismissed lightly.

There is a third distinctive value in agential anger's communicative component that is simple to state but may take a while—indeed, much of the rest of the book—to illustrate and defend sufficiently. It is this: agential anger and its emotional family are perhaps the most powerful manufacturers of the empathic

[31] Pereboom thinks many relationships can operate *sans* anger and resentment, and to illustrate he cites many parent–teenager relationships, where anger at their disregard is often replaced by disappointment. He also rightly recognizes, however, that these are not the equal adult relationships on which I have focused. Of them, he only remarks, "My sense is that some such adult mutual relationships are free from resentment and feature disappointment and sadness instead" (Pereboom 2014, 185). He does not, however, speak to the health of such relationships.

glue generating and preserving the moral community. Let me lay out some of the basic ideas here.

The specific communicative message of anger is necessarily emotional. It is to tell the target about his poor quality of regard *angrily*. But why? What is really missing if one just informs him of this in an emotionally neutral tone?[32] There are two reasons the anger adds significant value to the message, I think. First, the angry tone has a much more memorable dramatic impact. To really get across a message, it makes sense to say it in a way that will make the target more liable to pay attention to and remember it, and the angry tone does just that. The second reason is that the message aims to get the target to acknowledge his slight, which, as I noted above, is the only way to make possible his genuinely apologizing, making restitution, and/or attempting reconciliation for it. But his acknowledgment requires that he be made to appreciate, as fully as possible, what it is that he did to the angry one, and he cannot be gotten to appreciate that without having been gotten to *feel what it was like* when he did it. Now the crucial motivational link between acknowledging and rectifying a slight is *guilt*. Guilt is what generates the sincere desire to apologize, restore damaged relationships, and so forth. So how does the angry tone of the communicated message generate guilt in its target?

The moving day case with which we began is actually not very typical, insofar as it involves active ill will, an explicit, carefully choreographed attempt to hurt you. Many cases of poor regard, though, are of the "pure" inconsiderate variety, flat-out failures to see facts about others' normative perspectives as even seeming to be reasons. So suppose we have a case like this, wherein I have promised to help you move, but on moving day I do not show up simply because I forgot about it. You will likely still be angry with me, and you may make me well aware of it via the angry tone of your predicted response: "How could you be so inconsiderate?! You promised to help me move this morning!" So what happens? Your anger makes it very clear that this is a big deal, that I had best pay attention to you. What follows is a step-by-step description of what should be a very familiar (but rapidly occurring) phenomenological picture when things go as we expect: I suddenly realize that I did indeed promise to help you; I then entertain the image of you this morning, discovering me posting something stupidly trivial on Facebook while you looked around helplessly at all your furniture; I then, crucially, imagine what it must have felt like for you at that moment by stepping

[32] This is the sort of non-angry response Margaret Holmgren (2012 and Forthcoming) seems to urge. Pereboom 2004 (97–8) and 2014 suggests such a response coupled with moral sadness instead of anger.

into your emotional shoes (emotional empathy), that is, by thinking about how I would feel had this been done to me (where I share your cares); I come to fully appreciate, via this empathic leap, the anger you are now feeling at me, and *I now feel it too* in sharing both your perspective and your concern about promise-keeping; I then maintain this anger at myself in returning to my own perspective; and this self-directed anger is a crucial constituent of my guilt, motivating me, as the source of your hurt, to beat myself up, to grovel, and/or to do what I can to restore our relationship.

As I said, much of this happens quite rapidly, and not all of the steps always occur or even need to be taken. I may, after all, in being reminded of my broken promise, just go directly to feeling awful and apologizing. In that case, though, I would already have been well-habituated, a habituation that is a matter of fully internalizing those intermediate steps, such that my emotional triggers (in this case, guilt) respond directly to the perception of my inconsiderateness. But moral training clearly aims at engaging our capacities for each of the intermediate steps. "How would you feel if someone did that to you?" is one of the most ready-to-hand parenting prompts, an attempt to get our children to begin learning the crucial moral skills of empathic emotional engagement and of recognizing the irrelevance of differences in perspective for the appropriateness of certain emotional responses (this last is the attempt to blunt egoism in moral training).[33]

I intend to illustrate and develop these points as we go, especially in my extended discussion of psychopathy and high-functioning autism in Chapter 5. But for now just note that developing our fellows' capacities for empathy is a task we take on far beyond their childhood (see, e.g., Shapiro, Morrison, and Boker 2004; Pinderhughes 1984; Kremer and Dietzen 1991; Feshbach 1979 and 1983; Feshbach and Feshbach 1982). Getting them to understand and feel what it is like for others is a regular part of the project of building and preserving moral communities (Shoemaker 2014b). It has been an explicit strategy of moral theorists trying to get us to expand the boundaries of our communities, pushing us, via empathy, to go beyond thinking that the boundaries defined by just our intimates, tribes, states, or even species determine the range of our relevant concern (e.g., Singer 1981). But it is also part of our everyday, more mundane, lives with one another, an appeal—"Have you thought about how *she* would feel about that?"—that lends foundational structure to moral deliberation and, when

[33] For a fascinating look at the different forms of projective imagination that is in line with the story I am telling here, see Batson, Early, and Salvorani 1997. On teaching empathy to children and the feeling prompt, see Brooks and Goldstein 2001. Although see Prinz 2011b for considerations against the necessity of this practice for moral development.

successful, binds us more closely together (cf. Maibom 2007). Agential anger, to the extent that it is perhaps our most dramatic demand for this sort of acknowledgment, does far more to establish this empathic glue, I suggest, than anything else in our arsenal, including coercion, disappointment, contempt, protest, and unconditional love or forgiveness.[34]

Accountability vs. Attributability and Answerability

How, then, do we get from agential anger to a stand-alone type of responsibility? Agential anger fits slights, that is, poor quality of regard. It is clearly a sentimental response to responsibility of some sort, and it has a confrontational, communicative component built in to its action tendency, unlike the other responsibility sentiments we have examined.[35] What it aims to communicate is a demand for acknowledgment, a demand that the slighter take up the slighted's normative perspective in order to fully appreciate how the slighter made the slighted feel. In order for the anger both to fit and to serve as a form of intelligible communication, then, it must meet two conditions: (a) it must accurately represent quality of regard as poor; and (b) it must be able to secure uptake in the slighter. The slighter must correspondingly, therefore, have two capacities to be the fitting and intelligible object of agential anger: (a) he or she must be generally capable of quality of regard, and (b) he or she must be capable of understanding the demand being communicated and be able to accede to it, that is, be able to take up the perspective of the slighted in the way demanded. As the confrontational demand of agential anger comports best with our notion of *holding to account*, call the type of responsibility agential anger reveals *accountability*.

Now once we see these contours of accountability as revealed by agential anger, we can also see the ways in which many other responses to accountable agents might be appropriate. So resentment, if it is indeed a "cognitively sharpened" form of anger (D'Arms and Jacobson 2003, 143), also fits only those who are capable of the relevantly evaluated (as poor) quality of regard and are also capable

[34] I should note that Jesse Prinz (2011a and 2011b) lays out several arguments against empathy as central to, or as a precondition of, morality and moral judgment, and he rightly notes how harmful empathy can actually be, as it tends to spark favoritism, bias, and even hatred and violence. But he does not discuss empathy's role in accountability, and the harmful effects he discusses typically arise because of one-eyed empathy, empathy restricted to those within one's group, and so would presumably be eased or eliminated with *more empathy*, empathy cutting across the in-groups. I discuss Prinz, and my response to him, in detail, in Shoemaker 2014b.

[35] Again, this is why I think Macnamara's (2013b) otherwise plausible communicative account of the reactive attitudes is too sweeping: it claims for *all* reactive attitudes a communicative function that obtains for only a subset.

of understanding the emotional demands, and taking up the perspective, of the slighted party, who in this case is the same as the resentful party. Indignation, also a cognitively sharpened form of anger, requires the same capacities, although the relevant demand in this case is to take up the perspective of the one slighted, not the indignant party. But there are positive forms of accountability as well. Consider anger's opposite, gratitude. This emotion (which is also a sentiment) is fitting for what I have elsewhere called *heights*, and these involve taking another's perspective *more* seriously than he or she may demand or expect (Shoemaker 2013c, 117). It too has a communicative component built in, namely the request that the targeted agent take up one's own perspective to appreciate how (good) the heighter made one feel. The full formulation of accountability is thus as follows:

Accountability: *One is an accountable agent just in case one is liable for being a fitting target of a subset of responsibility responses to one—a subset organized around the paradigm sentimental syndrome pair of agential anger/gratitude—in virtue of one's quality of regard. To have quality of regard an agent must be capable of either (a) coming to see facts about others' (or the agent's own) normative perspectives as putative reasons in the agent's own normative deliberations, as a function of evaluational empathy, or (b) coming to feel what others feel in a simpatico fashion, as a function of emotional empathy. An agent is accountable for some specific attitude or action just in case it accurately displays either or both of these features of the agent's quality of regard.*

In attempting to account for the fact of our ambivalence toward marginal agents, I have advanced an overall theory of responsibility that is pluralistic, maintaining that there are three independent types of responsibility. I have just articulated the third, accountability, so to complete the theorizing of Part I of the book, I need to say just why it is independent of both attributability and answerability.

First, some attitude may be attributable to me—expressive of my deep self—without my being accountable for it. This is most obvious in cases of attitudes that do not have anything to do with slights, nonmoral behavior if you will. I may be a coward in fearing frogs, or slothful in wanting to watch TV all day, but in either case I may not slight (or height) anyone, so accountability is not even implicated. Second, attributability is also unnecessary for accountability (contra Watson 2004, 278), as anger may be fitting to me for some attitude or action even if it does not express one or more of my cares or commitments. One example is whims (Lippert-Rasmussen 2003): I may be moved by a desire to steal something of yours, where this desire is not dependent on either my emotional dispositions or my evaluative stance. It is thus not attributable to me, my deep self. Nevertheless, the action revealed an (out of character) lack of regard. Similarly, I may say something mean off the cuff without being a mean person.

Turn, next, to the reasons why accountability and answerability are independent of one another. First, one could be answerable without being accountable. This is quite obvious, as we have seen, in nonmoral cases: I may be answerable for my artistic decision to splash a huge swath of red across my otherwise dainty and precise portrait painting, but I am not accountable for doing so insofar as I am just not in a practical arena where regard to others is even implicated (other things equal). But what of cases in which we *are* in such an arena? Answerability without accountability may obtain here as well, for those capable of critical rationality but incapable of one or the other forms of empathy. One may be an excellent judge of some reasons about how to treat others, for example, without being able to see any of the reasons as flowing from others' normative perspectives. Psychopaths might fit this bill, as I will discuss in Chapter 6. This might also be true of adolescents, given differential development between critical capacities and empathic capacities. Or someone might be able to make rational judgments and to feel deeply as well but nevertheless fail to understand the emotional communication as such of the accountability demands for acknowledgment. This is perhaps the case for high-functioning autistic people, as I will discuss in Chapter 5.

It is, second, possible to be accountable but not answerable. On the one hand, in the "pure" case as I have described it, one might be able, but fail, to perceive facts about someone's normative perspective as even seeming to be reasons. In such a case, one could not be answerable for a failure of judgment, as judgment is not implicated when nothing even appears to be a reason to one. Nevertheless, to the extent that one was able but failed to take up another's perspective and have facts about it appear to be reasons, one could be accountable for one's disregard. On the other hand, one might be a deeply feeling creature, capable of emotional empathy but not evaluational empathy, for example, and so incapable of picking up on other-regarding reasons while nevertheless able to pick up and respond emotionally to the emotional plights of others. Here one's sensitivity may *height* them, displaying excellent quality of regard, and so render fitting their gratitude, without one's being answerable for anything, as one is incapable of recognizing the sorts of (evaluational) regard-based reasons one's judgment might be about. This, as we shall see in Chapter 6, might be the case for some adults with mild intellectual disability.

These last cases do raise an important question, though, namely, why should we think of "pure" (dis)regard as being something for which the agent is *responsible* in any familiar sense? Pure regard is certainly not subject to immediate volitional control: I cannot, as a mere act of "will," *see* the relevant facts of your normative perspective as reasons. But pure regard is also not subject to *rational* control, sensitive to evaluative judgment (the label is given in Smith 2005). Whether some fact about someone's normative perspective appears to me to be a reason, or whether I am disposed to respond emotionally in sync with the emotional plight of another, these things are not governed by one's evaluative judgments, even, I would contend, in the ideally rational. But then if pure regard is sensitive to neither volition nor judgment, in what sense could it be "up to us"?

Pure regard is what I will term *empathy*-sensitive, subject to our (indirect) empathic "control." That is to say, it is in attending to someone's normative perspective that the relevant sorts of facts appear as reasons or give rise to the relevant sorts of emotional responses. Of course, sometimes these things just do not bubble up. When this happens, familiar excuses may apply: "I'm just distracted by work," say, or "I'm stressed," or "I'm exhausted," or "I've been upset about what happened to my friend." These are the sorts of things that dull empathic sensitivity, and they may get one off the hook. But there remains a space between excuse and incapacity for genuine disregard, where one's sensors are functional but unproductive, and this is the zone in which agential anger, say, finds its fitting target. This is a *failure* of regard, and while it is not a matter of volitional or rational control, is still indirectly sensitive to a certain sort of perspective-taking, and to the extent that it is, it is subject to empathic control, and so may be up to us in a way that warrants its falling under the responsibility rubric.

Importantly, though, most cases of (moral) answerability will *also* be cases of accountability, and that is because taking someone's perspective seriously often does reveal reasons about that perspective whose worth one must then go on to judge. The key to understanding their difference, though, is once again to remind ourselves of the different objects of fitting response for each, which are, respectively, judgment and regard. And when these responses to different qualities of will come apart, we get the kind of ambivalence motivating this book.

Concluding Thoughts

The building of the tripartite theory of responsibility is now complete. I have covered too much detailed ground to summarize everything, but I do want to retrace the basic dialectic and note some reminders of what has been achieved. What motivates the enterprise are our ambivalent responses to several marginal agents, the sense that some responsibility responses are appropriate whereas others are not. Theories of responsibility attempting to account for *all* of our appropriate responsibility responses have received their best expression as Strawsonian quality of will theories. But all such theories, to the extent that they adopt a monistic understanding of "will," are hamstrung by our ambivalence in the marginal cases, I argued, ambivalence which is a function of our wide variety of emotional responsibility responses. While ordinary agents are typically eligible for all of them, marginal agents seem eligible for only some of them. And so, as it turns out, while the monists can each account for some subset of these responses, they individually cannot account for the whole set. The road most often taken in the light of such problems is to abandon the quality of will approach. I have taken a different, pluralistic road, however, incorporating all three of the different *qualities* of "will" identified by the monists, and showing how they give rise to three different types of responsibility.

To do so, I needed to articulate and categorize the wide variety of responsibility responses we have to the marginal cases, and I adopted Strawson's suggested methodology of leaning primarily on the "moral sentiments." Corresponding to, and evaluating, the three qualities of will are our sentimental pairs, three characteristic, pan-cultural, emotional *syndromes* and their oppositely valenced counterparts. These are the sentiments around which all of our other responsibility responses and practices tend to be organized and understood. The characteristic sentimental syndrome pair evaluating quality of character is agential admiration/disdain, and close examination of agential admiration's fitting deployment reveals that having the capacity for cares, commitments, or care-commitment clusters (which together make up one's deep self) renders one an attributable agent. The characteristic sentimental syndrome pair evaluating quality of judgment is agential pride/regret, and close examination of agential regret's fitting deployment reveals that having the capacity for judgment about the worth of various "instead of" reasons renders one an answerable agent. The characteristic sentimental syndrome pair evaluating quality of regard is agential anger/gratitude, and close examination of agential anger's fitting deployment reveals that having the capacity for regard of either the evaluative or emotional variety renders one an accountable agent. The host of other emotional responses we associate with responsibility (e.g., contempt, shame, disappointment, disapproval, embarrassment, hurt feelings, resentment, indignation, gratification, warm feelings, approval, elevation, esteem, and so forth) target one or more of these three types of will, perhaps with varying degrees of cognitive sharpening. These emotional responses, I have claimed, are a function of our caring about three distinctive features of agency—character, judgment, and regard—and they are what structure the world of responsibility for us.

Admitting the three types of responsibility into the mix enables us to resolve the motivating problem: we can now account for the fact of our ambivalence toward marginal agents. What is going on in such cases is that we tend to feel that these agents are the appropriate objects of some of our many responsibility responses but not others in virtue of their having capacities for some qualities of will but not others. Some of our responses evaluate quality of character, others evaluate quality of judgment, and still others evaluate quality of regard. Some marginal agents may have the capacity for emotional regard but lack the capacity for judgment or character, so agential anger or gratitude (to a limited extent), but not agential regret or disdain, would be fitting. Others may be capable of making excellent or regrettable decisions but lack the capacity for regard or character, so they would be eligible for agential approval or disapproval, agential pride or regret, but ineligible for agential anger or gratitude, and agential admiration or disdain. And still others may lack the capacity for judgment or regard, but still have the capacity to express their characters, rendering them eligible for agential admiration and disdain but ineligible for agential disapproval or anger. If there are actually three distinct qualities of will, grounding three distinct types of responsibility, then we can easily account for our ambivalence with a Strawsonian qualities of will theory in a way all previous monistic quality of will theories could not, revealing how marginal agents may be responsible in some ways but not others.

What we have accomplished in Part I, therefore, is to account for the fact of our ambivalence in marginal cases. But as this last paragraph suggests, with all of its hedged and vague language, we have yet to really fully explain or vindicate our ambivalence in any of the specific marginal cases. That is, what is the precise *source* of our ambivalence in any given case? Is, for instance, our ambivalence to a depressed agent or a psychopath the same sort of ambivalence we tend to have to a high-functioning autistic person? And if not, why not? In Part II, I address such questions. The tripartite theory of responsibility I have developed makes predictions about the kinds of responses that are going to be fitting in each specific instance. We can thus test whether the theory gets it right in light of our actual responses to specific sorts of marginal agents, at least once we fill in some crucial empirical details.

PART II

Ambivalence at the Margins

In Part I, I took seriously our ambivalent responses across a variety of marginal cases, ambivalence which consists in our tending to have some responsibility responses, but not others, to such agents. *Pure Quality of Will* theories cannot account for such ambivalence, however. Faced with the prospect of jettisoning the quality of will approach as doomed, therefore, I suggested a pluralistic theory instead, proposing three subcategories of responsibility responses that each track different qualities of will and so implicate distinct types of responsibility with very different agential requirements. Whether the latter move is more promising than abandoning a quality of will approach altogether will thus depend on the plausibility of the specific answers it gives in a wide range of cases. In what follows my basic strategy is to provide the tripartite theory with precise empirical details of the marginal agents in order to see what verdicts about their responsibility-status it will crank out and why. We can then test these verdicts for intuitive plausibility, although some of these intuitions may also be subject to revision, by our own lights, once certain empirical details are fully appreciated or consistency pressures are brought to bear.

In the chapters to follow, I will discuss several marginal cases, agents having clinical depression, scrupulosity, psychopathy, high-functioning autism, mild intellectual disability, poor formative circumstances, and Alzheimer's dementia. I will provide an inventory of each disorder sufficient to enable us to articulate what kind of ambivalence my theory predicts, for the most part, in each case (information I have boiled down into a diagram that shortly follows, for ease of reference). I do this, though, not only to see if the tripartite theory captures all of our specific response-intuitions, and not only to explain the precise source of our ambivalence, but also to vindicate fitting responses and provide a framework for counseling away from *unfitting* responses. To explain this last point, some loved ones of those with these disorders feel guilty about *being* ambivalent, about having mixed responsibility emotions to their depressed teenagers, for example, or to the demented loved ones in their care. If I am right, however, their ambivalence may be vindicated in some cases: There may be fitting grounds for it, explained via the tripartite theory, such that their guilt about the ambivalence itself would be inappropriate. In addition, some people in the throes of these disorders have responsibility responses to *themselves* which are unfitting, a function of some sort of mistake or misfire that my theoretical apparatus can identify and correct. These may be agents who beat themselves up because they view themselves as responsible, full stop. The tripartite theory implies a much more nuanced verdict in such cases, one that I believe fits much more closely with our fine-grained intuitions on these matters: While such agents may be responsible in some sense, they may not be responsible in the way their beating themselves up would license. The tripartite theory provides us with a mechanism by which we may counsel them away from such self-destructive (and misguided) responses.

But as we are about to delve into the details of real-life cases, I must start with a crucial caveat. As I laid it out in Part I, the tripartite theory may seem simply to yield a "yes" or "no" verdict to the question of responsibility among the three types, depending on the capacities of the agents in question. For example, if someone is capable of cares and commitments and having them issue in attitudes, then she is capable of quality of character and so is an attributability-responsible agent (eligible for fitting agential admiration/disdain). If she is capable of judgment with respect to the worth of the relevant "instead of" reasons, then she is capable of quality of judgment and so is an answerable agent (eligible for fitting agential regret/pride and their third-person analogs). And if she is capable of evaluational and/or emotional empathy and so able to see facts about others' normative perspectives as putative reasons in her own deliberative perspective and/or feeling what others feel in sync with them, then she is capable of quality of regard and so is an accountable agent (eligible for fitting agential anger/gratitude). But in real-life cases, capacities are not necessarily "on/off" switches; instead, they may come in degrees and so may also be merely *impaired*. What, then, does this in-between category mean for responsibility and our investigation into real-life marginal cases?

It means that matters can get pretty complicated. First, some non-exempt agents might still be less responsible than others, proportional to the degree of impairment to their relevant capacities. But they might not be, as what one is responsible for may still be well within the range of one's impaired capacities.[1]

[1] If both a master mathematician and I give the wrong answer to a simple arithmetic problem, then the fact that I have an impaired mathematical capacity relative to her does not reduce my

Second, *if* the degree of reduced responsibility is proportional to the degree of the relevant capacity impairment, this may or may not mean that such reduced degrees translate into reduced degrees with respect to fitting responsibility *responses*. Full-on agential admiration may be fitting for greater or lesser attributability-responsibility, as long as its structural conditions cross some threshold of adequacy. Nevertheless, third, it is difficult to know just how such translation from degrees of responsibility to degrees of response should even take place. Suppose I were to find that you had reduced regard capacities and that this meant you were less responsible than a normally capacitated regarder would be. What would this mean for my responses to your disregarding attitudes? Are you eligible for agential anger, just *not as much* as would be fitting for someone else? And if so, how would that translate into the relevant action tendency (if at all)? If I am fittingly less angry than I would otherwise be does that mean I have a motivation to demand less *acknowledgment*, am I less *motivated* to communicate the demand, or am I motivated to less *communication*? Or should I be *less inclined* to anger, or perhaps be fittingly (fully) angry at you but only in a smaller range of cases?

As should be obvious, these are very difficult questions, and I am simply unequipped to answer them.[2] But for my purposes, these are less important questions to answer than the following: How does talk of merely impaired capacities affect my theoretical reliance on our *ambivalence* toward marginal agents? I cannot dodge this question, as it goes to the motivation for the whole project, and it will be important for the chapters to follow. So what can be said about it?

One tempting route is to say that I am, and will be, discussing fictional, *idealized* versions of the agents in question, and that the real-life cases are just more complex but nevertheless approximate the ideal in various ways.[3] I do not want to take this route, however, because to motivate the project I am relying on our ambivalent natural responses to the *real-life* marginal cases in our midst. These cases will be familiar to many of us, and so should be our ambivalence. Idealizing the cases loses the motivational impetus of the enterprise.

What I want to say instead, then, is that, when marginal agents (or any other agents) are "merely" impaired, but not exempted, our ordinary responsibility

responsibility for the mistake relative to her (Ryberg 2014). That particular problem was within the range of my limited mathematical capacities, after all. Indeed, it seems as if both of us would be the fitting target of roughly equivalent (answerability) responses in such a case.

[2] For some of these issues I am tempted simply to point the reader in the direction of Kadri Vihvelin's recent discussion of abilities (Vihvelin 2013, Ch. 6) and move on. Thanks to Eddy Nahmias for the tip.

[3] Talbert 2008 is explicit that this is the approach he is taking in his discussion of the responsibility of psychopaths. Thanks to Terry Horgan for this suggested route in response to Shaun Nichols' forceful articulation of the issue.

responses tend to be (fittingly) *mitigated* in notable ways. So while it may not be clear precisely what about the syndrome of agential anger is to be altered by someone's regard-impairment, it is nevertheless recognizable that *something* about it should be; it at least seems clear that its ordinary deployment would be unfitting. So what matters for motivating my enterprise is that some of our responses toward marginal agents are recognizably, fittingly, altered, such that full deployment of some responsibility responses remains fitting whereas *full* deployment of other responses is not. It thus matters less (for my project) whether, in the latter cases, we altogether suspend our responses or just notably diminish them.

What this recognition allows me to do, then, is to maintain focus on *real-life* marginal cases in what follows, without worrying so much about whether they have exempted or merely mitigated status. Nevertheless, there will be one bit of idealization going on. That is because the disorders and disabilities I discuss admit of a wide *spectrum* of instances, so I do have to pick (and articulate, and justify) which ones I am targeting. What I will be discussing are the kinds of agents who are at the point on their relevant spectrum where they tend to generate the kind of ambivalence motivating my overall project, agents located in what I will call the "perverse sweet spot."[4] Consequently, they will usually be agents in the early to middle range of the spectrum for their particular disorder or disability, e.g., those with high-functioning autism, mild intellectual disability, moderate dementia, and so forth. These are agents who are not completely disabled and so may yet evince *some* qualities of will. Of course, matters will still be messy and complicated, but that is just how real-life agents are. In any event, the messiness will not prevent us from learning about the predictive plausibility of the tripartite theory, or the conditions for full-fledged membership in the responsibility community, which are our main tasks.

In each of the next four chapters, then, I focus mostly on the one feature of the different types of responsibility that I take to be the most interesting source of ambivalence in several marginal cases: Chapter 4 focuses on the nature and boundaries of the deep self for attributability; Chapter 5 focuses on empathic regard and accountability; Chapter 6 focuses on judgmental impairment and answerability; and Chapter 7 focuses on the role of agential history in all three types of responsibility. In the concluding chapter, after drawing out and weaving together the main threads of the book, I will discuss some possible limitations of my account, and then I will suggest some additional virtues of the tripartite theory, including how it might dissolve some long-standing disputes in the philosophy of agency and responsibility.

[4] I owe this apt phrase to Justin D'Arms and/or Dan Jacobson.

Marginal Ambivalence: A Chart

The chart below lays out the predictions of the tripartite theory of Part I for the responsibility status of the specific sorts of marginal agents to be discussed in Part II, once crucial empirical details are filled in. Real-life marginal agency admits of a very wide spectrum. I have in mind those who suffer mild to moderate forms of the relevant disorders or impairing backgrounds, those in what I call in the Introduction to Part II the "perverse sweet spot." Nevertheless, as the responsibility-relevant impairments of even these agents may range widely, their status in the chart below (and in the chapters to follow) may correspondingly range from *exempt* to *mitigated* to *unmitigated*, depending on a host of considerations.[5]

Agential condition:	Attributability	Answerability	Accountability
Clinical depression	*Mitigated to Exempt*	*Mitigated to Unmitigated*	*Unmitigated to Mitigated*
	Depends on the extent to which the agent's care-commitment clusters have been eliminated or disrupted	Depends on whether the disorder impairs judgment	Depends on the extent to which empathic capacities are preserved or apathy saps emotional responsiveness
Mania	*Unmitigated to Mitigated*	*Mitigated to Unmitigated*	*Exempt to Mitigated*
	Depends on whether relevant care-commitments clusters are intact and expressed	Depends on whether the disorder impairs judgment.	Due to empathic incapacitation or impairment (of both kinds)
Scrupulosity	*Unmitigated*	*Unmitigated*	*Exempt to Mitigated*
	For "pro" or "con" attitudes toward the thoughts, their expression, and the	For many attitudes *Mitigated* For some attitudes, to the extent to	Depends on the extent to which obsessions cloud or block regard

(*continued*)

[5] Where one of these terms precedes another in the chart, it is because I lean toward the first term as probably being the more accurate diagnosis for most cases.

Agential condition:	Attributability	Answerability	Accountability
	agent's general moral orientation *Mitigated to Exempt* For disruptive thoughts unconnected to cares or commitments	which a loss of a sense of attributability may implicate an impaired ability to recognize or judge the worth of certain "instead of" reasons	
Psychopathy	*Unmitigated*	*Unmitigated* For nonmoral judgments *Exempt to Mitigated* For regard-based judgments	*Exempt to Mitigated*
High-functioning autism	*Unmitigated*	*Unmitigated* At least for judgments where they have access to the relevant "instead of" reasons	*Mitigated to Exempt*
Mild intellectual disability	*Unmitigated*	*Exempt to Mitigated*	*Unmitigated* In some (caregiver, familial) contexts *Mitigated to Exempt* In nonfamiliar contexts
Poor formative circumstances	*Unmitigated*	*Unmitigated*	*Mitigated* For empathic difficulties
Dementia	*Unmitigated* For expressions of some persisting care-commitment clusters	*Exempt to Mitigated*	*Exempt to Mitigated*

4

Depression and Scrupulosity

The Boundaries of the Deep Self

In this chapter, I will discuss two real-life marginal cases to test whether the tripartite theory yields an intuitively plausible story about our ambivalence toward them. Although I will touch on all three types of responsibility, my focus will mostly be on attributability in this chapter, as I think these two marginal cases yield their most interesting insights with respect to the deep self and quality of character. I begin with what is, to my mind, the most complicated of all the marginal cases to be discussed: clinical depression. The complications are, in part, due to the facts that clinical depression manifests in a variety of ways, its etiology is still something of a mystery, and its "polar" opposite, mania, has some curiously disanalogous features. But I think the complications help reveal an especially valuable feature of the tripartite theory, namely, its nuanced flexibility. There are, for example, different types of ambivalence that the clinically depressed tend to generate, depending on their symptoms, including different types across third- and first-person respondents. If the tripartite theory rightly predicts and plausibly explains these differences (by focusing on the different perceptions of quality of will reasonably attributed to the different parties), then the theory is buttressed.

The second marginal case to be discussed is one in which certain agents are so obsessed with morality that they engage in all sorts of rituals and behaviors to ensure that they have not violated any of its tenets. Unlike many others with Obsessive Compulsive Disorder (OCD), however, these agents fully embrace their moral obsessions as their own. When their obsessions lead them to ignore those they love, though (as often happens), so that they violate other demands of morality (like their promises to these loved ones), we would tend to have ambivalent responses to such agents, I think. Again, the tripartite theory gains in plausibility if it correctly predicts and adequately explains these responses, once the empirical details have been laid bare.

"She's Just Not Herself": Clinical Depression

The DSM-5 lists the symptoms of Major Depressive Disorder (MDD) as follows, where a diagnosable episode requires five of the symptoms to be present during a two-week period (representing a change from previous levels of functioning), at least one of the symptoms is either (1) or (2) below, the symptoms cause significant social or interpersonal impairment, and they are not directly due to substance abuse:

1. Depressed mood
2. Significantly diminished interest or pleasure in most activities
3. Marked weight loss or gain (independently of efforts to bring about either)
4. Significant changes in quantity of sleep (either insomnia or hypersomnia)
5. Increased feelings of restlessness or slowing down almost every day
6. Loss of energy/fatigue almost every day
7. Feelings of worthlessness, or excessive or inappropriate guilt
8. Decreased ability to concentrate/indecisiveness almost every day
9. Recurring thoughts of death/suicide (American Psychiatric Association 2013)

Given the requirement of only five of the nine symptoms for diagnosis, it should be obvious how the many different possible combinations will generate many different "kinds" of MDD, that is, among the clinically depressed there will be many people who manifest it in very different ways. Now there are at least some generalities in the literature that afford us a toehold in discussing at least a significant number of people who suffer from the disorder. Very clearly, though, there will be plenty of clinically depressed people to whom my remarks simply will not apply. This is just a function of the messiness of the disorder. When relevant, though, I will remind the reader of this point and also mention different manifestations of the disorder when they are significant.

Let us start, then, with accountability. My tripartite theory predicts that if MDD appropriately exempts from agential anger (and the other responses organized around it), it would have to do so insofar as the depressed agent's capacity for regard—evaluational or emotional—was impaired. Is this the case? Seeing the relevant "reasonish" facts about, or being emotionally in sync with, someone else's normative perspective is enabled by (evaluational or emotional) empathy. According to recent psychological literature, though, many depressed people are, surprisingly, quite able to empathize with others, often at normal levels, and sometimes at elevated levels. Indeed, those with relatively high levels of empathy at a young age are more likely to become depressed (O'Connor et al.

2007). So how does empathy relate to their depression? From what I can tell, their empathy (and subsequent regard) is both evaluational and emotional: they fully recognize, feel, and appreciate the pain of others, say, and the pain of others both seems to be a reason to resolve it and is something they typically go on to judge to be a reason of significant worth. The tripartite theory would thus seem to predict that they are eligible for accountability and fitting agential anger. Yet that will seem to many to be the wrong answer. If our depressed friend fails to show up at a pre-appointed time, many of us would tend to suspend our anger, at least once we knew the facts about her. So is such a suspension fitting, and what could be its source? Is it just that the clinically depressed have a psychological disorder? If so, then the tripartite theory is otiose. We need to investigate further.

The problems of those with MDD (again, of a certain type) often begin with a malfunction of causal recognition: they come to believe that the pain of others is actually pain for which they themselves are causally responsible, given that they did not prevent it (Shafran and Rachman 2004, 98–100).[1] This perception of their own "failure" generates guilt, sometimes crippling, which itself generates downward assessments of their own worth (and so often leads to the desire to commit suicide). This downward tailspin then undercuts their motivations. While in some cases the other's pain could not actually be prevented because the depressed patients were not in any position to prevent it, at other times the "failure" to do so is due to the collection of their additional psychological impairments: they cannot think clearly about what to do to help due to the cognitive clouding of hippocampus shrinkage (affecting memory), amygdala over-activity (leading to hyperemotionality), and various prefrontal and orbitofrontal cortex dysfunctions (leading among other things to increased inhibitions) (O'Connor et al. 2007, 56). Their withdrawal from the world and general passivity, therefore, while often taken to be a matter of self-absorption or selfishness, is more often a result of feeling utterly ineffectual. They remain "highly attuned to others, but unable to effectively help them" (O'Connor et al. 2007, 56).

With these new details, we can apply a feature of the tripartite theory not previously wielded, albeit drawn from monistic quality of will theories of responsibility. Again, were the psychological problems just cited the totality of symptoms suffered by those with MDD, the tripartite theory indeed predicts that they would not be generally exempt from accountability. Nevertheless, the theory also predicts that they would, by contrast, be *excused*, as their lack of activity would not reflect any actual lack of regard. Rather, their deficiencies would just be

[1] As we will see, this malfunction is also shared by the scrupulous agents we will discuss later.

primarily *volitional*, with their causal misperceptions producing a downward spiral ultimately blocking either the formation of some intentions or any expression of those intentions (as symptoms 2, 5, and 6 above suggest). But they would still seem quite capable of pure regard.

This last capacity is surely impaired in many of those with MDD, however, in virtue of their disorder-caused *apathy*. Although some scientists view them as distinct syndromes, apathy and depression are closely correlated, and apathy is viewed as one of the two key symptoms of MDD.[2] It is operationally defined in the psychological literature as a "lack of motivation relative to the patient's previous level of functioning or the standards of his/her age and culture" in tandem with "at least one symptom belonging to each of the following three domains: (i) diminished goal-directed behavior (lack of effort, dependency on others to structure activity); (ii) diminished goal-directed cognition (lack of interest, lack of concern about one's personal problems); and (iii) diminished concomitants of goal-directed behavior (unchanging affect, lack of emotional responsiveness) . . . " (Robert et al. 2002, 1099–100). The aspects of apathy directly relevant to our enterprise are obvious: lack of motivation (sometimes described revealingly in the literature as "absence of will" [Barrios and Gili 1995]), and what is known as "emotional blunting" (Robert et al. 2002, 1100). These impairments are surely not coincidentally co-occurrent: the fact that the depressed are often not moved to action is naturally explained by the fact that they just do not *care* about anything that might otherwise move them, even if they are capable of evaluational regard. If so, then their *emotional* regard might be impaired after all: if their ability to care has been blunted, then they are less able to respond emotionally in sync with the up-or-down fortunes of possible targets of care. To the extent that these impairments obtain, my tripartite theory implies that such agents' accountability is actually impaired to a significant degree and agential anger toward them should be, if not suspended, then reduced. This seems the right answer.[3]

[2] On apathy and depression as distinct syndromes, see Levy et al. 1998. On the correlations between apathy and major depression, see, Marin, Firinciogullari, and Biedrzycki 1993.

[3] There is a variation of MDD that may give us some pause, however. It occurs when some depressed agents project their negative evaluations of themselves onto others. They may thus see others through a dark lens and lash out at them with what looks like ill will. As this lashing out may include intentionally poking at sore spots, a suspension or reduction of agential anger may not seem all that fitting. Still, I am tempted here to side with the normative recommendations of the tripartite theory and suggest that agential anger ought at least be reduced, primarily because of what I suspect are either empathic impairments or an apathy-sourced loss of mattering. I fully agree, though, that equanimity could be very hard to maintain in the face of such treatment.

My main interest in what follows, however, is depression and *attributability*.[4] Attributability ranges far beyond the mere "moral." All sorts of non-moral attitudes (and dependent actions) may be attributable to agents, including patterns of cowardly social choices, bold aesthetic moves, and conservative athletic decisions. This is an important fact, as it enables us to explore cases in which regard is not implicated and so is not potentially confounding either. Consider, then, a nonmoral fault—laziness—and let us structure our investigation around the following question: When a depressed patient remains in bed all day, refusing to get up or bathe or even eat, are her attitudes (of refusal, say) attributable to her in a way grounding fitting agential disdain or contempt? Is she, in other words, *lazy*?

On the tripartite theory, the answer depends on whether her refusal to get out of bed expresses her character in a way sufficient to render fitting these sorts of aretaic emotional responses, which evaluate quality of character as poor. For most people familiar with clinical depression, the answer seems to be no, such an agent is not lazy.[5] Why not? The explanation yielded by the tripartite theory would be that she neither cares about, nor is committed to the worth of, lying in bed; rather, its causal source must be something else (e.g., her depression). Indeed, staying in bed all day likely *betrays* her cares or commitments. So is this the right explanation?

One worry about it is that this third-person suspension of responsibility responses seems to be in tension with the persisting self-directed responses of those who have suffered through the maelstrom of depression (see, e.g., Styron 1990), for they tend *not* to suspend aretaic predications and sentimental responses toward themselves. Indeed, shame—a first-personal sentimental evaluation of character here—tends to be heightened in those with depression.[6] This

[4] What about answerability? The answerability of those with MDD will depend, according to the tripartite theory, on the extent to which their judgmental capacities are impaired. So can they make judgments about the worth of reasons, and can they recognize the relevant "instead of" reasons? From what I can tell from the psychological literature, sometimes they can do these things and sometimes they cannot. In either event, the tripartite theory's predictions strike me as plausible.

[5] A survey of blogs and counseling sites, anyway, overwhelmingly suggests this answer. For just a taste, see: <http://well.wvu.edu/articles/eight_myths_depression>; <http://psychcentral.com/lib/depression-myths-and-facts-demystified/0003777>; <http://amanicworld.com/2013/12/09/dont-confuse-laziness-with-depression-and-vice-versa/>; and <http://www.tigerfreedom.com/lazy-or-depressed/>. There are surely many who tend to have a different response, however, one that is in the ballpark of disdain. That they would have such a response is perfectly compatible with my theory's predictions, however, as long as they are taking their target's attitudes to express her cares or commitments. The correct answer about which side's responses are fitting then becomes, in part, an empirical matter (albeit not an empirical matter about what aretaic standards are in play).

[6] This may actually be a function of the fact that those more prone to shame are more prone to depression (Tangney, Wagner, and Gramzow 1992; and Kim, Thibodeau, and Jorgensen 2011).

fact should give us pause. Are their responses unfitting, or are the third-person responses to them unfitting? Or are fittingness conditions relative to perspective?

There is an interesting prima facie asymmetry that presses the puzzle more forcefully: While depression often tends to at least dampen various of our responsibility responses, certain high-flying *positive* states do not. Suppose I find out I have won the lottery and I kiss everyone around me, something I would never do ordinarily. Or during the bliss of a splendid meal, perhaps I offer an olive branch to a long-hated colleague. We do not think that the attitudes expressed are not attributable to me in such cases; rather, this is just *how I am when blissed out.*

Sarah Buss notes and exploits this asymmetry to make a case that the fundamental condition of autonomy is healthy human flourishing (Buss 2012, 661–2). By "autonomy" she has in mind something like the self-governing relation necessary for being *accountable* for one's actions, which she describes as being the appropriate target of praise or blame (Buss 2012, 649). So we are not seen as accountable, she argues, when we do bad things, if what is fundamental to situating us in our normative perspective is a disease, a malfunction for a representative member of the human species. This certainly includes depression, for Buss. But we are seen as accountable when our normative perspective is a product of our joy or giddiness. Buss thinks the best explanation for the asymmetry is the flourishing model, as joy and giddiness are not a function of *sickness.*

But of course MDD is part of a syndrome that may also include *manic* phases, and when it does, the disorder is characterized as bipolar.[7] Buss thus explicitly excludes mania from the "positive" list, as it can "prevent us from governing our behavior when it takes [this] extreme form..." (Buss 2012, 662). Now Buss's concern, as already noted, is accountability, and it may well be true that mania typically gets us to suspend our holding-to-account responses. Buss claims that the ground for exemption is the sickness, whereas my thought in developing the tripartite theory has been that it is not sickness *as such* that exempts; rather, it is a specific sort of incapacitation (or impairment), regardless of whether sickness is present. So which account is more plausible?

Shame is much more closely associated with MDD than guilt, in fact, except for what is called "maladaptive" guilt, which is either for events outside of one's control, as discussed above, or more generally for no specific actions or attitudes (Kim, Thibodeau, and Jorgensen, 2011, 68, 86). Indeed, it is rather surprising that guilt remains on the list of symptoms for MDD while shame does not, for it is shame, after all, not necessarily guilt, that is most closely associated with feelings of worthlessness. See Willa Goodfellow's post, "Depression and the Shackles of Shame," on the blog *Prozac Monologues*, <http://prozacmonologues.blogspot.com/2009/05/depression-and-shackles-of-shame.html>; and several of the essays in Clark 2008.

[7] There are varieties of bipolar disorder that need not concern us here.

I do not believe that Buss's sickness account is either sufficiently informative about why someone would not be accountable, or nuanced enough to deal with an ambivalence in our overall responses. Manic patients tend to think there just are no rules for them, that nothing they do is wrong.[8] Now what would explain their exemptions from (or mitigated) accountability, on my story, would be their incapacity (or impairment) for regard, and not just their rejection of the rules. But although the science on this score is still very new, it does suggest such an incapacity: While depressed patients tend to retain their empathic abilities, *manic patients tend not to* (Blumberg 2012; and Shamay-Tsoory et al. 2009). On my story, then, manic patients would have an impaired capacity for regard—grounding their exemptions or mitigations from accountability—in virtue of their impaired capacity for empathy. Nevertheless, as I suggested, I think there is an ambivalence in our responses to manic patients, for we still tend to rue their poor judgment—including their judgment of the worthlessness of the moral rules they reject—and so we take them to be *answerable* for what they do.[9] If I am right, we can explain the mixture of emotions we sometimes feel in dealing with manic patients as follows: disapproval and disappointment are fitting, even though agential anger is not. Buss's monistic account seems unable to account for this ambivalence, where it obtains.

But even if mania appropriately gets us to suspend our accountability responses, as Buss asserts, and even if it also appropriately gets us to suspend our answerability responses (as I doubt), it may not be sufficient to appropriately get us to suspend our aretaic attributability responses. Such responses are certainly experienced first-personally in the manic, as they are for those with depression (see Gruber et al. 2008; Gruber and Johnson 2009). When bipolar agents are in their manic phase, they often experience pride at who they are and the ideas they are coming up with left and right, and this is the opposite of shame in the character zone. They also tend to regret what they did in their manic state once they have come back down to earth (Leahy 1999). We might think, then, that because of the pervasive occurrence of such first-person responses that corresponding *third*-person aretaic responses are appropriate as well. After all, it still seems that *something* of the manic patient may be revealed during her manic state. Often manic patients—at least those not at the furthest extreme of the disorder—do accomplish rather extraordinary things. Their disregard for

[8] In this respect, they have many of the symptoms of pathological narcissism. See, e.g., Stormberg et al. 1998; and Fulford, Johnson, and Carver 2008.

[9] For an interesting discussion of the deployment of poor judgment in manic patients, see Leahy 1999.

others perhaps frees them up to devote their time, focus, and energy to a variety of creative tasks for which they may have some aptitude. It is hard to see why agential admiration would not be appropriate for their accomplishments in this state, then, such that certain of their traits would properly be evaluated as excellent, even if they were not accountable for the disregard that opened the door for those traits to be expressed.[10] But then if third-person attributions could be appropriate for the manic patient, *why would they not be appropriate for the depressed patient as well*?

Let me make explicit the overall puzzle: While there tends to be symmetry in the first-person responses to both depression and mania, there tends to be asymmetry in third-person responses. From the first-person, many people in the grips of depression respond with shame (or guilt) to what they perceive as their character failures, just as many of those in the grips of mania respond with pride to what they perceive as their character excellences. But from the third-person, many people tend to suspend or dampen their aretaic responses toward those in the grips of clinical depression, yet they tend not to suspend or dampen much their aretaic responses to their polar opposite, the manic person. But if these are just different "poles" of the disorder, why treat them asymmetrically? If we reject the asymmetry, then either the first-person perspective is right on both poles or wrong on both poles. But in either event, one pole of the third-person responses is subject to revision.

Insofar as I am presenting a human sentimentalist approach to responsibility, I am loathe to advocate thoroughgoing revisions of our natural responses. If, by our own lights, there are arbitrary inconsistencies in the way we respond to different agents, then revision likely needs to be undertaken.[11] But otherwise, a sentimentalist should take them seriously, especially if they are quite widespread. I thus want to resist the most revisionary option, in which attributability responses to both poles of this disorder are unfitting. Instead, I will explore two options. The first leaves in place the fittingness of all the relevant responses. The second leaves most in place and has several other valuable features the first lacks. I will adopt the better overall package offered by the second option.

[10] Indeed, it is hypothesized by Hirsch 2011 that mania has only been categorized as a psychopathology because of the envy many psychoanalysts have about the accomplishments of their manic patients.

[11] Suppose, to take an example from Fischer and Ravizza, a group of humans like us tended not to respond to women and minorities with resentment or indignation in the way they did to white men (Fischer and Ravizza 1993, 18). If they take their responses to fit some kind of quality of will, then by their own lights they are being inconsistent in responding in differential fashion to these groups.

On the first, nonrevisionary, option, we would need an explanation of the different fittingness conditions of third- and first-personal responses. What could that be? The best account, I think, would be that third-person aretaic responses just have different objects of attribution than first-person ones. In the first-person-case, the relevant object may be the character presumed to be expressed in one's attitudes *at that time*. If I am depressed, I may see what I (think I) ought to do, but if I cannot bring myself to do it, I may evaluate myself as lazy or cowardly by my self-disdain or shame. The self to which I attribute the laziness is my present self, one that has simply *evolved* from the previous self, the one that was (let us assume) far more energetic. What I am *now*, therefore, is lazy, so my shame is fitting. By contrast, in the third-person case, observers might be taking some overarching *agent-as-a-whole* as the relevant object of attribution and so see the agent-at-a-time before us as disconnected from that overarching agent's character. To the extent that the depressed agent before us expresses an attitude, then, it is not viewed as an attitude of that agent-as-a-whole, which in the mind of the third-person evaluator is the *real* agent. Instead of an evolved self before us, says the third-person evaluator, we have a *deviated* self, one who is not an instantiation of the genuine (but silenced) overarching character, so disdain is unfitting. "She is just not herself," indeed.

This is a complicated analysis, but it has some attractive features. Its main virtue is that it leaves in place our differential first- and third-person responses in the depression case. But it has some problems too. First, it could not easily explain why third-person responses to *mania* tend to be in sync with first-person responses. After all, if depression deviates the third-person self, why doesn't mania? At the very least, this analysis leaves that asymmetry a mystery. In addition, this "two selves" explanation would imply that we are just talking past one another when we counsel depressed people not to beat themselves up, or not to be ashamed of themselves, as we and they would just be referring to different objects. In reality, though, it seems that we are all talking about the very same thing, a single agential target, and we (from the third-person perspective) do believe that the depressed person is making a genuine mistake in feeling this way. Revision of some group's responses is thus probably necessary. But whose, and why?

I think by appealing to some distinctive features of my theory of attributability we can preserve most, but not all, of our responses, in a way that fully explains third- and first-person disagreement while also vindicating the asymmetrical attributability treatment of depression and mania. The theory's explanatory power in this sort of case will thus also boost its plausibility. Here is the basic idea: The transition into both depressed and manic states correlates with a significant jiggering of the agent's care-commitment *clusters* such that, while attributability of a wide range of attitudes to her may still obtain, the nature of the *character traits* of which they were formerly a part may have changed. Recall from Chapter 1 what a care-commitment cluster is: it is a network of mutually supportive and tempering cares and commitments. These are what I for the most part take our character traits to consist in. It thus could be that the transition into depressive and/or manic disorders tends to cut the tempering tethers in these clusters, such that their agents' normal patterns of attitudes and volitional structures are significantly altered.[12] These attitudes and structures would still reflect (mostly) persisting cares and commitments, but given the changes effected in the *relation* between the cares and commitments from the original structure, the character traits originally possessed may disappear or be altered. So someone whose care about creative expression is normally tempered by his commitment to respecting others' boundaries may have that tempering tether cut when losing empathy during the transition to mania. The behavior expressed, then, could still be attributable to him, given that it reflects his persisting caring for creative expression, even if his empathic impairments may suspend our evaluating him as having the admirably *tempered* character trait he formerly had. Nevertheless, creativity might be admirable on its own and in a different way, even without being tempered by certain moral commitments.

By contrast, a clinically depressed patient's empathic tethering may persist, but her depression will often include apathy, which in turn may undermine many of her *cares*—she becomes affectless in certain respects and so is no longer emotionally disposed to respond to the fortunes of the formerly cared-for objects in those respects—such that what empathy tethers her commitments *to* disappears. She may thus still have attitudes and intentions formed by her commitments—to work, to engage in activities generally—and these may still be attributable to her (specifically, to her evaluative stance), but to the extent that she does not care about doing anything about them, her lack of volition may not be attributable to a *trait* of hers. Alternatively, she may be unable to think clearly about how to apply her evaluative stance in her concrete circumstances, in which case what attitudes she could form would not express her evaluative stance (and its attached care-commitment cluster/trait). In either case, though, no element of her deep self may be implicated by her failure to get out of bed. By contrast, the lazy person *cares* about staying in bed, or is committed to the worth of doing so, and so his staying in bed reflects a care-commitment cluster—a lazy trait—to that effect.

[12] Matters may be quite different for those for whom no transition takes place, those who have always (more or less) been in such states. These may well just be depressive or manic *people*.

This story has genuine explanatory power. First, as we have just seen, it gives a plausible account of *why* the depressed patient may be distinct from the lazy person: in the latter agent, care-commitment clusters are implicated, whereas in the former agent, they may not be (for what may be a variety of reasons). Second, it preserves as fitting many people's asymmetrical third-person responses at the poles by pointing out an important asymmetrical relation between depression and mania: in both, third-person attributability responses are directed to agents in light of their perceived care-commitment clusters, but depression and mania may alter these clusters *in different ways* and so ground different sorts of responses. In cases of mania, while tempering tethers between components of a cluster may be lost, individual cares and commitments may persist and continue to be reflected in the manic patient's attitudes in a way sufficient to ground various attributability responses (albeit without the previous character traits still being implicated). In cases of depression, specific cares and commitments may be *lost* (or be unable to be expressed), such that nothing relevant is left to which the expressed attitudes may be attributable.

Third, the account I have given allows for genuine disagreement between parties by revealing the source of a mistake being made in some first-personal attributability responses of those who are depressed. In the most straightforward case, shame would be unfitting if it were the direct result of a dysfunctional view of the agent's causal ability to prevent harm to others. The more complicated cases are those in which depressed patients have attitudes that may actually seem to express who they are. For example, suppose that I do actually assign genuine worth to relaxation and lounging in bed all day—it would make for an excellent day, I think. But on most days, I also judge that it would be much *better* to get out of bed and work, and I also care a lot about getting out of bed (that is, I would be emotionally wrought were I to lounge around all day accomplishing nothing). Now suppose that I become depressed, and my depression significantly dampens my caring about getting out of bed: while I still judge it would be better to get out of bed, I no longer care about doing so and am consequently not motivated to do so. My failure to get out of bed may, in my mind, seem to express my other everyday evaluation that staying in bed all day would be good, even if not best. To the extent that this evaluation—which is mine, after all—is taken by me to be what governs my attitudes and behavior, I may view who I am with disdain and shame, as perhaps *weak* in going against what I simultaneously judge best (getting out of bed).

These responses are not fitting, however, because part of the deep self that ordinarily governs my behavior—the care-commitment cluster consisting in my mutually buttressing stances regarding the worth and importance of getting out of bed—has been disabled by the depression-caused dampening of my cares. What is left is just inertia. The fact that what I do *conforms* to some second-best evaluative stance, and thus comes to *seem* to govern my attitudes, is just the result of its having been spotlighted in relief against the undercutting of my original care-commitment cluster. But to the extent that it does not actually govern matters, my remaining in bed is not attributable to me.

The tripartite theory's view of attributability, therefore, according to which the deep self is primarily a matter of care-commitment clusters, provides what I think is an intuitively plausible explanation of an asymmetry in fitting third-person responses to manic-depression. Those suffering from the disorder may have deep selves, but their exempted or mitigated attributability status may differ in accordance with whether those deep selves continue to be expressed.

As I said in the introduction to Part II of this book, I am going to focus primarily on marginal agents within a kind of "perverse sweet spot," a moderate stage within the spectrum of the disorder in which some responsibility responses, but not others, seem fitting. But at the farthest ends of these spectra, no responses are likely fitting. With respect to clinical depression, that extreme may look like this:

> It was as if the door to whatever part of the brain that housed creativity had locked. Clarity of thought, memory and concentration had all left me. I was slowly fading away.
>
> I would try to talk to my doctors about my vanishing self, but they didn't have much to say on the subject. Instead they focused on whether I could make eye contact or how much expression I showed in my face. They monitored my lithium and cortisol levels; they took an M.R.I. of my head.... Everything was scrutinized—except the transformation of my self and my experience of its loss. (Logan 2013, 57)

Here the deep self just disappears in depression and the fog of subsequent medication. Recovery of this self can take years, long after the depression itself has lifted (Logan 2013, 58–60). Shame and regret are not what is typically reported by such patients; rather, frustration, confusion, and a sense of rootlessness are more often experienced. And shame (or any aretaic attitudes) would be quite unfitting, insofar as the fundamental agential capacity for attributability—the *having* of a deep self—would have been destroyed.

Nevertheless, for moderate cases of clinical depression and mania, I have argued that my theory of attributability has the resources for offering the most plausible explanation of the asymmetry in our (third-person) responses. It also implies that the depressed person's self-directed shame or disdain may be unfitting, and we can draw from it the tools by which we may counsel against such responses, despite the depressed person's own endorsement of the attitudes (I will say more on this point in the conclusion of this chapter).

"Lust in my Heart": Scrupulosity

Until recently I had taken OCD to be without need of a distinctive treatment with respect to attributability. Indeed, in Chapter 1, I essentially took OCD to be a fixed data point of non-attributability. The repeated urges to check and recheck the door to make sure it is locked, say, surely could not be attitudes that belong to these agents in any way grounding aretaic responsibility responses. Case closed.

A specific type of OCD recently brought to my attention has reopened the case, however.[13] It is the perplexing and fascinating pathology of *scrupulosity*, whose symptoms include "pathological guilt or obsession associated with moral or religious issues that is often accompanied by compulsive moral or religious observance and is highly distressing and maladaptive" (Miller and Hedges 2008, 1042). While scrupulosity shares some general features of OCD, such as persistent, anxiety-producing thoughts and urges to reduce the anxiety via various rituals, it has several characteristically distinctive features, given its moral or religious nature. For example, scrupulous agents tend to have extremely high moral or religious standards; they are perfectionists, of a sort. They also have chronic moral doubt, in contrast with nonscrupulous agents with OCD, whose doubts are often about various household objects (e.g., whether the door was locked or the oven left on). Another distinctive feature is labeled "moral thought-action fusion." Thought-action fusion generally is the belief that one's internal thoughts may have some external effects or status, and it is present in those with OCD across the board.[14] The moral version of thought-action fusion is the belief that thoughts can have the same moral status as actions. So thought-action fusion is manifested in the scrupulous as the belief that the "immoral" thoughts that crop up in them are as bad as immoral attempts or actions, despite being uncontrollable and intrusive. A brief feeling of lust for an attractive passer-by may be sufficient to send someone with scrupulosity headlong into a series of religious rituals in order to respond to what he takes to be the wrongful thought (Nelson et al. 2006).

[13] The case was brought to my attention in various forums by Tim Schroeder, Walter Sinnott-Armstrong, and Jesse Summers. See Schroeder Forthcoming, and Summers and Sinnott-Armstrong 2014.

[14] There are actually two general forms of thought-action fusion (Shafran and Rachman 2004, 87–8). Likelihood thought-action fusion is the view that certain thoughts about possible events increase the likelihood of their actually happening. When the thoughts are about oneself ("If I think about getting sick, I will be more likely to get sick"), it is called Likelihood-Self thought-action fusion, and when the thoughts are about others ("If I think about you getting sick, you will be more likely to get sick"), it is called Likelihood-Other thought-action fusion. The other general form of thought-action fusion is the moral version I am concerned with in the text.

Scrupulosity takes two different forms, however, and only one form piques my interest here. When the obsessions of someone with OCD are religious or moral, then their scrupulosity is a form of OCD. One of OCD's defining features is that the obsessive thoughts and urges are *unwanted*—"ego-dystonic"—and some scrupulous agents' religious or moral thoughts are indeed of this ilk. Their rituals are meant to eliminate or neutralize the offending thought (just as the rituals of the nonscrupulous person with OCD are meant to eliminate or neutralize the repeated thought, say, that the door is still unlocked). But in Obsessive Compulsive *Personality* Disorder (OCPD), the obsessions are experienced as wanted or endorsed—"ego-syntonic"—and so they are neither feared nor resisted (Nelson 2006, 1072, n. 1; Stein and Hollander 1993). Scrupulous OCPD agents view themselves as moral people in an immoral world. Their conviction in this matter presents a worry for our "fixed" data point, then: Given that the moral desires and obsessions *are* experienced and embraced as their own, perhaps we should not be so quick to view OCD generally as undermining attributability. Perhaps a fervid endorsing of one's desires is sufficient to render them one's own.

There may seem to be a parallel in the scrupulous to Harry Frankfurt's example of the willing addict, someone who loves the addiction that structures his volitions and would do what he could to stoke it were it to wane (Frankfurt 1988, 24–5). I am not sure this is a helpful comparison, but the reasons why it is not helpful will themselves be helpful to survey. The willing addict's craving structures his volition in a way that is different from that of the person with scrupulosity. In general, an addict's desire to take the drug, given its overwhelming strength, becomes his will, that is, it simply becomes his effective desire, regardless of his attitude toward it. What the willing addict does, though, is endorse this desire; in Frankfurt's terminology, the addict forms a second-order desire that the desire to take the drug be his will. His will is thus overdetermined, determined by both his addiction and his endorsement (Frankfurt 1988, 25). In contrast, the scrupulous agent's will is to engage in some behavior as a *response* to an obsessional thought. Perhaps, while praying, various distracting thoughts intrude, so the scrupulous agent becomes obsessed with praying correctly and without distraction, in part to make up for the perceived failing. Or perhaps the scrupulous agent is assailed with thoughts of Jesus on the cross with an erection (Abramowitz 2008, 157). Because of the fear of hell aroused by these thoughts, the agent is moved to pray or engage in various religious rituals to properly atone for his "sin" (and so note that, in a crucial difference from the scrupulous OCD agent, this OCPD agent does not engage in the ritual in order to eliminate or neutralize the thoughts; rather, he is moved to do so as the proper way to *atone* for them). So the scrupulous agent is moved by a desire for atonement, and this desire constitutes his will, but the will is not determined by any other source, so it lacks the overdetermination distinctive of the willing addict's will. There is no real *compulsion* in such agents, then.

There is obsession, however, albeit endorsed. But what exactly *is* ego-syntonic in the scrupulous OCPD agent, the precise object of endorsement? This issue is repeatedly glossed over in the psychological literature, much to my frustration. With closer inspection, we can see that many things probably qualify as ego-syntonic: the behavior required to atone for the perceived sin, the intention to atone, the commitment to the worth of religious/moral purity, and the care about avoiding immorality (such that scrupulous OCPD agents are disposed to get very emotionally wrought at the thought that they have somehow fallen into sin). But as with responsibility generally, one can properly atone only for those actions or attitudes that are *also* one's own. This means that scrupulous OCPD agents must take those obsessional, impure, or distracting *thoughts* to be attributable to them as well. Our question: Are they correct to do so?

I cannot see that they are. Consider how the contemporary cognitive-behavioral psychological account of scrupulosity goes. Imagine, first of all, sitting in church. If you are without OCD or OCPD, many thoughts, images, and desires—lewd, amusing, violent, or generally contrary to your convictions—may cross your mind during the service. This is normal, and we typically hardly notice it. But these may become obsessions when the person believes them to have a particular sort of significance or constitute a threat. Scrupulous people have two features that enable this belief: first, they have moral thought-action fusion, and second, they tend to believe that they have the capacity to *control* these thoughts, images, and desires. The first generates the scrupulous agent's belief that what he is thinking is immoral/sinful: to have the image of one's children lying dead on the floor of the sanctuary is just to believe that one genuinely *wants* them dead on the floor of the sanctuary, and this is just as bad (given the moral thought-action fusion) *as having killed them oneself* (Abramowitz 2008, 161). One thus ought not have such thoughts, and if ought implies can, it is one's failure to control those thoughts that is at the heart of one's *being* an immoral—disdainful—person, one who desperately needs to atone.

I have already explicitly allowed that one might be attributability-responsible for attitudes over which one has no volitional (or even rational) control—attributability is about how one is, not how one might have been—so to the extent that "attributability does *not* imply can" (at least in these familiar senses), I cannot locate the mistake the scrupulous agent is making about attributability in the second feature above. Self-disdain and the motivation to alter one's character may be appropriate even if one lacks a capacity to control (volitionally or rationally) the formation or persistence of one's attributable attitudes. The mistake, then, seems like it must have its source in her moral thought-action fusion, her belief that thoughts may be just as immoral as actions.

But *aren't* they, at least sometimes? If "thoughts" includes a wide range of familiar *attitudes*, then of course they are! Indeed, that is what my *qualities* of will theory is all about: I have maintained that one is responsible for actions only derivatively, that is, only when they reflect a certain quality of will, which may consist in attitudes of regard, judgment, or more general character traits that structure one's expressed attitudes. So when it comes to attributability, many attitudes will certainly be the appropriate targets of moral (and general normative) evaluation. The bungling assassin's intention to kill his target may be just as bad as the successful assassin's intention. And famously, some such attitudes are laid out in the Bible: "You have heard that it was said 'you shall not commit adultery'; but I say to you, that everyone who looks at a woman with lust for her has already committed adultery with her in his heart" (Matthew 5:27–8; New American Standard Version).[15]

Now without going too deeply (or at all) into Biblical exegesis, this actually seems to be a point about *accountability*: it is less a dictate about quality of character or quality of judgment than it is about quality of regard, and it counsels against an attitude for which one may be appropriately held to account (via, say, anger). But at any rate, one could easily expand this to be a dictate about character and attributability: married men who *tend to* look at other women with lust in their hearts are disdainful (on this religious construal), as they seem to be failing in the love and trust department with their own spouses. If they really loved their spouses, they would not have these feelings of lust for other women. This pattern of (mere) attitudes reflects poorly on such men's characters. And we have such evaluative responses to attitudes in many other arenas as well.

And yet there is an important difference between these sorts of attitudes and mere thoughts or images. Having in my head the mere image of kissing someone who is not my spouse is surely not just as bad as actually doing so (assuming the latter is bad), even if intending to do so is. But it does not seem as if—and it would be surprising were it true—scrupulous (OCPD) agents *merely* have the thought or image in question. Suppose what I see in my mind is my lips meeting those of someone to whom I am not married. It would be remarkable if moral anxiety

[15] Quoted also in Abramowitz 2008, 162. And when it comes to the perfectionism of the Scrupulous, they may at least seem to have the right motivations after all: "Therefore you are to be perfect, as your heavenly Father is perfect" (Matthew 5:48; NASV).

arose without my also imagining *intending* to kiss this person.[16] And even intending to kiss a girl is not sufficient; one also has to *like* it.[17] Indeed, the psychological literature assumes that it is genuine attitudes like this last complex that are the subjects of moral thought-action fusion. One clear-cut example comes from studies done on scrupulous agents about their views of the badness of a thought like "I hope __________ is in a car accident," where they insert the name of a friend or relative in the blank (Shafran and Rachman 2004, 94). Here a (wrongful) hoping attitude has already been packed into the "mere" thought. It thus cannot be that some image in and of itself is ostensibly bad and so anxiety-producing; it must instead be that it is one's attitude *in* the image that is deemed bad and anxiety-producing.

Consequently, I do not want to locate the malfunction of the scrupulous person in her moral thought-action fusion, as I am not at all convinced that thought-action fusion—at least where it concerns actual attitudes—is even a *malfunction* when it comes to attributability. Where I locate the malfunction instead is in the scrupulous person's indiscriminately taking the entire set of the (attitudinally loaded) thoughts and images that cross her mind *equally* as her own, in virtue of their all being perceived as incorporating some immoral/irreligious pro-attitude.[18] That is to say, the scrupulous person lacks a discriminating *sense of attributability* for those thoughts and attitudes that express her cares or commitments (her deep self). Normally, I think, we automatically discriminate amongst the wide variety of thoughts and attitudes that arise in us via a sense of what matters, a sense that, sometimes roughly, tracks the expressions of our deep self. Many of the thoughts and attitudes that arise in us are simply dismissed or fade away as irrelevant to what we care about or judge worthy. But others stick, arising to the level of the attention-worthy, and these are typically the ones that connect up to our cares or commitments in some way. What I am suggesting is that scrupulous agents lack this discriminating sense of what is genuinely important to them, and so the religious or moral thoughts about which they obsess are those that arise which they (mistakenly) view as having an attached pro-attitude, and so which they take to implicate *who they are* in a way that warrants attention, generates anxiety, and motivates atonement.

Crucially, though, some of the religious and moral thoughts that arise *are* attached to their deep selves (and so are attributable to them). To see what I have

[16] I am assuming here that scrupulous agents are on a spectrum with the rest of us, and so that the source of their anxiety is akin to ours, only cranked up several levels in salience or strength.

[17] See, e.g., Katy Perry, *One of the Boys* (Capitol Records, 2008).

[18] As Shafran and Rachman 2004 put it (p. 97), "[U]ndue significance is placed on the meaning of their thoughts by people with obsessional difficulties."

in mind, imagine an opposite disorder, *unscrupulosity*, where those who have it are committed to bringing about harms, boils, and plagues to those around them, but who are often assailed by anxious images of doing kind things for others instead (and liking it!), or comforting them when they suffer, so these agents are motivated to pray to Satan obsessively to atone or to make sure their praying style for the deliverance of the boils and plagues is done correctly and so gets through to Satan. Let us assume that these people have the OCPD variety of the disorder, so that they consider the thoughts their own, and they also embrace the required rituals, not as a way to neutralize the thoughts, but as the best way to atone for them. We would, I think, have a deep ambivalence about such people: While agential anger would probably not be appropriate for them, some other negative responsibility responses surely would be. They are deeply morally flawed, after all, and this fault is reflected in their general stance toward others. To the extent that they have unscrupulosity, though, on my diagnosis above they have no discriminating sense of which thoughts and attitudes reflect their cares and commitments and which do not. Nevertheless, their *moral orientation* still seems quite attributable to them, and it seems to render appropriate various aretaic responses, for example, agential disdain or contempt. The fact that they are assailed by anxious thoughts about *whether* the evils they want to be delivered will in fact be delivered, thoughts producing the motivation for obsessive rituals and prayers, may just be irrelevant to such aretaic responses, for these latter simply depend on the obtaining of the structural "expression" relation between the agents' attitudes and their deep selves.

By the same token, then, we would also seem to have reason to think that the *scrupulous* agent could be the fitting target of agential admiration for having such a persistent and proper moral orientation (to the extent that we believe this, anyway), that is, for having the ongoing concern for others that makes her kind or considerate, traits reflected in her intention to pray or to perform various rituals, an intention, not incidentally, that is produced by the considerate traits found in lots of nonscrupulous people as well. Now when that happens in the nonscrupulous, the anxiety they might feel about whether what they are doing will be effective or is sufficient to establish their moral aims normally goes away once they have thought about it or done a quick check. But this anxiety may not go away for a long while in the obsessed. This persisting moral anxiety could just be a function of their perfectionism: they have much higher standards for what it takes to get these things right. But then this general perfectionist stance on the world of moral/religious behavior is *also* likely attributable to them: that too is just who they are. A lot of the attitudes of (OCPD) scrupulous agents will be attributable to them, therefore, even if these agents are viewed as neither answerable nor accountable for what they do in light of those attitudes.[19] My theory of attributability explains and vindicates the kind of ambivalence we may thus have toward them.

Conclusion

My aim in this chapter has been to test the plausibility of the tripartite theory, and in particular the theory of attributability within it, with respect to the ambivalence we would tend to feel toward two complicated marginal cases. The first case was MDD, or clinical depression (as well as its polar opposite). I argued that, in light of the details of MDD, clinically depressed agents' attributability is (at least) mitigated. Considering manic agents raised a worry, however: Insofar as they sometimes seem fully eligible for attributability, and their disorder is just the flipside of depression, why are depressed agents not fully eligible for attributability as well? The best answer comes from the details of the tripartite theory: Attributability depends on expression of the agent's care-commitment *clusters*, and these may be affected in asymmetrical ways by mania and depression. We may thus be appropriately ambivalent to both depressed and manic agents, just in different ways.

The second case I discussed was the OCPD version of scrupulosity, wherein the agents' obsessions are ego-syntonic. Here I hypothesized that the scrupulous agent's attributability disorder has as its source the inability to discriminate between those attitudes that reflect her cares and commitments and those that do not. Combined with her (attributable) perfectionism and (attributable) moral thought-action fusion, this disorder sets the stage for the (attributable) intentions to atone or to pray until she gets it right. So while many of the originating obsessive thoughts and attitudes are not expressive of who she is, of her agential character, many of the things she does in response to them are.

Part of what these cases bring out is the need to precisify the target of our responses so as to determine as clearly as possible just what is and is not

[19] I have not really said much about these other two types of responsibility here. My tripartite theory predicts that scrupulous agents are probably neither answerable nor accountable, at least in their obsessional zones. They would probably not be answerable to the extent that an impaired sense of attributability, combined with an obsessional anxiety, would likely impair their ability to recognize, or make accurate judgments of the worth of, various relevant "instead of" reasons. To the extent that their obsessional anxieties would cloud or block their regard for those not in the sights of their atoning rituals, their accountability would be impaired as well. This again strikes me as the intuitively plausible answer in both cases, as they seem eligible for neither agential anger nor disapproval.

attributable to these agents.[20] The tripartite theory is nuanced enough to explain all of these complicated features in a way that no pure quality of will theory is able. What these cases also bring out, bit by bit, is the precise nature of the capacities needed, as well as those *not* needed, for attributable agency. One very important lesson drawn from consideration of the cases in this chapter is that the subjective stance agents take toward various of their attitudes is just not what generates the attributability of those attitudes. Instead, attributability is entirely a matter of agents' objective attitudinal and volitional structures.

Indeed, this last point may enable us more forcefully to counsel against the unfitting shame and self-disdain sufferers of these syndromes may heap upon themselves. Those in the grips of depression may spiral downward given what they take to be *their* "shameful" attitudes. If we can show them instead how these attitudes bear no relation to their current care-commitment clusters, and so express nothing of their true characters, we have at least one method for attempting to block the self-destructive spiral.[21] Importantly, though, our fitting ambivalence to some such agents may reveal other avenues for counseling and connection: to the extent, for example, that their capacities for judgment remain functional, they may still be answerable, and to the extent that their capacities for empathic regard also remain functional, they may be accountable as well. They may thus still be members of the moral responsibility communities in key respects, and this knowledge may also better enable constructive exchanges between us; they are not aliens to some of these communities, and so should not be treated, or treat themselves, as such.

Similarly, there are also implications here for the treatment of scrupulous agents. They, like psychopaths, tend to be perfectly content with their condition (the scrupulous take themselves to be moral people in an immoral world!), so the hardest part is often getting them to see the need for treatment in the first place (see Huppert, Kiev, and Kushner 2007, 936). One way might be to get them to see how the attitudes they take toward the images that arise in their heads (attached to the pro-attitudes that generate their anxiety) have no real connection to their actual cares or commitments. "Do you really approve of—see anything good about—Jesus' having an erection on the cross?" we might ask. Or "Do you really

[20] I am grateful to Tamler Sommers for this way of putting it.

[21] Matters here are complicated, though, by the fact that shame *might* be fitting for some non-agential features, such as one's weight, complexion, parental backgrounds, and so forth. If so, then shame might be fitting for non-attributable attitudes as well. Whether it is, then, may depend on some subjective factors after all, such as whether the ashamed agent does actually view the attitudes as expressive of her character, and this stance is what grounds her shame. Thanks to Justin D'Arms and Dan Jacobson for discussion.

think it would be good if your children were dead?" Appealing to their actual evaluative stance might enable them to see its disconnection from the sorts of pro-attitudes they find themselves having with respect to these images, and so may provide a means of recognition that something is actually going haywire for them.

I am no therapist, of course! But I nevertheless think that once we move beyond the deeply entrenched all-or-nothing model of responsibility, the tripartite theory opens us up to a new, nuanced set of tools for both those who treat and those who suffer from (at least some of) these disorders. I am hopeful that those better positioned than I will be able to develop and take advantage of these tools.

5

Psychopathy and Autism

The Limits of Regard

While the previous chapter focused on how the tripartite theory—informed by precise empirical details—predicts and explains our ambivalence in some marginal cases primarily with respect to attributability, this chapter will focus on how it does so primarily with respect to accountability. I will begin with psychopathy, which I think is a particularly rich and revealing case. As I suggested in the Introduction, it seems that many of us would tend to have ambivalent responsibility responses to psychopaths, at least once we know the full details about them. Explaining and vindicating this ambivalence is part of my project here (to be continued in the next chapter as well), but in this chapter I will show why I think psychopaths are appropriately exempt or significantly mitigated from accountability. Now some theorists agree that psychopaths are exempt/mitigated, but most of them, I will argue, do so for the wrong reason, relying on psychopaths' purported poor performance on a task designed to test whether they can distinguish moral violations from conventional norm violations (the "moral/conventional task"). Not only will I show that this task (and "the" distinction on which it is based) is deeply problematic, but also I will show why any lessons we can plausibly draw from it are quite different than what others have taken it to show. My basic conclusion will be that psychopaths lack sufficient regard to be accountable, ultimately because of their empathic impairments. I will then explore two challenges to this conclusion, one coming from a recent attempt to run a cleaned-up version of the moral/conventional test on psychopaths (a version they do much better on), and the second coming from a comparison between psychopaths and those at the high-functioning end of the autism spectrum, both of whom seem to have the same empathy-based regard impairments the tripartite theory deems relevant, but who are nevertheless thought by some to have differential accountability statuses. Both challenges may be resisted. Ultimately, I think the empirical details, in combination with the tripartite theory, yield the tentative, yet rather plausible, verdict that those with high-functioning autism are (at least) impaired for accountability, and for similar reasons as psychopaths.

The Moral/Conventional Task and Moral Responsibility

In 1978, Nucci and Turiel developed a test to see if preschool children could track what was taken to be a crucial distinction between "social conventional" and "moral" events (Nucci and Turiel 1978; see also Nucci and Herman 1982; and Nucci and Nucci 1982a and 1982b).[1] Social conventions were defined as "behavioral uniformities which coordinate interactions of individuals within social systems," and "in themselves are arbitrary in that they do not have an intrinsically prescriptive basis" (Nucci and Turiel 1978, 400). By contrast, "within the moral domain actions are not arbitrary, and the existence of a social regulation is not necessary for an individual to regard an event as a (moral) transgression" (Nucci and Turiel 1978, 401). Because the original "moral/conventional task" was on children, its 263 scenarios involved regulations with which children would be familiar, so examples of conventional transgressions included playing or working at the wrong time or in the wrong area of a classroom, failing to engage in an assigned group activity, or violating various other classroom rules (e.g., standing, rather than sitting, while eating a snack). Moral transgressions included hitting another child, stealing another child's belongings, or refusing to share (Nucci and Turiel 1978, 402).

The task was eventually designed to elicit four sorts of judgments in response to questions about scenarios describing a child's transgression. First, was what the child did *permissible* ("Was it right or wrong for X to do Y?")? Second, how *serious* was the transgression ("On a scale of one to ten, how right [or wrong, depending on the first answer] was it for X to do Y?")? Third, what was the *justification* for the answer to the permissibility question ("Why was it right [or wrong] for X to do Y?")? Fourth, if what X did was wrong, how *modifiable* were those first judgments upon the removal of authority from the equation ("Would it be OK for X to do Y if the teacher says X can?")? (Blair 1995, 15)

Regarding the first two questions, the children took moral transgressions to be more serious than conventional transgressions roughly just as adults did, and while both sorts of transgression were generally judged impermissible by both sets of subjects, conventional transgressions were "more likely to be judged *permissible* than moral transgressions" (Blair 1995, 15, emphasis in original; see also Smetana 1985). Regarding justifications, children (and adults) typically

[1] Some material in this and the next few sections has been drawn from Shoemaker 2011c.

appealed to what are called "normative" reasons—"those are the rules," or "it's just not acceptable"—to justify the impermissibility of conventional transgressions, whereas they would most often refer to the welfare of others to ground their reasoning about the impermissibility of moral transgressions (Blair 1997, 735). Regarding modifiability, conventional transgressions were judged to be more *authority-dependent* than moral transgressions, that is, if the teacher said it was OK for the child to perform the act, conventional "transgressions" were then thought to be permissible, whereas moral transgressions were not (Blair 1995, 6). Children worldwide have been found to make this moral/conventional distinction from as early as 39 months (Smetana 1981; Hollos, Leis, and Turiel 1986).

In 1995, the psychologist James Blair published the fruit of his insightful idea to study how psychopaths did on the task (Blair 1995; Blair et al. 1995). What, though, is psychopathy? It is still not officially recognized as a disorder, even in the recently released DSM-5, but it is nevertheless recognized by many psychologists as such. In the DSM-5, the only place for psychopathy—as was the case in the DSM-IV[2]—is under the more general rubric of Antisocial Personality Disorder (APD). In the DSM-IV, the symptoms of APD were primarily behavioral, including failure to conform to social norms, aggressiveness, repeated arrest, and so forth. In the DSM-5, many of the *personality trait* symptoms several theorists have taken to be distinctive of psychopathy have finally been included. This includes most of the "Factor 1" traits of Robert Hare's famous psychopathy checklist (the PCL-R; see Hare 2003), and these are the ones on which I will focus in my discussion. Some background, then, is in order.

Drawn both from Hare's work with male prison offenders in the 1970s and Hervey Cleckley's clinical profile of psychopaths in 1941, Hare's checklist essentially tests for likelihood of both criminal behavior and recidivism. There are twenty items on his checklist, and they are divided into Factor 1 traits and Factor 2 traits. Hare's Factor 1 (core personality) traits of psychopathy are essentially those of "Aggressive Narcissism": glibness/superficial charm; grandiose sense of self-worth; pathological lying; cunning/manipulative; lack of remorse or guilt; shallow affect (genuine emotion is short-lived and egocentric); callousness; lack of empathy; and failure to accept responsibility for his or her own actions. The Factor 2 items are those indicative of a "socially deviant lifestyle," and so include the need for stimulation/proneness to boredom; parasitic lifestyle; poor behavioral control; lack of realistic long-term goals; impulsivity; irresponsibility; juvenile delinquency; early behavior problems; and revocation of conditional release. Through detailed questionnaires and verification methods, investigators assign a

[2] Yes, they changed from Roman to Arabic numerals with the DSM-5.

score for each of the traits: 0 for "doesn't apply," 1 for "applies somewhat," and 2 for "applies fully." One's overall PCL-R score is a function of one's score on all the items in both Factors. Indeed, both Factors are highly correlated, and there is strong, albeit not conclusive, evidence that they have a source in a single disorder (Harpur, Hare, and Hakstian 1989; Cooke, Kosson, and Michie 2001). I will assume that psychopathy is in fact such a disorder, as most psychologists currently do. It obviously admits of a spectrum, however, with those closer to a 40-point total being higher risks for criminal behavior and recidivism. Clinical diagnosis of psychopathy typically requires a 30-point total or higher, although some clinicians will diagnose it in someone with a total of 26 or higher (Aharoni, Sinnott-Armstrong, and Kiehl 2012; Gacono and Hutton 1994; Haapasalo and Pulkkinen 1992).

As I said, I primarily have in mind those with higher Factor 1 scores, those who tend to be callous, manipulative, unempathic, egocentric, deceitful, impulsive, hostile, impervious to risk, and seemingly incapable of intimacy (Hare 2003). These are the features distinguishing them from the "merely" antisocial criminals, and when a high Factor 1 score is combined with a lower Factor 2 score, there is greater potential for a "successful psychopath," someone often capable of negotiating the world without incarceration (at least for a while). These tend to be charming, manipulative agents, capable of mimicking human emotional reactions but generally not feeling them. These are the kinds of agents represented by "Skip" from the opening pages of this book. Interestingly, psychopathy is also one of the few disorders in which those affected are perfectly (smugly) content that they have it. "How low and pitiable those feeling creatures are," psychopaths seem to think about us, "so susceptible to exploitation given their trusting and caring vulnerabilities." We are ants in their magnifying glass.

Blair originally studied ten incarcerated psychopaths and ten (incarcerated) controls, giving them the same moral/conventional task with some of the same stories from the early studies on children (Blair 1995, 13–14).[3] The details here matter, so I will quote from Blair:

> The four moral stories involved a child hitting another child, a child pulling the hair of another child and the victim cries, a child smashing a piano and a child breaking the swing in the playground. The four conventional stories involved a boy child wearing a skirt, two children talking in class, a child walking out of the classroom without permission and a child who stops paying attention to the lesson and turns his back on the teacher. (Blair 1995, 14)

Here is how they did, relative to nonpsychopaths (see Table 5.1):

[3] Blair's population of psychopaths was actually drawn from those with scores of 26 or higher on the PCL-R.

Table 5.1. Psychopaths vs. nonpsychopaths on the moral/conventional task

	(Im)Permissibility*		Seriousness†		Modifiability (Im)permissibility‡	
	Moral	*Conv.*	*Moral*	*Conv.*	*Moral*	*Conv.*
Psychopaths	.98	.93	8.28	6.42	.95	.80
Nonpsychopaths	1.00	.75	8.04	4.72	1.00	.38

	Justifiability											
	Others' Welfare		Normative		Disorder		Lack of Change		Rudeness		Other	
	M	*C*	*M*	*C*	*M*	*C*	*M*	*C*	*M*	*C*	*M*	*C*
Psych.	17.5	0.0	52.5	42.5	0.05	22.5	12.5	7.5	0.0	17.5	12.5	10.0
Nonpsych.	52.5	0.0	35.0	25.0	2.5	32.5	2.5	12.5	2.5	17.5	5.0	12.5

* The numbers here reflect the percentage of respondents who said the transgression in question would not be OK.
† Mean responses, on a scale of 1 to 10.
‡ The numbers here reflect the percentage of respondents who continued to say the transgression would not be OK, even if the teacher said it was OK.

There were two significant findings. First, unlike both nonpsychopathic children and adults, psychopaths typically did not make much of a distinction between "moral" and "conventional" violations after modification of the latter's permissibility by the teacher (Blair 1995, 18). Second, and more surprisingly, while psychopaths evaluated moral and conventional transgressions under the authority modification as more or less on a par, they "treated conventional transgressions like moral transgressions" (Blair 1995, 20) and so viewed them both as authority-*independent* (Blair 1995, 17; see highlighted columns of Table 5.1).[4] This result was taken merely to have been a function of the inmates' desire to prove they had reformed and learned the rules (that is, they were aiming at impression management). These general findings were replicated in another study of incarcerated psychopaths with more subjects (Blair et al. 1995), and it was also replicated to some extent in children with psychopathic tendencies: When authority was removed from an act's prohibition, while subjects did tend to note a distinction between the moral and conventional transgressions, it was far less marked than it was for controls (Blair 1997).

Several theorists have taken these findings to have great import for moral philosophy. While most have deployed them in investigations into the debate between internalists and externalists about moral judgment (Nichols 2004; Kennett and Fine 2008a and 2008b; Roskies 2008; and M. Smith 2008), some have been tempted to explore what they mean for questions of moral

[4] In his statement of this finding, Blair writes that psychopaths judged "conventional transgressions as moral on this criterion judgment; i.e., not *authority independent*" [emphasis in original]. This is a typographical error, however, confirmed by Blair in private correspondence. What he obviously meant given the surrounding context is that they viewed these as "authority independent."

responsibility, with widely varying results (Levy 2007; Fine and Kennett 2004; Glannon 2008; and Haji 2010). For example, Neil Levy takes psychopaths' failure to track the moral/conventional distinction as evidence for a crucial failure of moral understanding. While the results of the task reveal that psychopaths know their actions "are widely perceived to be wrong..., they are unable to grasp the distinctive nature and significance of their wrongness" (Levy 2007, 132). In a similar vein, Cordelia Fine and Jeanette Kennett suggest that, "while psychopathic offenders certainly appear to know what acts are prohibited by society or the law (and therefore know that their transgressions are legally wrong), they do not appear to have the capacity to judge an act to be *morally* wrong" (Fine and Kennett 2004, 432, emphasis in original). In both cases, then, what psychopaths are taken to lack is the capacity for moral understanding. Fine and Kennett think that this—the failure to meet the *epistemic* requirement—in and of itself is the source of psychopaths' lack of moral responsibility; Levy thinks that their lack of moral understanding excuses them from moral responsibility by preventing them from meeting the *control* condition (Levy 2007, 136). In addition, both sets of authors point to psychopaths' lack of empathy as an important source of their failure of moral understanding.

Heidi Maibom rejects this thought, arguing that even if psychopaths lack empathy, this does not yet show that they lack moral understanding. Indeed, one might come to moral understanding in a variety of ways, justifying not harming others via appeal to, for example, God's law, Kantian duties, or declarations of rights, but none of these moral justifications require empathy (Maibom 2008, 174–5).[5] If, then, their poor performance on the moral/conventional task does not reveal their incapacity for coming to moral understanding via *alternative*—non-empathic—routes, then it is insufficient to undermine their status as responsible agents (Maibom 2008, 182).

Over the course of this chapter, I will advance two arguments. The first is intended to show that, while the moral/conventional task (and "the" distinction on which it is based) is too problematic to bear the weight moral philosophers like this have put on it, there might still be a way to rescue something valuable from the remnants of these studies for our enterprise, revealing a heretofore unappreciated impairment of psychopaths. The second argument is intended to show, contra Maibom's suggestion, that the capacity for empathy alone *is* essential to accountability, and that its value is intrinsic, not merely extrinsic (as an

[5] Kennett 2002 presents a similar sort of argument for why a lack of empathy does not undermine some autistic agents' ability to arrive at moral understanding. I explicate and respond to Kennett's argument later in this chapter.

epistemic aid), contra Levy's and Fine and Kennett's suggestion. To do so, I will explore in depth the ways in which individuals with psychopathy both differ from, yet are importantly similar to, individuals with high-functioning autism.

Doubts about the Moral/Conventional Task and Distinction

Certain of the assumptions behind the moral/conventional task have come under serious empirical attack in recent literature. For example, many people actually view so-called conventional transgressions as serious and authority-independent (Nisan 1987), and many also view some so-called moral (specifically, harming) transgressions as less serious and authority-dependent (Kelly et al. 2007, 122–8).

But I think the foundational conceptual assumption of the task—that there is indeed a single, unified distinction between the moral and the conventional domains as presented in the literature—is untenable. There are four subdistinctions that make it up: the "permissible/impermissible" distinction (or, as it is put in the task, "the OK/not OK" distinction[6]), the "more serious/less serious" distinction, the justification distinctions, and the authority-dependent/authority-independent distinction. But these distinctions only occasionally overlap and they are actually orthogonal to one another. I have argued for this point in great detail elsewhere (Shoemaker 2011c), so here I will only mention the highlights. First, as is borne out by the empirical literature just mentioned, some impermissible "moral" acts are taken to be less serious than some impermissible "conventional" acts (e.g., an inconsequential broken promise versus a religious desecration). Second, when transgressions occur, the wrongness may be attributed to several possible justifications, including (a) welfare ("It will hurt him"); (b) rules ("It's against the rules/unacceptable to do that"); (c) rudeness ("It's bad manners"); (d) disruption ("It's distracting to the class"); (e) rights ("It's not his"); (f) justice ("It's not fair"); or (g) *other* (Turiel, Killen, and Helwig 1987, 170; Blair 1997, 734). But these sorts of distinctions do not necessarily map on to the seriousness or permissibility distinctions in the assumed way. To take just one example, welfare-based justifications may well attach to relatively nonserious (and what were typically taken to be "conventional") transgressions, for example, "One shouldn't slam a door in someone's face *because it might hurt him.*" Furthermore, it is quite possible that many subjects view transgressions as having

[6] Indeed, I think it obvious that the "OK/not OK" distinction is far broader than the moral rightness/wrongness distinction, given that the former may well apply in nonmoral domains such as the aesthetic, athletic, or prudential.

overdetermining justificatory sources. Thus some action may be both distracting *and* hurtful, both a violation of the rules *and* unfair. Where one justification seems more serious than another, then, that justification may be exclusively expressed, but that surely does not render it the exclusive justifier. Finally, there seems to be no necessary overlap between the authority distinctions and the other distinctions. As already suggested, some harming activities may be thought authority-dependent (e.g., a teacher spanking students), whereas some religious conventions, as well as some merely disgust-inducing activities, are viewed as authority-independent, and this may be true despite no obvious connection to harm, justice, or rights (see, e.g., Nichols 2002). It would also seem distinctly possible for there to be nonserious authority-independent transgressions (e.g., white lies) as well as serious authority-dependent transgressions (e.g., jumping the queue). And it could be that removal of authority does not alter permissibility but does alter *seriousness*: Perhaps hitting someone, while still impermissible, is actually viewed as less seriously wrong if there is no rule against it.

We have no good reason to believe, therefore, that there even is such a thing as "the" moral/conventional distinction as proposed, presupposed, or deployed for many decades in both the psychological and philosophical literature. Instead, there are just several specific subdistinctions, some of which sometimes overlap to some extent with some others. Now one might take this fact to vindicate what Kelly et al. call a "growing body of evidence justifying substantial skepticism about *all* the major conclusions that have been drawn from studies using the moral/conventional task" (Kelly et al. 2007, 129, emphasis in original). This would be too quick, though, for just because there is no single umbrella distinction that can bear any weight, that does not mean we cannot learn anything from deployments of the more specific subdistinctions. There is, after all, *some* sort of distinction we make that psychopaths seemingly fail to track, given the Blair results. So what is it, and can we learn anything from it?

Authority and Permission

I think the subdistinction that remains pertinent with respect to our interest in responsibility is the so-called authority-dependence/-independence distinction. In Blair's original studies, there are still two results of interest: first, psychopaths tended to view all the transgressions in these studies as roughly on an evaluative par, regardless of whether an authority said it was OK, and, second, they viewed them to be on a par in terms of being *impermissible* ("not OK"), regardless of the authority's ruling. Now this second point is the one discounted by Blair (and others), under the assumption that the incarcerated psychopaths responding this way were engaged in impression management. I will return to this discounting explanation in a later section.

Let us focus in the remainder of this section, though, on why psychopaths might view all transgressions given in the task on an evaluative par. Remember that the task described behavior in a child's classroom and that the relevant authority was the teacher. So when the teacher says it is OK to contravene the rule, why do we—normal agents—think it is OK to go along with the teacher in some cases but not others? I suspect the working assumption of most researchers is this: the *justifications* to which we appeal are different in the different cases. It is wrong for one child to hit another, regardless of what the teacher says, for reasons having to do with the victim's welfare, whereas it is typically wrong for a child to turn her back on the teacher solely because there is a rule against it. In the latter case, then, the teacher's announcement that it is OK purportedly eliminates this justification: Because he says it is OK, there is no longer a rule against it. But because psychopaths are "significantly less likely to justify items by references to the *victim's welfare*" (Blair 1995, 18, emphasis in original), their justifications for transgressions will not be that different from those on the so-called conventional side of the map, and so they will be more likely to rank all transgressions on an evaluative par despite the teacher's license to transgress.

The mistake in this assumption has already been exposed: The justification distinctions are just orthogonal to the authority distinction. In particular, some "conventional" transgressions may be thought to involve victims (such that welfare justifications become relevant). And as it turns out, it is quite plausible to think that there *is* a victim in all of the "conventional" cases presented to Blair's psychopaths (which, recall, were a boy wearing a skirt, children talking in class, a child leaving the class without permission, and a child turning his back to the teacher). For insofar as all of these would be disruptive to learning or classroom decorum, they could all be construed as instances of *rudeness to the teacher*.

Focus, then, on the back-turning case, where it is especially easy to think of the teacher as the victim. The fact that he could be viewed as both the classroom authority *and* the victim of the rude behavior yields the distinct possibility that, in the authority modifiability prompt, normal subjects judge the back-turning to be permissible because the teacher—in an exercise of his authority *as potential victim*—has granted permission to the behavior. But then to truly investigate the alleged authority distinction, we need to explore what would happen if the same sort of authority were exercised in the hitting ("moral") case: What if the potential *victim* there were to sincerely say that it was OK for the other child to hit her (or to pull his hair, or to smash her piano, etc.)?[7] In other words, what have been overlooked in the task are additional sources of authority that may well be essential to our making the modifiability distinction. And once we recognize these additional sources, it is no longer clear that even *non*psychopaths make the modifiability distinction in terms of authority-independence; they may actually view the so-called moral transgressions as authority-*dependent* as well.

So would it be OK (that is, not impermissible) to hit someone, or pull her hair, or smash her piano, or break her swing, *if she said it was OK to do so*? These questions have not been surveyed, to my knowledge, but in every case, my intuition is that the behavior, while certainly not obligatory, becomes permissible ("OK"). As long as the permission given was sincere, informed, and rational—the same implicit assumptions of the authority-exemptions provided in the standard moral/conventional task—it seems to alter the normative status of the behavior. This may not be true in all such "immoral" behavior, of course. Cannibalizing the German man who volunteered to be cannibalized is still going to be viewed as "not OK" by most.[8] But in the less severe behaviors of the task as administered to Blair's psychopaths, permission given would, I strongly suspect, make a big difference. Why? Performing the action post-permission could no longer ground much of a *complaint* on the part of the "victim." "You said I could!" is all the justification typically needed to block such a reply and to undermine any associated agential anger. What I am suggesting, then, is that we may not view many so-called moral transgressions as authority-independent after all. Instead, we attribute a very important kind of authority to the potential victim, as it is her voice that (at least partially) *determines* what counts as a moral—or at least anger-generating—transgression in the first place.

So what, then, grounds the distinction normal subjects make in the modifiability cases if it is not one between authority-dependence and -independence? I think that it has to do instead with the implicit or explicit directives of those with the proper standing to make accountability demands to us, that is, those whose angry demand for acknowledgment of a failure of regard for them would be fitting. In the "conventional" scenarios, then, the actual victim of the behavior—the teacher—has, in explicitly saying it is "OK," implicitly voiced his

[7] In the "olden days" (40 years ago), Physical Education teachers in the U.S. would sometimes have students resolve their differences by boxing. Whereas hitting one another might have been "not OK" outside of class, to the extent that all parties genuinely agreed to this method of resolution, hitting one another would have been rendered "OK" in the boxing forum. Thanks to Eddy Nahmias for this reminder of days (perhaps) gone by.

[8] See the story at: <http://www.guardian.co.uk/world/2003/dec/04/germany.lukeharding>. Thanks to Shaun Nichols, Steve Wall, Chad Van Schoelandt, and Daniel Jacobson for discussion on this point.

intention to withdraw all future expressions of anger for what would previously have been anger-generating behavior (e.g., turning your back on him), making it no longer count as *disregard*.[9] In the "moral" scenarios, however, the actual victims of the behavior—other students, presumably—have not withdrawn such future expressions by granting permission, which preserves the behavior's "not OK" status. This way of putting it explains precisely why the *teacher's* saying it is OK for one child to hit another is irrelevant for us to change our perception of its impermissibility, for the teacher's authority is not relevant to its impermissibility in the first place. But the fact that the impermissibility is not dependent on the teacher's authority does not mean it is not nevertheless *authority-dependent*. In fact, it is dependent on the authority of the actual victim, namely, the other child.

Given this discussion, therefore, the better way to describe what is being tested in Blair's "authority-modification" prompt is whether subjects make a distinction between actions with, and actions without, victim-authorizations. Blair's results would then suggest that psychopaths have serious trouble with this distinction. Why? Here is my proposed explanation: Psychopaths[10] have difficulty with the authority modification distinction as a corollary of their more general difficulty perceiving facts about people's normative perspectives as even *seeming* to provide (similarly valenced) reasons in their own deliberative framework, that is, they are impaired (or incapacitated) for *pure evaluational regard*. If psychopaths are impaired for evaluational regard, then the fact that someone may say that she will no longer count certain actions as disregarding, as anger-generating, will make no difference, just because it did not matter how this potential victim counted those actions in the first place! If this is the right explanation of the Blair results, then combining it with the tripartite theory yields the obvious verdict that psychopaths are impaired (or incapacitated) for accountability.

But is this the right general explanation, that psychopaths are impaired for evaluational regard? This is my made-up terminology, so what we need is a way to connect the concept up to the existing literature and then see what the evidence actually reveals. If there is an agreed-upon deficit in the literature on

[9] Contrast what our reactions would be in this case to one in which the *principal* said it was OK for students to turn their backs on teachers. I suspect we would be far less quick to think that such behavior would then be rendered OK, and if so, it would make perfect sense to explain this phenomenon by referencing the fact that the principal just isn't the *relevant* authority here, i.e., he has no standing to relax the teacher's demand not to treat her rudely.

[10] Along with Blair, I am simply taking "psychopaths" to refer to those diagnosed with a 26 or higher on the PCL-R.

psychopaths that is sufficient for what I construe as a regard-impairment, then we will have an argument for my conclusion about their troubles with accountability. As it turns out, there is such an agreed-upon deficit, but connecting it to my concept of regard will take some time.

Identifying Empathy

The psychological research overwhelmingly shows that psychopaths have serious *empathic* deficits (Blair et al. 1996; Jolliffe and Farrington 2004; Mullins-Nelson, Salekin, and Leistico 2006; Blair 2007, 387; Kirsch and Becker 2007; Bora, Gökçen, and Veznedaroglu 2008; Gao and Raine 2010). In this section I will show how these documented deficits are sufficient to impair what I call regard. If so, and given that impairments in regard explain psychopaths' scores on Blair's original studies (insofar as they include impaired abilities in recognizing agential authorizations and demands as at least putative reasons), then empathic impairments are sufficient for accountability impairments.

What, then, are the psychopath's precise empathic deficits? To see what they are, we first have to clear away some terminological confusion. There are, more or less, two senses of "empathy" in the (mostly psychological) literature. The first is "cognitive empathy," also known as "perspective-taking" or "theory of mind" (Smith 2006). This is an "imaginative process of simulation" generating "reciprocal awareness" (Kennett 2002, 345). On this understanding, empathy is a merely epistemic tool, one method of figuring out various sorts of moral reasons.

But there is also what is known as "affective" or "emotional" empathy (Losoya and Eisenberg 2001; Shamay-Tsoory, Aharon-Peretz, and Perry 2009). This is usually put (rather vaguely) as the ability to feel what others feel. Sometimes this is taken to refer to mere emotional contagion. Sometimes it is taken to refer to some more robust type of emotional synchronicity. And at other times it is put, quite problematically, as a kind of emotional concern for others.

Because of these very different understandings, some theorists prefer not to talk in terms of empathy at all (see, e.g., Nichols 2004). I agree that the very last sense discussed—emotional concern for others—does not belong under the rubric of empathy; it is a very different sort of attitude, one for which we do better to reserve the term "sympathy" (see, e.g., Darwall 2002, 50–3). But there is something that unites all of the other senses, namely, they point to some kind of experience "from the inside" of the psychological goings-on—whether cognitive, emotional, or both—of creatures very similar to, yet distinct from, ourselves. I prefer, then, to preserve umbrella talk of empathy, yet push for greater clarity about its distinct forms. This is what I tried to do in Chapter 3, and in what follows I will add to that discussion and show how my distinctions map onto the taxonomy of the contemporary psychological literature.

One of my theses in Chapter 3 was that empathy is more than merely an epistemic stepstool to regard; rather, empathy actually enables, or *activates*, regard in its "pure" forms, at least for the properly functioning. But which sort of empathy found in the psychological literature, if either, did I have in mind? In Chapter 3, I talked about *evaluational* and *emotional* empathy. These are both forms of *identification*, or identifying empathy. So let us begin the mapping project by contrasting these with non-identifying, or *detached*, empathy. This is mere perspective-taking of a very restricted sort. It is what tends to be engaged in, for example, by clinical psychologists or anthropologists purely as a means of *understanding* what their clients or study subjects are going through or thinking. This stance is quite compatible with viewing these clients or study subjects as *objects*, though, as mere puzzles to be figured out, and it requires no particular positive or negative attitude whatsoever toward them or their cares and commitments. Rather, detached empathizers are simply like spies in the target's head: While entirely maintaining their own set of cares and commitments, they are mere observers of the various psychological effects the world is having on their target.[11] This activity enables all sorts of explanations and predictions of others' behavior, but it is by no means what regard consists in. Sadists and manipulators do this too, after all. But detached empathy is actually just what most of those in the psychological literature refer to as "cognitive empathy." It is thus not what I have in mind.

Regard instead is typically enabled or activated by identifying empathy, that is, genuine engagement with others.[12] Rather than merely looking along the sightline of another's mind's eye and then observing the psychological effects in her of what one has seen her see, when I engage in identifying empathy with someone, I take up the normative perspective of her mind's eye *as my own* in certain crucial respects. In evaluational empathy, I actually see what the world looks like from her eyes with her set of commitments. Now when my own mind's eye rests on my own projects and goals, it does not view them dispassionately; rather, I (typically) view these interests as worthy of pursuit, as under the guise of the good. When

[11] This is just the sort of simulation empathy Gordon 1995 discusses.

[12] Always? Of course not. Much of the time we already have full awareness of what facts about others count as putative reasons, so actively taking up someone else's perspective may be unnecessary in any individual instance (for pure regard). But that awareness itself had to have its source, I am insisting, in identifying empathy at some point, as it is a perception of various "reasonish" facts found within the other's normative perspective, and seeing such facts as such is neither innate nor a function of judgments. See Chapter 3, fn. 14.

I engage in evaluational empathy with another, then, I adopt *her* perspective on her own projects, and in doing so I view those projects under the same guise as when I survey my own, namely, with the *worthiness-for-pursuit* built in. Crucially, I do not just see her projects as something *she* views as worthwhile; rather, I myself see those projects *as* worthwhile *from her perspective* (cf. Deigh 1995, 761).[13] Evaluational regard consists in subsequently coming to see those projects as providing putative positive reasons (e.g., reasons in favor of promoting, preserving, or respecting the projects) upon returning to my own normative perspective.

The other form of identifying empathy, namely, emotional empathy, very roughly corresponds to what those in the literature tend to call affective empathy. In my terms, when emotionally empathizing with you, I typically come to *feel* what the world feels like for you, as if what is (or will be) affecting you emotionally is affecting me emotionally. Here I must try on something more than (or something different from) your commitments (your evaluative stance); I must also (or instead) share your cares, your emotional investments. So emotional regard is a matter of coming to feel (at least a simulacrum of) what you feel, not as a matter of mere emotional contagion, but as a function of genuine engagement with your affective stance.

With these conceptual resources at our disposal, then, let us explore some of what we know about the relevant deficits of psychopaths. Many psychopaths, as it turns out, are quite capable of detached (cognitive) empathy, of bloodless perspective-taking, of looking down the sightline of the mind's eye of others, and of seeing what they see and *understanding* how they see it in a way they can use effectively to predict, explain, or manipulate their behavior (Dadds et al. 2009). In the unsettling documentary, *I, Psychopath*, the filmmaker follows Sam Vaknin, a self-professed narcissist and psychopath, around various parts of the globe as he is tested for these traits (it turns out his self-assessment is correct, as he scores very highly on the Hare PCL-R). During their travels, Vaknin is alleged to be berating the filmmaker off-camera, even though he is rather charming (if quite egocentric) on-camera. Finally, the filmmaker catches a Vaknin tirade with a secret camera. In it, Vaknin insistently and insightfully criticizes the filmmaker, homing in on weak spots and anxieties the filmmaker has only revealed to the audience. After the tirade, Vaknin then pedantically explains what he just did, pointing out how he manipulated the filmmaker emotionally in various ways and how he used that manipulation to engage in further twists of the emotional

[13] Doing so is perfectly compatible with my standing in evaluative disagreement with her once returning to my own perspective.

knife. He completely understands the specific sort of emotional turmoil he has caused the filmmaker to go through, and he uses his detached empathetic understanding to exploit and emotionally manipulate him some more. It is frightening to watch.

Psychopaths thus seem capable of (unimpaired) detached/cognitive empathy. Are they then capable of the two types of identifying empathy, evaluational and emotional, the types of empathy that I am claiming are essential to regard (and accountability)? Psychopaths are pretty uncontroversially impaired in emotional empathy—what the psychological literature means, roughly, by affective empathy—in virtue of their inability to feel anything other than the most superficial, fleeting emotions (Fingarette 1967, 24–6; Duff 1977, 191; Dadds et al. 2009; Jones et al. 2010).[14] What, though, about evaluational empathy? Are psychopaths able to make the transition from perceiving what projects another sees as worthwhile to perceiving her projects *as worthwhile from her perspective*?

I do not believe so, given two distinct disabilities, one about empathic motivation and the other about making the transition to regard. First, because of their emotional disabilities, psychopaths tend to be unable to *care about other people*, that is, be emotionally wrought at their up or down fortunes (see, e.g., de Oliveira-Souza et al. 2008, 156). But other people are the source of the normative perspectives that generate the sort of practical reasons relevant to accountability (see Chapter 3). If other people cannot matter (or if they matter very little) to psychopaths, then taking up their perspectives—and regarding them generally—cannot matter either (or matters very little). Nevertheless, lacking affective motivation to make the identifying empathic leap is not sufficient to impair pure evaluational regard, for perhaps one could, at least conceivably, be able to seek out the relevant practical reasons without taking an affective route (a possibility we will take up in the section on high-functioning autism).

Supplementing the analysis, then, is another disability of many psychopaths, namely, a *prudential* disability. Start with the anecdotal evidence of Hervey Cleckley's patient "Chester":

> Whatever strange goals or pseudo-goals there may be to prompt and shape his [Chester's] reactions as a member of the community, these too . . . fail to motivate him sufficiently, fail

[14] However, see Meffert et al. 2013, for a study suggesting that, while psychopaths are seriously deficient in spontaneous, or unprompted, emotionally empathic responses, they seem less deficient at it when explicitly instructed to feel with the actors in some videos. This is a very interesting finding, and it may go to the nature of the incapacitation or impairment of psychopaths. I doubt if it tells us very much about the kind of robust interpersonal empathic engagement I am concerned about here, but I of course await further study.

to induce decisions and acts that would give him the freedom to pursue them. It has been demonstrated to Chester repeatedly... that his characteristic acts put him in a situation [of confinement] he finds particularly disagreeable. This does not produce the slightest modification of his behavior. (Cleckley 1976, 134)

Or consider "Stanley":

[H]e easily obtained employment, usually as a salesman. While he worked, his income was ample for any ordinary needs. During one period of prosperity he was very successful selling small computers for household use. He later added as a sideline the enthusiastic promotion and sale of waterbeds, shortly after these were introduced and hailed as a stimulating erotic innovation. His profits from these enterprises were for a while spectacular until he lost both jobs through a combination of neglect and irresponsible conduct. On many other occasions he worked with what seemed to be real enthusiasm for periods of varying lengths. Then, without any particular reason, he would give up an excellent job at which he was distinguishing himself. On other occasions he would have to leave the valuable position to flee from prosecution for some legal offense. (Cleckley 1976, Section 19)

What "Chester" and "Stanley" and many other "successful" psychopaths[15] have in common is that, while they do seem to have occasionally persisting pursuits, they are more often quite impulsive, leaving projects behind with nary a look back in a way strongly suggesting that those pursuits do not *matter* to them. One's projects or plans may have, as a matter of some luck, no competitors, and so persist for a while in guiding one. But being guided in this way is very different from *guiding oneself* via a conception of what one construes as good or what one cares about (Watson 2013). And it starts to become clear from the evidence that psychopaths just do not care when their pursuits are derailed, nor does the prospect of prison alter their plans, even though they tend to hate being in prison (Newman and Wallace 1993; Lykken 1995; Hart and Dempster 1997). When they look through their own mind's eye, it would seem that the evaluative landscape they see is just flat. It would seem, in other words, that not only are psychopaths impaired in regard for others, but also they are impaired in regard for *themselves* (a point Watson 2013 makes as well). They are unable to see (or have great difficulty seeing) facts about their *own* normative perspectives in a "reasonish" way.

I am suggesting that psychopaths are evaluationally impaired generally. They tend not to have (or have poorly functioning) evaluative stances, stances from which various sorts of pursuits are viewed from the perspective of one *qua* persisting agent as worthwhile and are thereby transformed into prudential

[15] "Successful" only in the sense that they are not in prison... yet.

(guiding) ends (cf. Watson 2013). Additional evidence for this interpretation comes from what the PCL-R calls psychopaths' failure to accept responsibility for their actions, which includes being "without the slightest sense of guilt or regret" (Hare, Neumann, and Widiger 2012, 478). Regret, as we know, evaluates one's own judgment as poor and tends to motivate policy change. But regret is not on the table for just any old mistaken judgments: if I am killing time by idly multiplying two numbers and I make a mistake in calculation, regret would not be fitting. And this is because what I am doing *just does not matter*. But where I take my calculations to be important, to be worth doing (say, if I am an engineer), then I will surely (fittingly) regret making any errors. Why? Because I have undermined my *ends*, those pursuits to whose worth I am committed. If one is without regrets, though, then the most plausible explanation is that one lacks an evaluative stance, and this is what seems to be the case for (at least many) psychopaths.[16]

Psychopaths are thus, I think, deeply impaired (or perhaps incapacitated) for either emotional or evaluational regard, either to others or to themselves, an impairment having its main source in their empathic impairments. This empirical interpretation, in combination with the tripartite theory, yields the verdict that psychopaths have seriously mitigated (or are fully exempt from) accountability. The Blair studies, then, might be said to provide an illustration of one specific manifestation of psychopaths' impairments, namely, their inability to engage in an important domain of evaluational regard for others, wherein one comes to see facts about others' (implicit or explicit) authorizations as putative reasons in one's own practical deliberations. But as should by now be clear, I think their accountability impairments range much more widely to include impairments of non-authorization-related evaluational regard to others, emotional regard to others, and regard of either kind for themselves.

Moral/Conventional Task 2.0

There are two significant reasons to worry, however, about my conclusions about psychopathic non-accountability. In this section I will discuss the first. I was motivated to the larger discussion of identifying empathy by the idea that, even if there is no general moral/conventional distinction as assumed in the literature,

[16] Other possible explanations are that psychopaths without regret never fail to betray their evaluative stance, they do occasionally betray those stances but never (or cannot) recognize that they have done so, or they just aren't capable of negative attitudes to those betrayals (although they do make mistakes and recognize them as such). I have a hard time believing any of these possibilities, though.

and even if the moral/conventional task is quite confused, we might still be able to draw some significant conclusions about the responsibility of psychopaths by focusing on Blair's results just for the authority modification prompt in the original studies. But both Blair's methods and his results have raised red flags. Regarding the latter, Blair's incarcerated psychopaths failed to recognize authority modifications as significant, but not by treating all the transgressions equally as "conventional"; rather, they treated all the transgressions equally as "*moral*" (or at least as very serious wrongs). This is a strange result, though, and one might wonder why, if psychopaths pay no mind to authorities and authorization with respect to norms and rules, and all the relevant norms and rules on my construal are most plausibly viewed as authority-dependent, they do not simply *discount* the weight and seriousness of all norms and rules. And if it turns out, as Blair himself suggested, that they were attempting to manage the impression of those in "authority," then why should we trust their reports as being at *all* representative of their actual beliefs? Regarding Blair's methodology, there was a crucial ambiguity in the modifiability prompts, whose general form was this: "Would it be OK for X to Y if the teacher says X can?" (Blair 1995, 15) One understanding of the question could be "Do *you* think it is in fact OK for X to Y if the teacher says X can?" The other understanding could be "*Is it generally taken to be* OK for X to Y if the teacher says X can?" These are very distinct questions: the first asks for the subject's own moral judgments, whereas the second asks merely for the subject's judgment about *others*' (or perhaps "society's") moral judgments. Which interpretation did the psychopaths take up? Indeed, why should we think that "the" psychopaths all took up the same interpretation? As long as these worries linger, we may not be in a position to draw any firm conclusions from the Blair studies at all.

Aharoni, Sinnott-Armstrong, and Kiehl 2012 recently attempted to eliminate these red flags (and others) about the original Blair studies, along with some of the more general worries about the moral/conventional distinction and task I raised earlier, by developing a new way to deploy a restricted version of the moral/conventional task on a much larger sample size of incarcerated psychopaths.[17] To avoid the problem of incorporating multiple orthogonal distinctions

[17] They surveyed 109 inmates, and ultimately they compared the scores of those with less than a 15 on the PCL-R psychopathy checklist with those who got a 26 or greater (so they went with the more liberal diagnostic number to align with Blair, although Sinnott-Armstrong assures me, in private correspondence, that their results held for those in the population who scored over 30). This procedure yielded a comparison between sample sizes of, respectively, 24 and 22, over twice as many as in Blair's original study.

in the task, they focused solely on the authority modification distinction (the same one on which I have focused). To avoid the worry about whether psychopaths were engaged in impression management, they designed a forced-choice task, one in which the subjects were given 16 scenarios and then (truly) informed that exactly half of them fell under the "moral" rubric and the other half fell under the "conventional" rubric. (The prompts chosen had been run through an earlier survey of representative subjects to determine eight relatively clear-cut "moral" transgressions and eight relatively clear-cut "conventional" transgressions.) Finally, to avoid worries about whose judgments were being surveyed, the authors were explicit: In their prompts, "Moral wrongfulness was defined by acts that *society would consider wrong* even if there were no rules, customs, or laws against them" (Aharoni, Sinnott-Armstrong, and Kiehl 2012, 489; emphasis mine).[18]

What they found was that, under these new and more carefully specified conditions, there simply was *no significant difference* between psychopaths and nonpsychopaths in assessing whether various transgressions were morally wrong or merely conventionally wrong. In particular, the psychopaths seemed to have no difficulty judging that some transgressions count as wrong regardless of whether there are rules, customs, or laws in place against them whereas the wrongness of other transgressions depends precisely on such rules, customs, and laws. Consequently, as the authors put it, "psychopathy is not well-characterized by a distinct deficit in classifying moral as opposed to conventional wrongs" (Aharoni, Sinnott-Armstrong, and Kiehl 2012, 492). Instead, to the extent that there were variations in ability to distinguish the moral from the conventional, it was not psychopathy but *IQ* differences that seemed most relevant (Aharoni, Sinnott-Armstrong, and Kiehl 2012, 493).

This was a very cleverly designed study, correcting many problems in Blair's original studies. It might also seem as if it puts my story about the non-accountability of psychopaths in jeopardy, as it turns out they *can* make the authority modification distinction I was assuming from Blair that they cannot. There are several reasons, however, why I doubt that this is the right conclusion to draw. First, the authors seem to think that the ability to report how others ("society") classify moral and conventional transgressions manifests genuine "moral knowledge."[19] I have a hard time believing this. Imagine a modified

[18] The other red flags in Blair's original studies that the authors were at pains to correct included the fact that Blair included only men and used scenarios only about childhood schoolroom transgressions.

[19] See their gloss that psychopaths have "relatively accurate moral knowledge" and "normal moral knowledge" (Aharoni, Sinnott-Armstrong, and Kiehl 2012, 493).

Searlian Chinese room (Searle 1980), a *Moral Alien Room*, where we find ourselves with the job of sorting different depictions of the aliens' strange and elaborate rituals, hugs, ear movements, and the like into two different piles, based on a set of instructions pointing to subtle features of the interactions. We are then told that the left-hand pile includes their "schmoral" interactions, and the right-hand pile includes their "schmonventional" interactions. After lots of practice, we can classify and distinguish these interactions when we see them in public. Do we have schmoral (or schmonventional) knowledge? I doubt it. But psychopaths' abilities may consist in no more than this, and there is nothing about the newer study that suggests otherwise.[20]

Indeed, I would have thought that to eliminate the "impression management" explanation we would need to find out whether psychopaths *themselves* would think the various transgressions still count as wrong were there no laws or rules against them. But to find that out, one would need a more open-ended survey, not a forced-choice one, as the latter requires an objectively "correct" answer that could well be at odds with the psychopaths' subjective moral assessments. In other words, I may well think that *none* of the so-called transgressions are wrong, but if you force me to classify eight as wrong and eight as permissible, you will have made my subjective responses—what I *really* think about the "transgressions" in question—irrelevant. On this point, then, Blair's more open-ended studies may have been more likely to have revealed psychopaths' actual moral views.[21]

Second, *authorities* were not deployed at all in this study, contrary to the set-up in Blair's.[22] Instead, what was removed in the new study's modifiability prompt were rules, customs, and laws.[23] But I have not been doubting that psychopaths can recognize rules, customs, and laws (and probably even respond to them); rather, my doubts have been focused on psychopaths' abilities to recognize the significance of *agential authorizations* as determining the boundaries of regard or disregard for those in the position to hold others accountable. The modification in this new study thus neither tests nor refutes the basic datum in Blair's study around which I offered my proposal: Just because psychopaths may be able to classify some transgressions as what members of society would deem "wrong if no rules..." does not mean that they would be able either to distinguish how

[20] The same may be true of those with autism, as we will discuss in the next section.

[21] Note that I am not saying that Blair's study succeeded in doing so, only that his had a better chance of doing so.

[22] The authors admit this. See Aharoni, Sinnott-Armstrong, and Kiehl 2012, 494.

[23] Aren't these authority-based, though? Some may be, but surely most are not. Think of our many authority-less customs or the huge number of subtle, hardly-ever-remarked-upon interaction norms, like the appropriate way to shake hands or how close to stand to someone else during conversation.

people generally would classify behaviors-with-permissions-by-potential-victims or how they themselves would think of such behaviors.

So what is the takeaway here? Despite my serious worries about the overall moral/conventional "distinction" and task, I have suggested that there may still be some noteworthy data from Blair's original studies from which we could draw in figuring out the empirical details about psychopaths relevant to responsibility, namely, that when it comes to the authority modification distinction, psychopaths do seem to be drawing different conclusions from the rest of us. I have proposed a provocative explanation for this difference, namely, that psychopaths may have trouble recognizing the normative significance of agential authorization as part of their impaired regard for others, impairments having a source in their empathic deficits. Combined with the tripartite theory, this story yields the verdict that psychopaths are impaired (or exempted) with respect to accountability. Now nothing about the Aharoni et al. results undermines this story. But it is still true that the data in line with this story come from an older study with several red flags, so my proposal must remain tentative. What I would like to see, then, are new studies focused just on *authorization*-modification. In particular, I would like to see how permission-granting affects assessments of the permissibility of certain sorts of targeted behavior, for both psychopaths and nonpsychopaths. If, for example, nonpsychopaths view hair-pulling as permissible once the victim grants (rational and informed) permission, but psychopaths do not, then such a result would tend to favor my story. In addition, although this would be much more difficult to test, we would need to know whether psychopaths *themselves* view various transgressions as OK, rather than merely trying to find out whether they are classifying various transgressions in conformity with societal classifications. Of course, what we find out here might well be that they rate *every* transgression as OK, regardless of its status. But that would surely tell us something valuable (and scary) as well.

Empathy and High-Functioning Autism

Even if the Blair results are unusable, however, my general argument about psychopaths' empathic deficits being the source of general regard-impairments could be sound. Nevertheless, this argument might have a troublesome implication, revealed by a question Jeanette Kennett poses in an important paper (Kennett 2002): If psychopaths are amoral agents, lacking moral concern and motivation in virtue of their empathic impairments, then why aren't autistic persons amoral agents as well, given *their* empathic impairments? Her own answer was that empathy, while it typically does matter for normal moral agents, does not matter so much for moral agency per se; that is, it is not the sole entrée into moral agency, and indeed, other abilities are more fundamental. One could compensate for one's lack of empathy and still be a (perhaps clumsy) moral agent. What is critical, then, is being able to find an alternative (non-empathic) way to see that others' interests are reason-giving in the same way one's own interests are. And as it turns out, according to Kennett, some people with autism—in particular high-functioning autistic adults and those with Asperger's syndrome—are capable of doing so, while psychopaths are not. Members of the former group take what Kennett calls a "Kantian approach to moral thinking" (Kennett 2002, 350), developing "moral rules and principles of conduct for themselves by reasoning... on the basis of patient explicit enquiry, reliance on testimony and inference from past situations" (Kennett 2002, 351). While they may be unable to read from facial expressions just what is wrong with someone, they nevertheless do have a general moral concern to do the right thing. Their empathic impairments make it difficult for them to figure out just what that is, but such impairments do not disable them from moral agency, whose sufficient condition Kennett locates in their *concern*, a sense of (Kantian) duty that psychopaths are thought to lack.[24] Consequently,

> [i]t is not the psychopath's lack of empathy, which (on its own, at any rate) explains his moral indifference. It is more specifically his lack of concern, or more likely lack of capacity to understand what he is doing, to consider the reasons available to him and to act in accordance with them.... His indifference to reasons is the key to his behaviour, not (or not solely) his lack of empathy. Those who lack empathy may miss finding out about things which *constitute* reasons for action, but they need not thereby exhibit *indifference* to reason. (Kennett 2002, 354–5; emphasis in original)

Kennett is explicitly discussing moral agency, but what she says might easily be adapted to our discussion in this chapter, especially if we think of "moral agency" as "eligible for accountability." I have suggested that psychopaths could be exempt from accountability to others in virtue of their failure to recognize the authorizing demands (implicit and explicit) of others as (even putative) reasons, and that this failure is very likely a function of their empathic impairments. But individuals with high-functioning autism and Asperger's syndrome allegedly share this incapacity.[25] So either they are also exempt/mitigated from

[24] Additional support for this last point comes from Kennett's unpublished paper "What's Required for Motivation by Principle?"

[25] There are important differences between those with high-functioning autism and those with Asperger's. But given their relevantly similar empathic impairments, I will be grouping them together under the heading of "those with high-functioning autism" just for ease of reference during our discussion.

accountability, despite their general moral concern for doing the right thing, their general conformance with morality, and the accountability responses both they and others may level at them, or they are not exempt/mitigated, in which case empathic impairments do not have the importance for regard and accountability I have taken them to have. The former is thought to be implausible, whereas the latter bodes ill for my theory of accountability (according to which regard is crucially a function of empathy).

At the end of the day, I will lean toward grasping the first horn of this dilemma (and so attempting to undermine the description of it as implausible), although there are defensible arguments on both sides of the issue, given in part the fact that the relevant empirical work is still in its adolescence.[26] In what follows, I will advance one argument in favor of thinking that those with high-functioning autism have limited accountability, perhaps being capable of one form of regard, and then I will advance two arguments in favor of thinking they are exempt or seriously mitigated from accountability. At the end of the day, I lean in the latter direction, but not quite as confidently as I do with respect to psychopaths.

To begin with, there is some good evidence that those with high-functioning autism are impaired with respect to *emotional* empathy. While they do have and express a wide range of emotions, and they can be and are frequently affected emotionally by the emotional displays of others, their emotional responses, it turns out, tend to be affective responses to *distress* cues in others. So the expressed fear or sadness of another will tend to trigger emotional responses in those with high-functioning autism (Rogers et al. 2006, e.g., 1791), but they tend to remain unaffected "by the other person's feelings *as* the feelings of another self with whom one is engaged" (Hobson et al. 2006, 135; see also Hobson et al. 2011). The impairment here does seem to rest on their inability to take up the perspectives of others in any real way, and so implies that accountability's emotional regard does at least require such a capacity.[27]

Evaluational regard, however, may not require such a capacity. I argued that the psychopath's exemption/mitigation from accountability may be a function of his inability to see worth in *any* projects, starting with his own. But those with high-functioning autism tend to have all sorts of projects they view as worthy, as ends that guide their normative deliberations. Temple Grandin is the exemplar here, a high-functioning autistic professor of animal science at Colorado State

[26] I took a much different (and more stridently contra-Kennett) stance in Shoemaker 2007, 94–7.

[27] Although see Nathan Stout's dissertation-in-progress for some reason to doubt this interpretation.

University who has contributed to many improved standards at slaughterhouses and livestock farms. But there are many others as well who have life plans around which they organize various of their more short-term interests and goals. Now even if this sort of end-setting solely involves seeing worth in their own projects, they would at least have a tool that psychopaths seem to lack, namely, the psychological foundation to transition from evaluational self-regard to evaluational other-regard *even in the absence of perspective-taking*. The key would come in an ability to acknowledge—with great difficulty, surely—that others have ends worth taking seriously in their own deliberations. The difficulty here is well-captured by a quote from an autistic adult that Kennett also cites:

> I really didn't know there were other people until I was seven years old. I then suddenly realized that there were people. But not like you do. I still have to remind myself that there are people. I could never have a friend. I really don't know what to do with other people, really. (Hobson 1992, 165; quoted in Kennett 2002, 348)

While difficult, though, those with high-functioning autism may be able to *remind* themselves of the existence of other people. And to the extent that they take their own ends to be worth consideration, they may also be able to infer the worth of acknowledging and considering the ends of those other people. This could be a kind of alternate route to universalization, albeit one that does not get the person with high-functioning autism there via empathy, so it is an example of why Kennett thinks a Kantian moral psychology may ultimately be favored (Kennett 2002, 350–3).[28] It is made possible both by the concerns of those with high-functioning autism about being good and their attraction to "ideals of order and consistency and something like the golden rule..." (Kennett 2002, 351). Evaluational regard—considerateness—might thus be possible, although in a hard-earned fashion (and so would likely merit much gratitude).

The case here is possible but dubitable, for a couple of reasons. First, we might doubt that the relevant commitment of those with high-functioning autism is a

[28] I should register my deep skepticism about the Kantian move Kennett makes here. As she rightly points out (p. 349), because those with high-functioning autism are incapable of reading the motivations of others, they are incapable of deception. It is quite well-known that they take the utterances of others quite literally (so jokes and irony are also very difficult for them to get), and they intend their own utterances to be taken equally as literally. Now if one is incapable of deception, one is also incapable of manipulation. But the Humanity Formulation of Kant's Categorical Imperative—treat others as ends in themselves, and never solely as means—is interpreted by many as just a general obligation against the *manipulation* of others. If one is incapable of manipulation, however, it is unclear in what sense the Categorical Imperative could be said to apply to one, and so it is unclear in what sense one could be an actual Kantian moral agent or under the Imperative's rubric. "Oughts" against manipulation would seem to apply to neither angels nor the autistic.

moral concern. As Victoria McGeer points out, their ends may be less about doing the right thing or taking others' interests as reason-giving and more about their "need to abide by whatever rules they have been taught without sharing our understanding of the ends those rules are meant to serve" (McGeer 2008, 240).[29] If you found yourself in a world in which you could not read off from people's faces what they were feeling or the sorts of signs for interaction that others do without effort, it would likely be terrifying, especially if these other people increased the noise level in your head by yelling at you, or if they punished you for failing to conform. If so, you would surely grasp at whatever rules for such interaction that you could find and obey them rigidly. Change would be your enemy; rigid rules would give you comfort. Even if you had no idea what the grounding of those rules consisted in, or whether they counted as "moral," it would not matter.[30]

Those with high-functioning autism might, then, be like those in my *Moral Alien Room*, just mimicking the moral behaviors of those whose own ends and motivations they simply do not understand.[31] If so, their concern might be less moral than prudential: they may just want to avoid the fear that comes with change or the unknown. They would have what McGeer calls a "passion for order" that grounds and structures their lives, motivating "their rule-oriented behavior and encourag[ing] them to such virtuoso displays of reason in trying to enlarge their understanding of the kind of order that exists in the social world so that they might participate in it" (McGeer 2008, 244). And indeed, this passion

[29] I think McGeer's claim here is buttressed by the fact that, in some recent studies, adults with high-functioning autism "judged conventional and disgust transgressions to be significantly more serious than did [controls], and failed to distinguish disgust transgressions from moral transgressions along the seriousness dimension" (Zalla et al. 2011, 122). Further, while 77% of the control group cited welfare considerations for the wrongness of so-called "moral" violations (e.g., "it will hurt her"), only 37% of those in the autistic group cited welfare considerations. "In fact, as for both moral and conventional transgressions, they favored explanations in terms of 'Rules' and, accordingly, failed in drawing the moral/conventional distinction along the dimension of justification" (Zalla et al. 2011, 122). This result also reinforces my earlier complaints about the moral/conventional distinction and task. For years, psychologists have been claiming that those with high-functioning autism pass the task, when really what they were "passing" was the *authority modification* condition of the task. But these tests suggest that they may not "pass" the seriousness or justification conditions. All of these conditions just need to be treated separately, in my view, and without reference to "moral" or "conventional" at all, which just confuses the matter.

[30] McGeer 2008 (240) cites a revealing passage suggesting such an analysis by Therese Jolliffe, from Jolliffe, Lansdown, and Robinson 1993. I think this point is also revealed repeatedly throughout the fascinating "accountability" conversations recorded between parents and their high-functioning autistic children in Sterponi 2004.

[31] In his unpublished paper "Conversation, Responsibility, and Autism Spectrum Disorder," Nathan Stout advances an analogy like this against Michael McKenna's conversational theory of responsibility.

for order reveals itself in all sorts of other ways, from the obsession with train schedules to the lining up of toys and encountered objects to general attractions to organizational taxonomies in science (McGeer 2008, 245; also revealed in conversations in Sterponi 2004). But this would suggest that the parts they play in our responsibility conversations are just different from the sort of *regard* that matters for accountability.[32]

A second reason to doubt the Kennettian story comes from considering the function of holding-to-account responses. As I argued in Chapter 3, fundamental to agential anger is the action tendency to demand acknowledgment from those who we perceive to have (in)sufficiently regarded us. But this is precisely a demand for a kind of *identification*, specifically, for emotional empathy, a demand to feel what it was like for us when (dis)regarded. While the ultimate aim of doing so may be apology and reconciliation in the negative case, the most immediate aim is to get the offending party, when returning to his own perspective, to have his shared emotions with us transform into *guilt* for his trangressions. But given their deficits of emotional empathy, those with high-functioning autism would seem unable to adhere to the demand for acknowledgment. This point is buttressed by the fact that, according to both parental reports and experimental results, those with high-functioning autism tend to experience neither guilt nor pride (or experience them only in rare cases), despite perhaps being able to label expressions of the emotions in others (Hobson et al. 2006, 129–30).[33] Now if being accountable is just a function of being eligible for being appropriately held accountable, and the fundamental aim of holding accountable—expressing the accountability demand—is for acknowledgment and a certain emotional experience and transformation as a result, then because those with high-functioning autism tend to be unable to do either, it would not be appropriate to hold them accountable and consequently they would not *be* accountable (or at least their accountability would be significantly mitigated).[34]

[32] Of course, they might still be *able* to play the regard part, but if this characterization is correct, the fact that many of those with high-functioning autism simply do *not* play this part would, I think, suggest some sort of regard-impairment, especially given the (felt) pressure to conform in societal interactions.

[33] In Shoemaker 2007, I concluded that those with high-functioning autism could be accountable partially in virtue of its being likely that they experienced guilt (96). I had at the time cast about all over the place for psychological confirmation or disconfirmation of this claim about guilt, and I had not found any. Consequently, I inductively inferred that, insofar as these agents seemed quite capable of a wide range of other emotions (demonstrated by an abundance of psychological literature), they were also very likely capable of guilt. Since discovering Hobson's work, however, I have been disabused of this bad inference.

[34] I fill in this sort of argument a bit more in Chapter 7.

These last two arguments have me leaning in the direction of agreeing that those with high-functioning autism are not accountable (or their accountability is quite mitigated). Nevertheless, it is important to point out that if those with high-functioning autism are not accountable it is *not* in virtue of their being just like psychopaths. They do seem capable of a kind of evaluation of worth and self-regard that psychopaths are not, and perhaps such an evaluative ability is capable of being exploited—in combination with their love of order, rules, or sound reasoning—in a way that would generate significantly fewer social transgressions on their part than psychopaths. This way of talking, of course, clearly sounds like the taking up of an *objective* attitude to them that may be objectionable to many.[35] Nevertheless, it does seem that the impairments of those with high-functioning autism in *relating* to others—at least as psychologically developed non-autistic humans do—may ground such an attitude, at least to some extent (Hobson et al. 2006, esp. 131–40). Indeed, this is what must be so deeply frustrating for parents and caregivers who are continually moved to try relating to their charges in interpersonal terms and are continually (mostly) thwarted in doing so (see, e.g., Sigman et al. 1986).

Conclusion

My intention in exploring the cases of psychopathy and high-functioning autism in this chapter was not only to illuminate the nature of empathy, regard, and accountability, and not only to showcase the tripartite theory's facility in handling these cases, but also to demonstrate again why the empirical details of these real-life marginal cases matter so much to our investigation. I began by exploring many theorists' entrée into discussions about psychopathic responsibility, namely, Blair's studies of how incarcerated psychopaths allegedly did on the moral/conventional task. I expressed deep skepticism about both the task and the so-called moral/conventional distinction on which it is based, and so expressed deep skepticism about the incorporation of such results in constructing theories of psychopathic responsibility. However, I took some time to explore an original interpretation of the results for only the authority modification prompt. It could be, I argued, that how psychopaths responded there is explained by the fact that they have serious difficulty (or are even incapacitated for) recognizing agential

[35] Let me be clear that there is of course no connection whatsoever between being the object of an objective attitude and having diminished moral status.

authorizations, a corollary of their general lack of regard, which has its source in their deficits in identifying empathy.

There were two stumbling blocks to this proposal. First, there were the latest results from a cleaned-up study by Aharoni, Sinnott-Armstrong, and Kiehl suggesting psychopaths can pass the moral/conventional task after all. I tried to show in response that these results, due to various methodological and conceptual worries, would not undermine my case. The second stumbling block came in the form of Kennett's puzzle: Psychopaths are not moral agents, whereas those with high-functioning autism are, even though both have serious empathic impairments. Kennett's own resolution was to deny the importance of empathy for general moral agency. What I have suggested, by contrast, is that perhaps the premises of the puzzle are false, at least as applied to *accountability*, for given the evidence it seems more likely that neither psychopaths *nor* those with high-functioning autism are accountable (or at least they both have significantly mitigated accountability), and in both cases this would be true in virtue of their empathic impairments. Psychopaths tend not to be able to make the transition from detached to identifying empathy of either the emotional or the evaluational kind, which means they are also impaired for regard of either kind. Their impairments of emotional regard have their source in their emotional deficits generally. Their impairments of evaluational regard have their source in their general evaluative deficits—impairments in seeing the worth of any pursuits—yielding impairments of *self*-regard as well. Those with high-functioning autism are capable of self-regard, however, and they are at least capable of recognizing prudential reasons to navigate their way through social interactions in a way that will generate the least resistance. Their difficulties with identifying empathy have a source in their perspective-taking disabilities, which makes even detached empathy difficult. The question, then, was whether they might still be engaging in regard *sans* empathy, as Kennett argues. I have noted that this is unlikely, for two reasons. First, the available evidence suggests that those with high-functioning autism are concerned less with regard and morality than they are with rules and order. Second, their difficulties in adhering to the demands of our accountability practices—specifically, the demands for acknowledgment that are built into the motivations of the relevant accountability sentiments—suggest impairments in the capacities that generally render agents eligible for being held to account, and so suggest impaired accountability.

Notably, I have left it open that both psychopaths and those with high-functioning autism could still be both answerable and attributability-responsible for actions and attitudes. If so, this would explain and vindicate the specific sort of ambivalence many of us may feel about both kind of agents' overall responsibility (or moral agency). But as one might expect, the issues raised by their potential answerability and attributability are complex. In Chapter 6, I take them up, along with discussion of another type of marginal agent that will shed some important light on these phenomena.

6

Psychopathy and Intellectual Disability

Impairments of Judgment

In Chapters 4 and 5, we have focused on what the specific story I have told about attributability and accountability predicts, in combination with the relevant empirical facts (insofar as we can ascertain them), about several marginal cases. In this chapter we will engage in a similar project with respect to answerability, and so our focus will be on impairments of judgment. In the first section, I will return to psychopathy. While I have already argued that the tripartite theory implies that psychopaths are either seriously mitigated or fully exempt from accountability, it is not yet clear what the theory implies about their answerability. Figuring out their eligibility for this type of responsibility requires delving into some more of the details of their pathology. But as we will see, doing so threatens to undercut my motivating thought that psychopaths tend to generate a fitting ambivalence in many of us, for some of the empirical details might give us reason to believe that they are actually seriously mitigated or fully exempt from *all three* types of responsibility. Nevertheless, I will make what I think is a fairly plausible case for their being attributability-responsible in a wide range of cases, and answerable only in a much smaller range of cases.

In the second section, I will explore the regularly overlooked case of adults with mild intellectual disabilities.[1] What I will argue is that the tripartite theory, informed by the empirical details about the disorder, implies that these agents may be fully eligible for accountability and attributability, but their answerability tends to be (at least) impaired in virtue of fairly distinctive sorts of abstraction and judgmental impairments. To the extent that the objects of their actual regard

[1] This is what the DSM-IV and its previous versions labeled "mild mental retardation," as did I (in following their terminology) in Shoemaker 2007 and 2009.

are fairly limited, though (e.g., tending to deploy it primarily just to intimates), I will suggest one strategy for expanding their empathic range and so generating their greater inclusion in the accountability community.

Psychopathy Redux

In Chapter 5, I argued that the tripartite theory predicts that psychopaths are not accountable (or at least their accountability is significantly mitigated), as they are impaired for identifying regard of either kind. But I left open whether they might be answerable or attributability-responsible. In previous work, I argued that they straightforwardly meet the conditions for both remaining types of responsibility (Shoemaker 2011b). If right, this entails one sort of ambivalence toward psychopaths: while full-fledged accountability responses like agential anger (including resentment and indignation) and gratitude would tend to be unfitting for them, full-fledged attributability responses (e.g., agential disdain, admiration, and contempt) and answerability responses (e.g., agential disapproval, disappointment, pride, regret) could still be fitting for them. However, in this section, I will explore a tension for this account, stemming from the specific prudential deficits discussed in Chapter 5. Dealing with this tension will have me narrowing the range of psychopaths' answerability, as well as doing some clarifying work on the nature of answerability and attributability generally.

I begin, though, with the possibility that psychopaths are impaired for answerability in the *moral* domain. The capacity rendering one eligible for answerability, recall, is the capacity for judgment about "instead of" reasons, reasons in favor of doing something or having some attitude instead of some relevant contrary action or attitude. Now there seems no doubt that psychopaths have this capacity in many nonregard-based domains, such as mathematics, aesthetics, athletics, or standard means–end reasoning. But to the extent that my desire to avoid pain tends not even to appear to them to be a reason not to cause me pain, they are impaired in recognizing the relevant regard-based "instead of" reason to which we would refer in the fleshed-out version of our answerability demand as follows: "Why did you cause me pain (for example) *instead of respecting my preference to be pain-free*?" Insofar as the evidence suggests that the latter fact about me (as well as certain other facts about my normative perspective) is not something psychopaths (at least those at the far end of the PCL-R checklist spectrum) seem to be able to take as reason-giving, they would seem to be exempt from (or severely impaired for) answerability for regard-based actions or attitudes. Criticizing them for their failures here would be akin to criticizing someone in a strict liability case, for example, criticizing someone who sold alcohol to a minor with an undetectable fake ID. The law may do it, but in interpersonal morality we think it unfitting. This argument provides a prima facie case against moral answerability for psychopaths.

What, though, if psychopaths nevertheless actively judge that my preference to be pain-free (say) is *not* a reason not to cause me pain? This is the objectionable stance psychopaths ostensibly take on the Scanlonian construal articulated by Matthew Talbert in a series of papers (Talbert 2008, 2012a, 2012b, and Forthcoming). We might think it is one thing to be unable to see some fact as a reason, but something else entirely to actively judge that some fact does not count as a reason (even if one simply could not see it as such). It is this latter stance toward regard-based reasons that Talbert interprets psychopaths as having, and it is the source, for him, of the appropriateness of full-bore accountability responses to them like resentment.

In Chapter 5, I made my case for why I think psychopaths are impaired for identifying empathy and thus accountability. If they cannot really come to see certain facts about others' normative perspectives as even putative reasons in favor of promoting or respecting others' ends, then any judgments they may make about them will not be *regard*-based. If they are impaired for quality of regard, then the responsibility responses organized around agential anger will be unfitting for them. That is not to say, of course, that we will not tend to feel anger—perhaps lots of it—toward them, especially if they harm us. But once their agential (empathic) impairments are rendered fully salient, the inappropriateness of responding to them in this way ought to sink in.[2]

But even if anger and its like would be unfitting for psychopaths, we might still think that plenty of other negative responsibility responses would be appropriate, and we might well want to ground them by adopting Talbert's approach. So consider answerability responses. If you judge that my interests do not matter, then even if you cannot see my interests as reason-giving, your judgment that they are not reason-giving still seems criticizable, perhaps *especially* if you cannot recognize them as such. For comparison, suppose there were people who, while capable of seeing various descriptive facts about works of art, were unable to see these facts as reasons to admire or appreciate them. For example, they may full well be able to recognize when paintings have various compositional features or color palettes, but they are unable to see how these elements provide them with any more reason for admiration than would random splotches on a moldy

[2] Although we may also think that unfitting anger toward psychopaths when they harm your loved ones is actually a mark of your good character, similarly to Williams' lorry driver and his unfitting regret (discussed in Chapter 2).

basement wall. Call these people *aesthetopaths*.[3] Suppose, then, that one such person, Chris, went around actively judging and exclaiming that some beautiful works of art were in fact not beautiful, that she had no reason whatsoever to admire them. It would be deeply frustrating and irritating to deal with Chris (at least in art-related matters), and criticism of her would most certainly be warranted. So why wouldn't it be the same with the psychopath?

It would, but the reasons are subtle. Let us start by noting what a fitting criticism of the aesthetopath would actually be grounded on. We would not fittingly criticize Chris, it seems, for judging a work of art to lack beauty *instead of judging it to be beautiful*; after all, she cannot see aesthetic value as we can. Rather, we are criticizing her for calling the beautiful object nonbeautiful *instead of withholding judgment on its beauty altogether*. So the target of our criticism is her judgment that the reasons in favor of *coming to an aesthetic verdict* were more worth acting on than the reasons in favor of withholding judgment. But what could these latter reasons be, and why should she have judged them more worth acting on? Perhaps because she knows she is an aesthetopath, because she has been called wrong in her aesthetic assessments so many times before, and because people continually get irritated with her for blithely pronouncing her nonbeauty judgments, she has very strong self-interested reasons in favor of withholding judgment. But these are all reasons she *is* capable of seeing and judging as to their worth.[4] So while she is incapable of seeing the "instead of" reason in favor of calling something nonbeautiful rather than beautiful, and so is not answerable for failing to do so, she is nevertheless capable of recognizing the "instead of" reason for withholding judgment (or at least not announcing or acting on her verdict), and so she is answerable for failing to do that.

I think the same thing may be true for the psychopath. In regard-based scenarios, he may not be answerable (and so criticizable) for his judgment that the reasons in favor of ignoring facts about my normative perspective are worth more than the reasons in favor of treating those facts as simpatico practical reasons, as he is simply impaired for recognizing facts about my normative perspective as reasons in the first place. But he *might* be (fully) answerable for coming to a verdict about how to treat me, answerable for forming a judgment

[3] I have been unable to find anything in the empirical literature about the existence of aesthetopaths as such, but I have no doubt there are those who lack access to aesthetic values as a function of other impairments or disabilities. Psychopaths are perhaps among them.

[4] These are what Russell 2004 calls "external reasons." Compare to his discussion of Jill, who cannot feel fear but can still recognize when things are dangerous or harmful (Russell 2004, 294–5). Note that I have not said that Chris cannot feel admiration, however, only that she can never recognize reasons to feel it. Perhaps this amounts to the same thing, although I am not sure.

that the reasons in favor of treating my interests as nonreason-giving are worth more than the reasons in favor of *suspending any treatment of those interests one way or the other*. His answerability in the latter case would be in virtue of the fact that these second sorts of "instead of" reasons would not have to be regard-based; rather, they could merely implicate his self-interest. For example, people really get frustrated and upset with him when he judges their interests worthless. "Successful" psychopaths sometimes seem able to take these latter sorts of reasons seriously, as they tend to want to keep their other manipulative schemes alive and they cannot do so if people do not like to deal with them. To that extent, therefore, they could be morally answerable.

There is, then, a good case to be made for a limited sort of moral answerability for psychopaths, albeit not along the lines Talbert suggests. But when this possibility is combined with some of my previous remarks, it may look like a serious tension arises for my accounts of both answerability and attributability, and so ultimately a worry may arise about whether there ought to be any ambivalence at all in our responses to psychopaths. In Chapter 5, I argued that some psychopaths appear to lack even *self*-regard, so they are not only morally impaired but also prudentially impaired. But if they really are prudentially impaired, then would they even be able to see the self-interested reasons just cited? In other words, why think they are answerable at all where regard of any kind, self- or other-, is implicated?

The tension for attributability is related. Some theorists, including myself, have thought that it is perfectly appropriate to respond to psychopaths with disdain, and so to label them "cruel," "manipulative," "nasty," and the like (e.g., Watson 2011; Shoemaker 2011b). These are aretaic attributability assessments, and on my view they would have to be grounded in the fact that psychopaths' attitudes and actions somehow express their care-commitment clusters. But if psychopaths have impaired capacities for caring about anything *and* they have impaired capacities for an evaluative stance (given their deficits of even self-regard), then in what sense could they be said to have a deep self at all for such attitudes to express?

The tension for answerability is more easily resolved, I think, than the tension for attributability. As I have already suggested a few times in the early chapters, one might coherently judge some reasons more worth acting on than others in a way that is contrary to one's general evaluative stance. One example I gave was acting on whims, where one could be answerable for one's judgment that a whimsical desire was worth acting on, despite its being contrary to one's stably held values. Another example was drunk judgment. And rage may blind one to a class of reasons that one would, under ordinary circumstances, judge more worth adhering to insofar as they would express one's general evaluative stance. These are all examples of genuine "out of character" actions for which one might nevertheless be answerable. But the worry brought out by their prudential failings is that psychopaths seem to present a different sort of example, as they may judge some reasons more worth adhering to than others, not contrary to, but in the *absence* of, a general evaluative stance altogether. Of course, we have already allowed that they may have long-lasting, single-minded projects, guiding them just to the extent to which no contrary projects happen to arise. Such projects may still give them reasons to do various things, not in virtue of *their worth* (they are not ends, after all), but simply in virtue of the fact *that they happen to have them*. These would thus be reasons of self-interest only in the sense that they reflect the *interests of the self* at some point in time. To the extent that these interests may generate relevant "instead of" reasons, we might think, reasons the psychopath can recognize, he could be answerable for his poor quality of judgment with respect to them, even in the absence of an evaluative stance.

But if psychopaths indeed tend not to have a general evaluative stance, and if they tend not to have genuine emotional dispositions either, it would seem to follow that they would tend not to have the cares, commitments, or care-commitment clusters that I have argued constitute the deep self, so nothing could be attributable to them. If their specific judgments (e.g., that people's interests are not worth taking into consideration) do not flow from some feature of a deep self, then on my account disdain for them would not be fitting, nor would the host of aretaic predicates regularly heaped upon them. As I appealed to psychopathy at the beginning of the book to illustrate our ambivalent responses in marginal cases, leaning heavily on the fittingness of these aretaic responses to do so, I definitely need to address this tension.[5]

I think the answer starts with a recognition of the fact that judging another's interests unworthy of respect is often precisely the kind of attitude that, in part, makes agents *bad*.[6] Now I say "in part" because judging that another's interests have no worth might also be what a value nihilist would do. If *nothing* matters, then of course your interests do not matter. Nevertheless, it is surely possible for there to be kind or loving nihilists. The primary difference between these nihilists

[5] The tension I have just articulated is a genuine tension for Gary Watson's account of psychopathy as well, a view he has presented in Watson 2011 and 2013. My solution *might* work for him, but because he does not have the role for "mere" cares in his version of attributability that I do, I am just not sure.

[6] See Maibom 2008 for discussion of psychopaths as "the bad" (as opposed to "the mad"). For her, being bad seems sufficient to render psychopaths eligible for accountability. As I have shown, this is not the case, but one of the many valuable features of the tripartite theory is that her plausible remarks on their responsibility for badness might still be applicable, just with respect to a different type of responsibility, viz., attributability.

and our psychopaths would be that the latter have a desire to hurt others. Consequently, it is this desire, in combination with the judgment that others' interests do not matter, that makes someone *really* bad, that is, cruel.[7] And this seems to be the combination present in many psychopaths.

There are, then, two attitudes potentially attributable to psychopaths: the desire to hurt someone (say) and the judgment that that person's preferences not to be hurt (say) are not reasons against doing so. And here is where the narcissistic side of psychopathy rears its head, for it seems that, no matter what desires psychopaths have, there are typically *no* reasons they can see against satisfying them. What this suggests is that, despite their deficits in recognizing either moral or prudential worth, there still seems to be something that matters to them, namely, *that they satisfy their desires*. Now if this were the case, one would expect psychopaths to have some sort of negative response when their desires are not satisfied, a kind of response distinctive to a loss in value. And do they ever! As it turns out, the evidence is quite strong that psychopaths tend to be hyper-responsive to their own desire-frustration, experiencing and expressing lots of anger when they cannot do or get what they want (see, e.g., Blackburn and Lee-Evans 1985; Serin 1991; Morrison and Gilbert 2001; Blair 2010 and 2012).[8] As they tend to evince a stable pattern of angry response to frustration of their own desires, it seems safe to draw the conclusion that, even if they tend not to respond emotionally to the frustration of anyone else's desires or aims, and even if they have made no conscious commitment to the worth of satisfying their desires, they certainly behave as if they care about *doing and getting whatever it is they happen to want.*

But of course getting what we want matters to all of us, so what distinguishes us from psychopaths on this front? It is that psychopaths tend not to care about, or be committed to, *anything else*. Recall the discussion in Chapter 1 about care-commitment clusters, and in particular about the ways in which various cares or commitments tend to buttress or constrain one another. My example there was one in which, were I to care solely and single-mindedly about my wife, with no other cares about myself or commitments to morality, I would be disposed to do anything and everything to preserve and promote her ends. I am suggesting here

[7] Thanks to Angela Smith and Christian Coons for helpful discussion here.

[8] Whether they experience more anger than nonpsychopaths, or whether their anger is roughly comparable but they have more difficulty than nonpsychopaths in *regulating* it, is the subject of some discussion by Harenski and Kiehl 2010. Interestingly, because they tend to be impaired with respect to threat sensitivity, the reactive aggression they display is much more likely to be to goal-frustration than to physical or social threats, even though they tend to cast about for the source of their desire-frustration in a way that looks an awful lot like retaliation for threats (Blair 2010).

that psychopaths seem to have an analogously single-minded, unconstrained care, just with respect to their own desire-satisfaction. The only thing that matters is getting what they happen to want. So to the extent that we take Talbert's characterization of them seriously, their intentions to harm others, when a function of both their desire to harm others and their judgment that others' interests provide no reason against doing so, are attributable to—are expressions of—their *unconstrained* caring about their own desire-satisfaction. But that is just agential badness.

At the end of the day, then, I think there is a quite plausible story that can be told about how psychopaths are fully attributability-responsible: they *are* cruel, manipulative, etc. But if they are answerable in the moral domain, I suspect it is only with respect to the set of "instead of" reasons making reference to the worth of withholding judgment about regard-based reasons generally, and not the set actually incorporating such regard-based reasons. In other words, if psychopaths have deficits in perceiving facts about others' normative perspectives as even appearing to be reasons, then they have at least mitigated answerability for judging that those facts have no worth in their deliberation about whether or not to punch someone in the spleen, say (as opposed to poking them in the eye). Nevertheless, to the extent that such facts may be recognized as causing others to respond to their objects and oneself in certain ways, then they may appear to be (self-interested) reasons to withhold judgment on how to treat those facts, so some psychopaths still might be answerable for their decisions about whether to treat these seeming-reasons as reasons or about how much worth to ascribe to them. This is answerability of a kind, but we may well hesitate to call it *moral* answerability or think that it grounds moral criticism.

Mild Intellectual Disability

Among caregivers especially, there are deeply ambivalent responsibility responses to adults with mild intellectual disability (MID).[9] My aim here is to explain the source of, and vindicate, this ambivalence, especially with respect to answerability, by once again feeding the relevant empirical work into the tripartite theory. In doing so, it will once more behoove us to compare and contrast adults with MID to psychopaths. But it will also behoove us to compare and contrast them to children, with whom they are often (wrongly) grouped in the literature. By the end of the chapter, then, I will hope to have a much richer

[9] Some of the material in this section has been drawn from Shoemaker 2009.

understanding of answerability on the table, one that is more sensitive to the details of these real-world agents.

Being categorized as intellectually disabled used to be primarily a function of scoring a 69 or lower on an IQ test, but IQ is no longer appealed to. Instead, diagnosis is a function of assessment of adaptive abilities, and so includes deficits in the following domains:

1. Deficits in intellectual functions, such as reasoning, problem solving, planning, abstract thinking, judgment, academic learning, and learning from experience....
2. Deficits in adaptive functioning that result in failure to meet developmental and sociocultural standards for personal independence and social responsibility....
3. Onset of intellectual and adaptive deficits during the developmental period (American Psychiatric Association 2013).

There are, roughly, three general intellectual impairments involved: (1) not being able to learn as much or as quickly as nondisabled people; (2) not being able to store information as well as the nondisabled; and (3) not being able to engage in abstract thought or to apply principles or information from one situation to another very well (Evans 1983, 7). I will be focusing on the third. This disability obviously admits of a wide spectrum, and there are four standard categories of intellectual disability, based on adaptive function scores: mild, moderate, severe, and profound. By far the largest subcategory is "mild," whose members by some past estimates make up nearly 90 percent of the total intellectual disabilities population (Evans 1983, 24). The members of this group have generally failed to arrive at the stage of development wherein one becomes relatively proficient at abstract thought, deploying deductive reasoning, "and perform[ing] logical operations on abstract ideas" (Castles 1996, 4–5, 51).

People with intellectual disabilities are often thought to be "eternal children," and so discussions of moral responsibility that even mention them invariably lump them in with children and then suggest that, insofar as children are not morally responsible, neither are those with intellectual disabilities (e.g., Wallace 1994, 167, n. 14). This is a mistake, however, at least with respect to adults with MID, for there are significant physical and mental differences that emerge as they grow older that render them quite distinct from children. Specifically, adults with MID tend to be more mature physically (enabling many of them to work), emotionally (many are fully capable of, and experience, romantic love, grief, despair, guilt, and remorse), and cognitively (having had to negotiate an at-times very confusing world with a limited set of cognitive tools for far longer than normal children do, and having, quite simply, learned a lot more stuff). Because of these key differences in maturity level, then, we should not expect there to be much of an analogy between children and adults with MID regarding responsibility. And there is not. I will argue that these forms of maturity may compensate for or supplant some cognitive disabilities sufficiently to bring them into some of the worlds of responsibility.

Let us start by comparing and contrasting adults with MID to psychopaths. While some psychopaths are also intellectually disabled, in cases of no overlap there are at least three relevant differences. First, psychopaths have significantly diminished (or no) arousal to the distress of others, whereas adults with MID have no such impairments (Blair 1996, 577; Blair 1999a). Second, MID entails none of the emotional deficits of psychopaths (Blair 1996 and 1999a; Herpertz and Sass 2000), and, crucially, the capacities for mature responsibility emotions—e.g., guilt and remorse—that seem essential for both the development of a moral self and participation in our interpersonal accountability exchanges tend to be fully operative in adults with MID. The third difference regards empathy. Psychopaths, recall, are capable of detached empathy, the most basic form of perspective-taking, but they remain significantly impaired for either form of identifying empathy (evaluational or emotional). Adults with MID seem fully capable of identifying empathy, however. Note the following observation of interactions among adults with MID in a workshop:

> [W]orkshop members are exquisitely sensitive to situations or remarks that might damage the self-esteem of their fellow workers. They protect one another from derogatory remarks and rush to provide comfort when a friend is upset. Indeed, people with mental retardation[10] are often more sensitive to the problems and feelings of their peers than are even the most sophisticated and well-intentioned of nonhandicapped individuals. (Castles 1996, 80)

I can only see such responses as exemplars of regard, displays of identifying empathy yielding simpatico emotional responses and recognition of simpatico reasons. If this is standard behavior, then it would seem that in virtue of their robust empathic capacities (capacities impaired or lacking in psychopaths), adults with MID are perfectly eligible for being the fitting target of accountability responses.

Is this a surprising result? It will not be for their friends, parents, and caregivers. From such parties, moral address of the sort demanding acknowledgment often seems perfectly sensible to those with MID, as the literature—what

[10] Again, this used to be the official diagnostic term for those with what is now termed intellectual disability.

scant literature there is, admittedly—suggests (Castles 1996, 78–9; Heshusius 1981, 98–110). Adults with MID seem generally able to understand the emotional communications of agential anger and gratitude as such, see and appreciate the distress associated with injuries and harms to others as reasons of the right sort, and *feel* what the injured or harmed party feels in being so affected. It seems they have the basic capacities to be regarding, accountable agents, and their accountability is taken for granted by those close to them.[11]

There are a few things to note here. First, what this point helps to bring out is that the conditions of accountability need not lean too heavily (or at all?) on the ability to apply abstract moral principles to concrete cases, contrary to what some have suggested (see, e.g., Wallace 1994, 157). As noted earlier (from the DSM-5), those with MID tend to have (mild) deficits in abstract thinking generally, so their full-fledged regarding responses to those within their intimate circle are unlikely to be the result, say, of applying a "respect humanity" principle, a "maximize happiness" principle, or even a "be nice" principle to the case at hand.[12]

However, second, their abstraction impairments, in combination with their impairments in judgment (again, as noted in the DSM-5), may have more of a mitigating impact when it comes to *answerability*. The key capacity for answerability is, after all, quality of judgment, and in particular the capacity to make judgments about the worth of various ("instead of") reasons. But to the extent that these evaluative judgments require the application of some abstract evaluative standard to the case at hand, adults with MID may have more difficulty with them. In order to judge that a reason is more worthy than another, one has to be able to apply whatever abstract standard of worth one has in mind to these specific reasons. For most of us, this standard will be grounded in our general evaluative stance. But if one has difficulty applying that abstract standard to the case at hand, then one will have difficulty making the requisite sorts of judgments about one's reasons. They may tend not to reflect one's actual evaluative commitments (and so perhaps will be quite inconsistent with one another across time). This is the sort of position in which I am suggesting adults with MID may find themselves. The tripartite theory, in combination with the details of the disability, implies at least mitigated answerability amongst adults with MID.

Nevertheless, to the extent that they seem unimpaired with respect to identifying empathy, they seem fully capable of pure regard, in both respects. First,

[11] It is not, however, to most others. I will return to and diagnose this point below.

[12] Indeed, it is difficult to believe that many, if any, people actually proceed in such a manner. See Arpaly 2003.

because of their emotional maturity and wide emotional arsenal, they look fully capable of emotional regard and so susceptible to the emotional address at the heart of (either form of) accountability's regard-based demand. So while it may be less than fitting to disapprove of or criticize an adult with MID for poor moral judgment, the demand that she "feel what she has done" may be fully fitting, precisely because it is a concrete appeal unreliant on judgment, and one she seems fully capable of undertaking.

Now it may seem as if it is only emotional regard of which adults with MID are fully capable, but I have been suggesting the possibility that they may be capable of unimpaired *evaluational* regard too, even if they are impaired for answerability. Recall Scanlon's two critical stages of judgment with respect to reasons: (1) deciding that what seems to be a reason is one, and (2) deciding that such a reason has a certain worth relative to other reasons (Scanlon 1998, 65–6). What I have called "pure" evaluational regard takes place at a pre-critical stage, however, when certain facts about others' normative perspectives come to seem "reasonish" as a function of evaluational empathy. One could thus "purely" regard someone but have difficulty with respect to one or the other critical stages, and thereby be fully accountable with respect to that form of regard while having mitigated answerability. I think this is often the case with adults with MID: they tend to be able fully to see and empathize with another's pain, say, but their judgments of what to *do* about it may be impaired. They may be inundated with seeming reasons by the facts of another's pain and decide the wrong ones are the genuine reasons, or they may make serious errors in assessing the worth of various genuine reasons (by the lights of their own evaluative stance). But at least their heart is in the right place, we are wont to say. They may still mean well in a way meriting gratitude for the quality of their evaluational regard.

The story of attributability for adults with MID seems straightforward. Given the evidence of their wide-ranging emotional capacities and experiences, they obviously care about many things, and to the extent that their attitudes express these cares, those attitudes would be attributable to them and various aretaic predicates could fittingly apply. There is also no reason to believe that they do not have general commitments, an evaluative stance providing them with ends, such as the worth of work, relationships, and contributions to community. So to the extent that these commitments are successfully expressed in attitudes, those attitudes would also be attributable to them and various aretaic predicates could fittingly apply.

In combination with the empirical details (and some speculation on my part, of course), the tripartite theory seems to predict the following (appropriate) ambivalence to adults with MID.[13] Two general categories of response (aretaic responses; agential anger and gratitude) may occasionally be fully fitting, whereas one (including moral disapproval or criticism) may be less so. I believe, however, that this will be an independently intuitive result only for those already in the circle of intimacy of those with MID. For many others, it may seem more intuitive that, while adults with MID are perhaps attributability-responsible, neither answerability *nor* accountability responses will be appropriate. What, then, would explain this different set of reactions?

In looking at our practices, it seems that adults with MID tend to be held accountable primarily just by those within their circle of friends, family, and caregivers because these are fellows with whom they already find themselves emotionally, interpersonally engaged. In intimate relationships like this, the gloves come off and anger and gratitude—from both parties—tend to be full-throated (Taylor and Bogdan 1989, 29 and 32).[14] However, strangers (who are aware of the relevant emotional and evaluational regard capacities in play) who are not in such relationships and find themselves in the regard-realm with those with MID may think that they may not be able to recognize them as a fellow member of the accountability community—as akin to their family, friends, and caregivers—and so do not view them as appropriately liable to expressions of the moral demand for acknowledgment. And such reluctance may be appropriate. Because of their developmental impairments, adults with MID may indeed have difficulty recognizing other unfamiliar members of the accountability community *as* members of that community. That is, they may have trouble accessing or appreciating abstract principles about mutual recognition and accountability amongst *all* members of the accountability community, or they may have trouble seeing (without serious prompting) how the practices of mutual accountability with which they are familiar ought to be applied to unfamiliar agents. What they can and do easily appreciate, however, are concrete appeals from those they care about, those with whom they are already emotionally connected, and they also

[13] On a more general ambivalence toward those with disabilities (cognitive and physical), see Soder 1990.

[14] Could this full-throated sort of accountability-assessment be explained by the assessor's failure to retain a proper perspective regarding the intellectually disabled adult with whom she is in a relationship? This is surely possible in some cases, just as it is possible for someone to be so enthralled by a charismatic psychopath that she treats him as though he were a fellow member of the accountability community. But in both cases a clear-eyed perspective on the agent in question will, I believe, yield the responses I have suggested. For most of those in relationships with adults with MID in particular, what evidence there is strongly suggests that their full-throated reactive attitudes are just as natural and proper-seeming (to both them and others) as their moral reactions to paradigm members of the moral community. And to the extent that their targets have the requisite regard-based capacities, this makes perfect sense.

have no trouble holding such familiar agents to account as well (see, e.g., Castles 1996, 75–80). Consequently, to the extent that their empathic abilities are limited in these latter sorts of ways, the tripartite theory can allow that adults with MID may not be eligible for full accountability in interactions with strangers, even if they are so eligible in interactions with their familiars.

Of course, one of the ideals for many caregivers is to extend the range of accountability for their charges, but how does this take place? Given the above discussion, it would have to involve some sort of empathic expansion, helping the adult with MID to recognize the wider range of those with whom he or she is capable of identifying. Here is one method of doing so (one that I hope resonates with those in this position). When an adult with MID interacts with, and injures, a stranger, the caregiver may express a kind of anger on behalf of the stranger (an exaggerated mimic, perhaps) followed by the familiar appeal, "How would you feel if someone did that to you?" In being susceptible to the accountability-responses of the caregiver—someone with whom he or she is already in an emotional relationship—the adult with MID may then come to feel the fitting guilt or remorse. So far, however, this person will merely be identifying with, and responding to the demand made by, the caregiver. But through repeated encounters like this, the hope is that this person will eventually come to see the face of the caregiver in the stranger, either through abstract generalization (which could be very hard) or by making some sort of direct empathic leap, that is, to see them both as one at least in terms of their both *having* normative perspectives to be taken seriously. In taking up the stranger's perspective, then, he or she will be in a position to respond appropriately, without mediation or antecedent relationships. This is *empathy training*, a way of expanding adults with MID's interpersonal engagement skills (Shoemaker 2014b).[15] It may be a nonstandard route to the extension of accountability relations, but the end result seems just as good as ordinary examples of these relations. And furthermore, to the degree that many adults with MID seem capable of some such extension, doing so would once again be a testament to their own nonstandard route to cognitive maturity.

Conclusion

In this chapter, I have attempted to shed some more light (primarily) on the nature of answerability by exploring two marginal cases, psychopathy and

[15] For other sorts of methods of empathy training in those with intellectual disabilities, see Matson and Senatore 1981. See Caparulo 1991 for a discussion of empathy training for adults with MID who are sex offenders.

intellectual disability. I have expressed doubts about the (full) moral answerability of each, albeit due to different sorts of judgmental impairments. Even for those psychopaths who judge that others' interests are not reason-giving, to the extent that they lack any access to the relevantly moral "instead of" reason—that is, to the extent that they have serious deficits in seeing facts about others' normative perspectives as "reasonish"—their answerability is (at least) mitigated for standard moral violations. But insofar as they may be able to make self-interested decisions about whether to come to some verdicts about how to treat others, they may be answerable for those decisions, and so may be the appropriate target of some answerability criticism. But this is a much smaller range of answerable attitudes than those who favor answerability for psychopaths will be happy with, I suspect. Whether this is the right answer bears reflection and more empirical detective work.

Many psychopaths, however, are very likely fully attributability-responsible for various of their harming intentions, as these are a function of their caring about getting whatever they happen to want. The evidence that they care in this way is provided by their well-documented stable pattern of anger at their (and only their) desire-frustration. The fact that they also judge others' interests not to matter (if they do so judge), in combination with this guiding care, is what makes them the fitting target of disdain for their cruelty, say, or general badness.[16]

To the extent that moral answerability requires applying abstract principles about wrongness to concrete judgments of moral worth, the tripartite theory implies that adults with MID impaired with respect to both abstract thinking and judgment generally would seem to have (at least) mitigated answerability. Given

[16] Paul Russell offers a "moral sense" condition on responsibility, namely, that a "responsible agent must be able to feel and understand moral sentiments or reactive attitudes" (Russell 2004, 293; for discussion see McKenna 2012, 81–3, and Nelkin 2011, 24–6). Psychopaths, he argues, tend to be unable to meet this condition and so are not responsible. He seems to have in mind just something like accountability, but I think psychopaths also fail to meet this condition with respect to answerability. In other words, not only are they unable to feel and understand specifically *agential* anger (see fn. 8 in this chapter), the characteristic sentiment of accountability, but also they tend to be unable to feel and understand regret, the characteristic sentiment of answerability. In neither case, however, do I think their violation of the moral sense condition is what *makes* them nonresponsible; rather, given my arguments, it is more likely a symptom of their more fundamental failures, namely, their impairments in evaluational and emotional empathy/regard and so their deficits in seeing the relevant "instead of" reasons. What I argued in this chapter, however, is that they may still be attributability-responsible, and this would be true even if they cannot feel and understand its characteristic sentiments of agential admiration or disdain. This may mean that the moral sense requirement applies only to two of the three types of responsibility. Perhaps it is not intended to apply to more than that. Alternatively, one might try and make the case that psychopaths *do* feel and understand something like these aretaic responsibility responses, so that they actually do meet the moral sense condition as applied to attributability. This move could then preserve the moral sense condition as a good heuristic for responsibility across all three types.

their generally intact capacities for identifying empathy and (both forms of) regard, though, we have what I think is a very interesting illustration of how full accountability can obtain even when answerability does not. Of course, adults with MID may be accountable only to a limited range of others: to their friends, family, and caregivers, or to those with whom they are in antecedently rich interpersonal emotional relationships. Nevertheless, there seem to be available methods by which such an accountability-domain may be expanded, and even though they may take a nonstandard route, it is the destination, we might think, that matters.

The tripartite theory does quite well, it seems, in explaining and vindicating our ambivalence in the cases of psychopathy and MID. In Chapter 7, I will make a different use of marginal cases by appealing both to agents from poor formative circumstances and to those with dementia in responding to a powerful objection to the ahistorical nature of all three types of responsibility.

7

Deprivation and Dementia

How History Does and Doesn't Matter

The three types of responsibility and their exempting conditions all make reference just to agents' current qualities of will. To be attributability-responsible for some attitude at t_1 is just for it to express one's character, that is, some of one's cares, commitments, or care-commitment cluster(s) had at t_1. To be answerable for some attitude or action at t_1 is just for it to be governable by one's judgments about the worth of various "instead of" reasons at (or just before) t_1. And to be accountable for some attitude or action at t_1 is for one to be eligible for accountability responses with respect to one's degree of regard at t_1. What seems irrelevant in each case, then, is the agent's history leading up to t_1: Regardless of what the agent's past consisted in—or even whether she had much of a past—she may be responsible entirely as a matter of how she is, and what she does or feels, *now*.[1]

One might insist (and many have insisted) to the contrary, however, that agential history matters for responsibility in a way ignored by the tripartite theory, and one might come at this point from two different directions. First, one might think that some agential histories motivate the inclusion of additional (ahistorical) conditions on responsible agency, conditions without which the tripartite theory will yield the wrong answer in key cases. Second, one might

[1] I am fairly permissive about what is to be included under the rubric of "now," intending this to refer to what we can think of roughly as *proximal* causes of actions or attitudes, so that we can include intentions, cares, or evaluative stances (which may be related to actions/attitudes by milliseconds or over several days). Contrast these with *distal* causes, which are at some more distant remove from the actions or attitudes in question. I have no principled way to distinguish these, and at their edges they will surely blend into one another, but in the cases in the text there is no need for a principled distinction, as it is quite clear which is which. In addition, the word "now" is somewhat ambiguous between the time of action and the time of assessment. For ease of discussion in this chapter, I will just consider these times to be extremely close to one another, so that an assessment responds immediately to some attitude's expression, say. Delays between expression and response complicate matters in interesting ways, but I will not address such complications here. I have addressed some of them in Shoemaker 2012b. See also Khoury 2013.

think that some agential histories directly motivate the inclusion of a historical condition on responsible agency in a way the tripartite theory abjures.

Both ways of objecting may emphasize and draw from the marginal agency of those who come from *poor formative circumstances.* Susan Wolf offers the first kind of argument by appealing to someone who comes from a deeply morally deprived upbringing, someone who has been raised, essentially, to be wicked. Our pretheoretic intuitions about this case, Wolf argues, motivate the addition of a normative competence (normative sanity) requirement to theories like mine.[2] The second kind of argument appeals to abusive childhoods to suggest that some cases of ambivalence toward violent adults may motivate the addition of a requirement that responsible qualities of will avoid a certain deviant causal history.[3] In either case, though, history matters to responsibility.[4]

[2] Hers is a normative competence requirement that is itself, I should stress, ahistorical.

[3] There is another very important causal-deviance objection to ahistorical theories of responsibility that I will not discuss, one drawn from worries about *manipulation.* These start with the intuition that when the current "time-slice" agential properties (like quality of will) have some sort of deviant causal route, having been implanted, say, by brainwashing, hypnosis, or direct neural stimulation, the agent cannot be responsible for them. Consequently, the fact *that one is the way one is* cannot be sufficient for one's being responsible; what is also needed is some kind of historical causal condition about how one *got* to be the way one is. These worries most often stem from consideration of science fiction scenarios, which hypothesize people whose values are switched by evil neuroscientists in some kind of immediate, wholesale fashion, people who exist for only a minute, or people who have been designed from their embryonic stage to develop in certain sorts of ways (for discussion, see, e.g., Locke 1975; Frankfurt 1988, 47–57; Mele 1995, 2008, 2009a, 2009b, 2013; Fischer and Ravizza 1998; Zimmerman 1999; Fischer 2004; Russell 2004, 300; Haji 2008; Pereboom 2008; and McKenna 2013). While there are a few real-life "manipulation" cases discussed in this literature, involving psychological transformations due to conversion, loved-ones' deaths, salesmanship, or injury (see, e.g., Arpaly 2006, 109–16; and McKenna 2008), manipulation generally is just not relevant to the ambivalence we have with respect to the real-life marginal agents I am focused on in this book, and that is why I am not considering this objection here, although I hope to do so elsewhere.

[4] Note that both of these are examples of a certain kind of psychological history. But one might worry that physiological—in particular *neuro*-physiological—history matters too. Consider, for instance, the 2002 case of the 40-year-old man who began having serious pedophilic urges but was then discovered to have an egg-sized tumor on his orbitofrontal cortex. Once the tumor was removed, the urges went away. The urges returned when the tumor regrew (see Batts 2009, 270). When he was in the midst of the pedophilic urges, would the tripartite theory imply that they were *his*, attributable to him in a way grounding disdain? If so, this would seem implausible, *given his history.* After all, if he and a "garden variety" pedophile had exactly the same sort of urges and character for a time, the former would tend to get off the hook (as he did in the actual criminal case) whereas the latter would not. I agree that this man is not the fitting target of aretaic predication, but saying why, in the language of the tripartite theory, is rather difficult. I think this is because it is just not clear to me how sexual urges are to be conceptualized and so just how they would fit into the character schema I have constructed. Are they attitudes? If so, are they attitudes to which we tend to have fitting responsibility responses, in and of themselves? Many people have had such responses, of course (feeling disdain for homosexuals, say), but it is hard to see these as fitting, primarily because these urges do not seem to express agential *character* in any interesting sense. Instead, the urges seem to reflect something antecedent to character, call it an *orientation*, a sexual prism through

It is my aim in this chapter to show just how and where history does and does not matter for responsibility. I will begin by resisting or qualifying both of these objections as applied to my tripartite theory. I will then turn to a final, quite different, marginal case—Alzheimer's dementia—in order to illustrate a significant role that history does play in one of the three types of responsibility, namely, as illuminating that someone may have a persisting quality of character.

Two Objections from Poor Formative Circumstances

The two potential poor formative circumstances-based objections to the tripartite theory could draw, respectively, from Susan Wolf's fictional JoJo and Gary Watson's real-life Robert Harris. The basic idea behind Wolf's case is that there may be morally deprived upbringings of such an extreme sort that they generate what she calls "normative insanity" in the adult inheritors of these deprivations (Wolf 1987). Watson's focus, by contrast, is on the sorts of horrifying abusive circumstances some children go through, horrors that somehow explain their eventually becoming "evil" adults (Watson 2004, 219–59). Their differing terminology reveals that they start in different corners on the issue, however. Normative insanity implies *exemption*, or significant mitigation, from responsibility. Being "evil," on the other hand, implies being *non*-exempt (and significantly unmitigated). And for the most part, this is how the authors view them, although Watson is more perspicuous. Our first question, then, will be this: Do poor formative circumstances of either sort exempt/mitigate from responsibility, that is, what does the tripartite theory actually predict about poor-formative-circumstances-based exemptions/mitigations? Our second question will be this: If there are some exemptions/mitigations for those from poor formative circumstances, what is their nature, what is their grounding, and so to what extent, precisely, does their agential history matter for their current responsibility status?

which one sees the world, a kind of filter or condition on the formation or preservation of various character traits. These are very sketchy thoughts, but to return to the case at hand, because of my uncertainty about the status of sexual urges, I am uncertain whether the tripartite theory *does* imply this man's attributability-responsibility, say. What, though, if he acted on these urges? To the extent that he did so by forming an intention with respect to the satisfaction of his urges (so that the urge did not simply bypass his intentional features altogether in causing his action in the way of some kleptomaniacs or people with Tourette syndrome, say), he could be both answerable and accountable, even if the urge he meant to satisfy was not among those eligible for attributability status. I am grateful to Frankie Worrell for discussion here.

In "Freedom and Resentment," Strawson does claim that poor formative circumstances exempt, noting that seeing someone with this background "tends... to set him apart from normal participant reactive attitudes on the part of one who sees him, tends to promote, at least in the civilized, objective attitudes" (Strawson 2003, 79). Strawson's suggested theoretical explanation for exemptions of this sort, recall, was that they were grounded in the lack of a capacity for quality of will, but we have already seen this idea to be problematic, and it is especially implausible for the purported poor formative circumstances exemption, as those from such circumstances sometimes seem to exhibit *terrible* qualities of will toward us. The person raised in a deeply racist family may spew racist hatred as an adult, just as Robert Harris actually killed people without compunction. Further, as Watson points out, there is a deeper problem for Strawson here: If the reactive attitudes are examples of "moral address," expressing the basic demand for goodwill, and intelligible moral address presupposes the possibility of moral interlocution, "then the paradox results that extreme evil disqualifies one for blame" (Watson 2004, 235). Evil people reject the basic demand altogether, so they have no reason to take our expression of this demand seriously. Without the possibility of moral interlocution with them, though, Strawson's view—if it is an expressivist view of the sort Watson interprets it to be—implies that our retributive reactive attitudes to the extremely evil are unfitting. This is surely absurd.

Or is it? On its face, my own Strawsonian view seems to have the same problem: If people cannot understand or properly respond to our moral demands—in my case, our angry demands for acknowledgment—then this failure manifests their lack of accountability, and if their evil is in fact the *source* of their inability to acknowledge what they do to us, then yes, evil would disqualify from (accountability) blame. To the contrary, though, I think my tripartite view actually resolves this problem for the Strawsonian, but the matter is somewhat complicated. To explain my resolution, I will begin with Wolf's version of the poor formative circumstances "exemption" before turning to Watson's Robert Harris.

JoJo and Moral Ignorance

Wolf aims to reveal as insufficient what she calls the "deep self view" of responsibility, one holding that an agent is responsible if (a) her actions are governed by her superficial self, that is, her will or intentions, and (b) her superficial self is governed by her deep self, that is, her second-order desires or evaluations. The deep self view in fact is the model for my own view of attributability, although Wolf takes it be about the whole of responsibility (more on this issue below). Wolf's complaint is that the deep self view (and thus the tripartite theory's view of attributability) fails to deal adequately with the following case:

> JoJo is the favorite son of Jo the First, an evil and sadistic dictator of a small, undeveloped country. Because of his father's special feelings for the boy, JoJo is given a special education and is allowed to accompany his father and observe his daily routine. In light of this treatment, it is not surprising that little JoJo takes his father as a role model and develops values very much like Dad's. As an adult, he does many of the same sorts of things his father did, including sending people to prison or to death or to torture chambers on the basis of whim. He is not *coerced* to do these things, he acts according to his own desires. Moreover, these are desires he wholly *wants* to have. When he steps back and asks, "Do I really want to be this sort of person?" his answer is resoundingly "Yes," for this way of life expresses a crazy sort of power that forms part of his deepest ideal. (Wolf 1987, 53–4)

Wolf's assessment of the case is this: "In light of JoJo's heritage and upbringing—both of which he was powerless to control—it is dubious at best that he should be regarded as responsible for what he does" (Wolf 1987, 54). Nevertheless, given that he meets both conditions of the deep self view, it implausibly implies that he *is* responsible, an assessment in conflict with our "pretheoretical intuitions" (Wolf 1987, 56). Of course, if we think he lacks responsibility in virtue of his lack of control over the formation of his deep self, then the rest of us are in precisely the same boat as him. So there must be something else that differentiates him and us, and Wolf finds it in the mundane consideration that he is *insane*. There are two ways one may lack sanity: one may lack either a minimally accurate non-normative, or a minimally accurate normative, conception about the world. Lacking the former constitutes cognitive insanity; lacking the latter constitutes normative insanity. JoJo is normatively insane, and this is why he is exempt. Wolf thus amends the deep self view to the *sane* deep self view by adding this crucial condition: one's deep self must be sane, that is, one must have "the minimally sufficient ability cognitively and normatively to recognize and appreciate the world for what it is" (Wolf 1987, 56).

Applied to my tripartite theory, the objection would be that, insofar as JoJo seems to meet the conditions for all three types of quality of will, the theory, like the deep self view, also mistakenly implies that JoJo is responsible. A Wolfian would thus likely claim that, at least for some types of responsibility, we must add a normative sanity condition. The agential history of the morally deprived agent matters, therefore, in revealing the need for an additional (ahistorical) condition for responsible agency.

The motivation for her sanity story gets its traction entirely from our responses to the JoJo case, specifically from what she labels our "pretheoretical intuitions" (Wolf 1987, 56). But as David Faraci and I have shown, people's pretheoretical intuitions are nothing like what Wolf claims about them (Faraci and Shoemaker 2010 and 2014). We demonstrated this by running a series of surveys.[5] In our control case we presented Jo the First (JoJo's father) and had him doing exactly what JoJo does—beating peasants on a whim and so forth—with no background story about his upbringing. We then asked subjects to assess Jo the First's blameworthiness, on a scale from 1 ("not at all blameworthy") to 7 ("completely blameworthy"). They did so quite sternly: the mean was 5.8, with half of the respondents assigning him the highest score of 7. We independently presented Wolf's JoJo case to subjects. Their mean response was a 4.77 on his blameworthiness scale. This is a statistically significant difference from responses in the control case, but it is still a high assignment of blameworthiness, and it is just not close to the "not at all blameworthy" assessment Wolf claims our pretheoretical intuitions would yield.

One important confound for these results is that there are three types of responsibility, so it is not clear which one (if only one) was being implicated by people's thoughts about "blameworthiness." Of course, Wolf uses the generic term "responsibility" herself, so if anything, her term is less clear than ours (and we defend the use of our terminology in our first paper [Faraci and Shoemaker 2010, 324, n. 11]). But *tu quoques* do not help advance the discussion. What is clear, at least, is that people think JoJo's morally deprived formative circumstances do not exempt him from responsibility altogether: there remains some dimension on which he is viewed as pretty blameworthy. Indeed, I believe respondents are actually *ambivalent* about JoJo's responsibility, viewing him as a marginal agent, and the tripartite theory offers the best explanation of this ambivalence.

To see why, let us explore what the tripartite theory actually predicts about JoJo's responsibility. Start with attributability. Gary Watson implies that JoJo could be responsible on (his version of) the attributability face of responsibility, insofar as his actions express his general evaluative stance (Watson 2004, 260–88).[6] Wolf does agree that JoJo's evaluative stance is expressed in his actions; her objection is to the sufficiency of this expression relation as a "deep" sense of

[5] Distributed not just to undergraduates, but to the widely diverse respondents of Amazon's Mechanical Turk, with the help of Yale's Experiment Month.

[6] Watson doesn't discuss the JoJo case explicitly, but he is responding in part to Wolf's essay that includes the JoJo example, and he clearly has it in mind in spots.

responsibility. Recall from Chapter 1 Watson's response: Insofar as one is *committed* to one's actions as declarations of one's ends (as is true for someone like JoJo), those actions express one's very identity as an agent, and because the aretaic appraisals of attributability "implicate one's practical identity, they have ethical depth in an obvious sense" (Watson 2004, 271). This sense of responsibility is as "deep" as any other. As should be obvious, I completely agree. Attributability in my sense covers both Watsonian evaluative commitments *and* cares (emotional dispositions), and so if anything it implicates a more robust—deeper—sense of practical identity and responsibility.

Negative aretaic assessments are probably not what those surveyed have in mind by "blame," however.[7] Instead, they are likely thinking of moral criticism or angry confrontations, and these are primarily the domain of, respectively, answerability and accountability. So how does JoJo fare on these types of responsibility? Start with accountability. There is nothing about JoJo's history that indicates that he lacks any capacity for regard, for evaluational or emotional empathy. One could plausibly think, for instance, that he would be very considerate and sensitive toward his father, whom he idolizes. Nevertheless, he does seem less anger-worthy than his father, so here is where JoJo's history may strike us as relevant. In other words, doesn't his history at least serve to mitigate his accountability? I do not think so. Rather, *if* his accountability is mitigated, it will be so solely because he has impairments in the capacities wholly captured by the tripartite theory's conditions for accountability (and so Wolf's additional normative competence requirement is unmotivated). Faraci and I have recently put forward the following *Difficulty Hypothesis* as the best explanation of what is actually going on here: "Childhood moral deprivation may mitigate blameworthiness assessments in virtue of the difficulty agents are viewed as having in overcoming their morally deprived upbringing to grasp the relevant moral reasons" (Faraci and Shoemaker 2014).[8]

There is some precedence in the literature for including difficulty in exercising a capacity in the criteria for moral responsibility, but the focus has typically been on difficulty in exercising *volitional* capacities.[9] It is difficult for the unwilling addict, for example, to resist taking the drug because his counter-desire, his craving for the drug, is so strong. To the extent that we cut him some slack,

[7] David Faraci and I are, with Joshua Knobe, attempting to determine empirically whether this is actually the case.

[8] The next few paragraphs draw some material from that essay.

[9] See, e.g., a recent thread kicked off by Dana Nelkin on the agency and responsibility blog Flickers of Freedom: <http://agencyandresponsibility.typepad.com/flickers-of-freedom/2013/01/difficulty-and-degrees-of-blameworthiness-and-praiseworthiness.html>.

then, we may do so because we think it was just too difficult for him to overcome that volitional obstacle, as it also would be for comparably situated agents.

JoJo, however, has no counter-desires making harder the exercise of his volitional capacities; indeed, his volitional capacities are exercised far too easily. Rather, his difficulty is both *empathic* and *perceptual*: he has difficulty identifying with certain others and so seeing their interests as "reasonish." More importantly, perhaps, he has difficulty seeing this difficulty *as a difficulty*. And that is because he has been raised, essentially, to be an exceptionalist: his (and that of his father) is the only perspective that matters. Because all those peasants are not him, it is difficult for him to take their perspectives seriously.[10] Yes, he can engage in detached empathy with them, looking along the sightline of their mind's eye, but, he thinks, so what? "I can also 'understand' what it is like for a dog about to be kicked, or for a sow about to be slaughtered," he might say, "and while this may give me reasons to kick harder, or to increase the terror (for my own amusement), *their* interests give me no reasons whatsoever to refrain."

Subjects cut him some slack for this difficulty, but not much. Why not? It is because, I suspect, they believe he is able, and ought, to identify with others and see the reasons flowing from their value as fellow rational creatures. Identifying empathy is not *that* hard. If JoJo is torturing someone on a whim, the peasant's tortured cries ought to pierce JoJo's soul, and as long as JoJo is a fellow human being, a failure to have his empathic shell penetrated in this way reflects poorly on him (Faraci and Shoemaker 2010, 329). His is ultimately a failure of human *sensitivity*.[11]

Thus construed, JoJo may have difficulty regarding others, and so his accountability to them may be somewhat mitigated. Anger to him is fitting, we tend to think, but to a somewhat muted degree. What, though, of his answerability? Here is where the importance of "instead of" reasons again—as with the psychopath—comes to the fore. Suppose you were an anthropologist visiting JoJo's island and you (foolishly) confronted him about his treatment of the peasants, demanding

[10] The analogy Faraci and I run is to my having been shown the famous image of the "duckrabbit" repeatedly since childhood, and also having been taught over and over that what I am looking at is a duck, and only a duck. When, as an adult, I meet you, and you insist that the image can also be seen as a rabbit, it will be no surprise if, given my upbringing, I have a very hard time coming to see it as a rabbit, or seeing why I should take your claims about it seriously. Certain features of the picture have been drilled into me as exclusively salient (e.g., the bill), so it is quite difficult for me to come to see other features (e.g., the little "rabbit mouth" indentation on the back of the duck's head) as salient in my assessment of the image. Nevertheless, I'm *capable* of seeing it as a rabbit, as I have the same perceptual and conceptual mechanisms as you.

[11] Christian Coons rightly suggests that this might well be a reason to be *more* expressively angry with someone like JoJo, in order to "get it through his thick skull."

to know why he whipped someone on a whim. JoJo's glib response, "I thought it would be fun," will not suffice as a genuine answer, for it seems to ignore the implied "instead of" demand, which you might helpfully fill in: "No, why did you whip that peasant *instead of* responding to him in a more respectful way?" JoJo's puzzled silence would be all we need to realize how he simply does not seem able to see any reason to treat the peasant respectfully; he is a *peasant*, after all! If JoJo really cannot see the relevant regard-based "instead of" reason against whipping the peasant, though, he is not answerable for any judgmental failure in this specific case. For him there were no decisions to make about whether some peasant-fact that appeared to him as a reason really was one or whether one of those peasant-reasons had more worth than another. Because of his difficulty with regard, his quality of judgment is simply not implicated here and now, and so he may be *excused* from the range of answerability responses. But because he fully retains the general *capacity* for judgment, he remains an answerable agent.[12]

In combination with the relevant facts about moral deprivation, the tripartite theory predicts that poor formative circumstances with respect to such deprivation render fitting an intuitively plausible sort of ambivalence. Full-blown aretaic (attributability) responses will tend to be fitting, whereas in certain cases full-blown angry (accountability) responses will not (and while quality of judgment may be fully intact, it may not be implicated in such cases, so answerability responses are also off the table). The best explanation for JoJo's mitigated accountability, I have suggested, is his difficulty in coming to empathize with others in the appropriate regarding ways. But then there is yet no need to appeal to JoJo's *history* as mitigating or as motivating an additional sanity clause. Rather, all his history does is shine a light on the difficulty of his currently making the requisite empathic leaps already explicitly required by the tripartite theory of accountability.

Robert Harris and Childhood Abuse

If poor formative circumstances of the moral deprivation sort do not exempt, what about poor formative circumstances of the childhood abuse sort? The Robert Harris case is horrifying on all kinds of levels. As an adult, Harris killed two teenagers, essentially for the fun of it, then calmly ate the fast food they had

[12] He could surely judge, for instance, that he ought to help his drought-stricken farmers now *instead of* letting them go bankrupt and starve, as doing so will keep his army fed. Thanks to Eddy Nahmias for the example.

just purchased. He joked about impersonating some police officers to tell the boys' parents what had happened, and he also talked aloud about killing some cops. He was sentenced to death in California, and even the other prisoners on death row hated him. But as a child he went through the kinds of horrors very few can imagine: he was abused physically and psychologically throughout his entire childhood, both at home and at school, sent to a youth detention center by 14, raped repeatedly there, and so on. As his sister said, "He had no feeling for life, no sense of remorse. He reached the point where there wasn't that much left of him" (Corwin 1982; quoted in Watson 2004, 241).

When reading or hearing the details of the brutality of his crimes, most people's responsibility responses tend to kick into high gear: anger, disdain, condemnation, and the like will easily brim up to the surface. But when we hear Harris's horrible back story, we are given genuine pause. Our question, then, is what function the pause serves. One might think the pause suggests that Harris's poor formative circumstances in fact exempt (or mitigate) him from the range of our angry reactive attitudes and practices. If this is the case, then, first, we have the problem Watson articulated: extreme evil, absurdly, would seem to disqualify (or mitigate) from accountability. Second, we might also have the basis of a different sort of history objection to the tripartite theory: if Harris is exempted, it would only seem to be in virtue of his horrifying agential history. If so, then it looks like we would have to add a non-horrifying-agential-history requirement to the tripartite theory to handle such cases.

But does the pause in our reactive attitudes suggest Harris is exempt? Watson claims that what Harris's back story generates instead is a kind of *ambivalence*, and I think he is right: "[T]he biography forces us to see [Harris] as a *victim*, and so seeing him does not sit well with the reactive attitudes that are so strongly elicited by Harris's character and conduct" (Watson 2004, 244; emphasis in original). Watson's diagnosis here is that we come to have sympathy for the boy Harris was, but this rests uneasily with our (persisting) antipathy for the man he is. We thus lack a coherent, unified response to him. In later work ("Two Faces of Responsibility"), however, Watson suggests that our response is perhaps less incoherent than he originally thought, for it could instead just consist in simultaneous, distinct responses to different faces of responsibility: our antipathy is to "brutal" Harris, whose actions reflected his practical identity; our sympathy—pity—for him is grounded in our worries about the fairness of blaming him, given that he "has already suffered too much and that we too would probably have been morally ruined by such a childhood" (Watson 2004, 281). The former response suggests Harris's full-blown attributability-responsibility; the latter response suggests Harris's eliminated or, more plausibly, his mitigated accountability.[13]

Obviously, I am sympathetic to the multiple "faces" of responsibility approach to this case, and I agree that the muted responses are, if anything, to Harris's accountability (and perhaps his answerability, although I will not discuss that here). So suppose we say that Harris is not exempted from accountability but that his accountability is somehow mitigated. Watson's treatment of the case still grounds (as he seemed to intend) a version of the second objection above to an ahistorical theory like mine: If an agent's degree of accountability depends on the fairness of certain angry expressions, it ultimately would depend on all sorts of past considerations, such as the extent to which the agent has previously suffered, and so an ahistorical theory of responsibility will be incomplete. To illustrate the worry, suppose that Agnes and Anastasia are exactly alike psychologically and have each disregarded me in an exactly similar way. Suppose the only difference between them is that Anastasia has suffered too much in the past (although she doesn't remember having so suffered), in a way that it truly would be unfair to express my anger to her. If her degree of accountability is mitigated thereby, my theory of accountability has to incorporate a historical condition to account for it.

The objection succeeds only if an agent's degree of accountability depends on the extent to which it would be *fair* to hold her to account. But it does not. Recall that accountability (on the Strawsonian sentimentalist construal I have adopted throughout) is about the *fittingness* of various holding-accountable responses, not their fairness. To appeal to the fairness of responses as a condition of accountability is to appeal to a *wrong kind of reason*:[14] While it may be immoral to resent Anastasia for her disregard, given her past suffering, that does not mean her disregard was not angersome. So to say that Anastasia is not *accountable* solely in virtue of her past suffering is a mistake. She *is* accountable, but it could just be morally wrong to do something that might make an accountable person suffer some more, like being angry with her (cf. Smith 2007), and this moral reason might win the day, all-things-considered.[15] Still, she slighted me, so there remains *a* reason (a reason of fittingness) to be angry, even if it is ultimately overridden by other types of reasons.

[13] Watson is careful to note, however, that mitigated or exempted moral accountability may imply nothing whatsoever about whether Harris is still subject to various legal sanctions. See Watson 2004, 281.

[14] Recall the discussion of wrong kinds of reasons and the moralistic fallacy from Chapter 3. In addition, I am not saying that Watson's account commits this fallacy, only that it risks doing so.

[15] Although as I intended to make clear in Chapter 3, I think the so-called connection between anger and suffering has been considerably overblown in the literature.

But if unfairness-tied-to-history is not what mitigates an agent's accountability, what does? Let us compare Robert Harris to a nondeprived killer, someone with a "normal" childhood who nevertheless brutally kills someone as an adult with a kind of amusement. Call this completely made-up person Spector. I think Spector will get our full-throttle angry responses, and this anger is fitting in virtue of his complete disregard of his victim. But if that is what makes our anger fitting, why would it not also be fitting for Harris, as he has seemingly expressed an identical quality of will? To the extent that our angry response to Harris nevertheless does become somewhat muted in light of his biography, I think that it is solely because of the epistemic value of his history, which reveals to us just how Harris might have had the *empathy* beaten out of him. We can understand how much easier it sometimes is, in light of the various stresses of the day, to retreat into our own heads and cease venturing into the heads of others, to view others, in Strawson's words, from the objective stance. Once we become aware of Harris's upbringing, we may begin to understand how a more or less permanent (nonvoluntary?) retreat might have occurred: he could well have come to view everyone from the objective stance via a deeply ingrained defense mechanism. If so, then I do not think we view Harris as even *having* an identical quality of will to Spector; rather, insofar as we see Harris (and not Spector) as having come to be seriously impaired for identifying with his victims, given his emotionally ravaged self, he may be much less accountable after all. But his mitigated accountability would now be a function of the lack of fittingness, not the lack of fairness, of our emotional demands to him, and so no agential history condition would yet be motivated.

Nevertheless, some uneasiness remains on this story, as many will still see anger to Harris as fitting, in a way that it may not be to the psychopath. The psychopath seems genuinely less capable of empathy, and so our anger has little to no communicative point to him, whereas Harris seems more *reachable*, we may think. But this may simply reflect the difference between an impaired capacity and a dormant capacity.[16] If Harris just has the latter, where his activation of the capacity has been rendered more difficult by his traumatic childhood (making him roughly akin to JoJo), then we may think that our anger could still serve a forward-looking function, which includes aiming to *restore* Harris to the moral community, by demanding and attempting to rebuild

[16] Michael McKenna suggests that this may be what is going on with Harris, so that while he is not a member of the moral community, he nevertheless retains a *capacity* for membership. His extreme evil does not, therefore, exempt him from the reactive attitudes, despite "the practice of holding responsible and the actual demands of morality [being] constituted by the moral community" (McKenna 1998, 129).

in him the empathic glue that serves to bind the rest of us. Our regard-based emotional demands may ultimately break through his hardened heart, we may hope, even if his level of accountability is as mitigated as the psychopath's.[17] And as Watson's postscript on the Harris case suggests, this is precisely what seems to have happened in the end. He had some close friendships in the final decade of his life, and on the day he was executed, he mouthed "I'm sorry" to one victim's father. As Watson writes, "Harris either remained, or became once again, capable of friendship and remorse. His crimes were monstrous, but he was not a monster. He was one of us" (Watson 2003, 259).

This is a tragic and difficult case. There could be a variety of appropriate responses to someone like Harris. All I have attempted to do in this section is show how the tripartite theory predicts one sort of plausible ambivalence toward Harris, depending on how certain details of his case are filled in, and in so doing the theory can remain ahistorical: All that matters is Harris's current quality of regard. To the extent that agential history does matter for accountability, its value can remain merely epistemic, just like with JoJo. I see no reason to worry about the ahistorical nature of my account, therefore, from the so-called threat of poor formative circumstances.

Dementia

To this point, I have been deflecting worries about ahistoricity generated by a couple of famous marginal poor formative circumstances cases. In response, I have offered plausible interpretations of the responses we tend to have to the cases according to which agential history, at the most, serves an epistemic function with respect to responsibility: it sheds light on the agent's true, current, qualities of will. But history may also serve a slightly different valuable function: it sometimes enables us to see that the agent *has* a current quality of will in the first place. This point is best brought out by considering our final marginal case, dementia.[18]

"Dementia" is a catch-all term for a number of different symptoms caused by a wide variety of brain disorders. The official DSM-5 statement about it has

[17] On McKenna's interpretation of the case, Harris is already engaged in a form of moral dialogue with us, one that is, as he puts it, "a terrible and contemptuous form of dialogue," namely, one of "icy silence" indicating that "the conversation is over" (McKenna 1998, 132). There are real attractions to this interpretation, although the metaphor may be a bit off in Harris's case, as he might more plausibly be construed as simply refusing to acknowledge us and our attempted conversation at all. But I agree that there is an important sense in which he could retain the capacity to do so. And at the end of the day, both McKenna and I are aligned in defending ahistorical views of responsibility against Watson's challenge.

[18] Some of the material that follows has been drawn from Shoemaker 2014a.

replaced the term "dementia" with "major or minor neurocognitive disorder,"[19] and its diagnostic criteria for the generic major form are as follows:

A. Evidence of significant cognitive decline from a previous level of performance in one or more cognitive domains (complex attention, executive function, learning and memory, language, perceptual-motor, or social cognition)...
B. The cognitive deficits interfere with independence in everyday activities...
C. The cognitive deficits do not occur exclusively in the context of a delirium.
D. The cognitive deficits are not better explained by another mental disorder (e.g., major depressive disorder, schizophrenia) (American Psychiatric Association 2013, Code 331.83).

By far the most insidious and widespread purveyor of these evils is Alzheimer's disease, which affects one in ten Americans over the age of 65, and nearly half of those over the age of 85. Because of its increasing familiarity in people's lives, I will focus on it here.[20] What makes this form of dementia distinctive is first, of course, that its etiology is Alzheimer's disease, but second, that, in its major form, it requires both memory impairment *and* impairment in at least one other of the specified cognitive domains: language function (aphasia); the ability to activate or execute intact motor capacities (apraxia); complex attention; impaired social cognition; or a disturbance in planning, organizing, sequencing, or abstracting abilities (executive functioning) (American Psychiatric Association 2013, Code 331.9).

My starting datum is this: As with most of the other disorders discussed previously, there is a stage in the progression of Alzheimer's dementia where dementia sufferers (DSs) typically stop being the fitting target of one subset of responsibility responses yet remain the fitting target of a different subset of responsibility responses. This is the "perverse sweet spot" relevant to our discussion. It is

[19] "Dementia" is thought to be both stigmatizing and insensitive to the fact that the condition is a matter of decline, not deficit. For my part, I doubt the claim about stigma is true; indeed, as Alzheimer's dementia in particular has come to the fore of public consciousness, "dementia" seems to me to have become much less stigmatizing, and far more medicalizing, than it had been. Further, changing the term now runs the risk of desensitizing people to dementia's potentially devastating effects. (See: <http://todaysgeriatricmedicine.com/archive/110612p12.shtml> for discussion.) Regarding the insensitivity-to-decline point, I will make clear in the text just what a matter of degree the decline is, as it will play a crucial role in my argument. I will thus continue to use the term "dementia" here, for the sake of clarity, familiarity, and ease of exposition.

[20] While most forms of dementia have numerous features in common, one form of dementia—frontotemporal dementia (FTD)—has some striking differences. Specifically, patients with FTD seem to behave much like psychopaths. They have lost a kind of emotional empathy that makes it very difficult for them to make a variety of moral judgments (Mendez et al. 2005). I will set these fascinating cases aside here, although I would think the responsibility profile of such agents would more or less match those of psychopaths.

the realm of a distinctive and familiar sort of ambivalence both caregivers and family members have toward DSs. In what follows, I will first discuss what the former subset consists in and why the suspension of our responses in that domain is fitting. Then I will discuss the latter subset, which carves out a domain in which DSs may still be responsible. It is in this second subset that we will find the additional epistemic role played by agential history, a role brought out by discussion of a possible objection to my view.

Accountability and Memory

I think it fairly obvious that DSs (in the "sweet spot") are exempted or significantly mitigated from both accountability and answerability. The reason for the latter is simple: answerability depends on a capacity for judgment about the worth of reasons, so when this capacity for reflective deliberation and decision-making has become sufficiently impaired, answerability is impaired. Impairment in judgment is straightforwardly a matter of executive functioning impairments, which eventually always occur in Alzheimer's dementia. And the reason for the exemption or mitigation from accountability might seem equally straightforward: if your ability for social cognition, say, or language, is impaired, your ability to understand the emotional communication of accountability's demand for acknowledgment is also likely going to be impaired.

Nevertheless, I think this last move may be too quick. Impairments to one's social cognition do not necessarily involve impairments to one's understanding of emotional demands; rather, they could just involve impairments to one's ability to avoid various priming or attribution biases in reasoning or to one's solving of cooperative problems. And impairments to one's language abilities are typically verbal or signal impairments, not necessarily emotional impairments, that is, losses in one's ability to understand the point of emotional demands like anger. And it is less than clear that impairments to the other cognitive domains would be doing the exempting or mitigating work either. Why, for instance, would impairments in my ability to name objects, or recognize faces, or move my arms, or organize and plan have any implications for my ability to understand your emotional communications to me? The only impairment left is that to memory, which must occur on any diagnosis of Alzheimer's dementia.[21] But memory loss alone surely is not sufficient for exemption from accountability: just

[21] Technically, the impairment is to memory *and learning*, but as this impairment is conjunctive, and as I think what people would tend to regard most important to responsibility is memory, I will focus primarily on it.

because you forget that you did something does not mean you are off the hook for doing it. So it is just not clear why DSs should get off the accountability hook after all.

It is for this reason that I think the diagnostic requirement of at least *two* impairments is crucial. So what is the relevant exempting combination? I want to begin with a deeper exploration into the role of memory in accountability. Let us start by considering why exactly memory loss alone is not exempting. Suppose that I take a sleeping pill that takes an hour to knock me out, and I know that its only side-effect is that I will not later remember anything that happens during the half hour prior to its knocking me out.[22] Crucially, this pill does not alter my ordinary cognitive, deliberative, or volitional abilities in the least. Suppose, then, that during that last half hour after taking the pill one night, my simmering hatred for my slightly noisy neighbor reaches its boiling point, so I decide to beat him up before going to bed. The fact that I genuinely do not remember doing this the next day is irrelevant to my accountability, as already noted. My neighbor will surely, and fittingly, be angry with me for beating him up and will be motivated to communicate that anger to me.

But why? If expressions of the accountability emotions are essentially communicative, and I do not remember what I did to cause them in this case, how could their intelligibility be sustained through this sort of memory loss? The answer lies in the fact that there are multiple communicative functions involved in the deployment of our accountability responses. Remember, these emotional demands are for acknowledgment. Most of the Strawsonians who have a communicative theory of the reactive emotions emphasize that they serve a backward-looking function, getting the agent to see how he violated the basic demand for good will. But I think that such communications also, importantly, serve a *forward-looking* function.[23] I do something more than merely demand that you acknowledge what you did to me in expressing my anger; I also communicate an additional demand: "You are to treat me with goodwill, *and you will be well-served to heed this demand in the future.*" Consequently, even if your loss of memory of some past action undermines the first communicative function, it does nothing to undermine the second. To the extent that expression of an accountability emotion may be intelligible as long as it fulfills *either* communicative function, it could still be intelligible strictly with respect to its forward-looking

[22] So I will later at least remember taking the pill. This case is an adaptation of one presented in Parfit 1984 (287–8), to very different effect.

[23] McGeer 2014 does stress the forward-looking functions, but she is in the distinct minority, and she may also go too far in the other direction. I favor an account that emphasizes the importance of both functions.

aspects when directed at the person who has genuinely forgotten performing the action that sparked such a response.[24]

This is not yet to say, though, that the backward-looking communicative function is even missing in the sleeping pill case. Imagine two variations on our case. In the first variation (A) my neighbor and some bystanders respond immediately after the assault with resentment and indignation, respectively. In the second variation (B) they do not respond as such until the next morning (perhaps the assaulted neighbor is unconscious until morning, and then he tells others straight away upon waking up). At the time of their response in (A), I still remember assaulting the neighbor, but at the time of their response in (B) I do not. In (A), my neighbor's expressed resentment presumably meets both communicative aims: it serves to communicate his demand that I acknowledge my wrongdoing, and it serves to dramatically reiterate the demand for goodwill as something to which I should pay closer heed in the future.[25] Why, though, could this not also be the case with the neighbor's expressed resentment the next morning in (B)? If the backward-looking aim of the expressed resentment is to communicate his anger at me for assaulting him and to get me to acknowledge what I did, that aim can still be met as long as there is some sort of essential connection between me in the morning and the action the night before, something that ties the assault to me-now. Memory is typically what would *reveal* this connection to me, providing me with a sense of identity with the agent of the assault. But my neighbor's communicated message could also well resonate with me in memory's absence, particularly if I can still fully *identify* with the assaulter of the night before, that is, to fully appreciate what it was like for him at the time from the inside, to feel what he was feeling, and to understand and endorse the considerations that moved him—that is, *me*. Where my current volitional structure is continuous with, and causally dependent on, his, I can actually "see myself" doing what he did in a way that both provides me with a relevant sense of identity and renders any actual memory of having done so redundant. This is how the communicated message of my neighbor can still intelligibly maintain its backward-looking force. And as it obviously meets the conditions of its

[24] To the worry that bringing in a forward-looking communicative function returns us to the objectionable social efficiency justification for our responsibility practices to which Strawson initially objected as lacking in humanity (Strawson 2003, 89–90), see Shoemaker 2014a, in which I explain why this particular forward-looking feature of our emotional demands actually plays an essential role in reinforcing interpersonal *engagement*.

[25] As it turns out, I *won't* remember it, but that is irrelevant to whether his expression serves its forward-looking communicative function, namely, to dramatically impress on me the importance of the basic demand in a way that I can understand and take up with respect to its forward-looking dimension *at the time of the expression*. More on this point below.

forward-looking aspect as well—I can understand the emotional force of his expression of the demand in a way that can get me to reshape my present and future deliberations about how to treat him—such emotional expression may fulfill both of its communicative functions in the sleeping pill scenario regardless of the time at which it is deployed. Identification, therefore, plays a robust role in accountability: not only is my ability to identify with others essential to regard and the emotional demands for acknowledgement they might make, but my ability to identify with my past and future selves is essential as well in order for me to make sense of those emotional demands.

Turn, then, to the memory impairments of Alzheimer's dementia. To this point, I have focused solely on memory loss with respect to some specific past action. But the memory impairment of dementia is much broader, applying to one's actions, experiences, and judgments, and it constitutes an ongoing problem. One can never be sure that what is experienced will ever be remembered again. But now we can see how *both* communicative aims of expressions of the reactive emotions may be undermined in such patients. If I can neither remember what I did *nor* be expected to remember your remonstrations of me when engaged in future deliberation, then it looks as if it there would not be any communicative point in you expressing your accountability emotions to me in the first place.

But can't we at least get a story about identification like the one above that could work to establish DSs' accountability? After all, at the time of remonstration, couldn't the memory-impaired patient at least *identify* with the past agent, even if she could not remember precisely what she did, such that she-now could still be tied to the action in a way that makes her victim's expressed anger (at this later point in time) a sensible form of communication to her? She could, it would seem, *without any additional impairments*. But of course memory impairments alone are insufficient for a diagnosis of Alzheimer's dementia. While the impairments of Alzheimer's ultimately run in varying degrees across all of the named cognitive abilities, the two likely suspects for combining with general memory impairment to exempt DSs—when they are so exempt—are impairments to social cognition or executive functioning. The reason is that these cognitive domains typically govern the ability to engage in identification of the sort necessary for the intelligibility of the accountability emotions, in the absence of memory, to achieve both their backward- and forward-looking communicative aims; in particular, they include the deliberative, abstraction, and/or emotional capacities that are implicated in the ability to place one's feeling self either in the position of some future affected self or in the position of some past acting agent. To the extent that one's ability to imaginatively project oneself forward or backward in this way is damaged, though, so too will be the point of any communication presupposing that ability. What the combined impairments of Alzheimer's dementia wipe out, then, is one's *sense of one's own agential identity.*

It is pointless as a form of communication to hold DSs accountable. Is it thereby *unfitting*? In other words, if there is no point to holding DSs accountable, does that also mean that they are *not* accountable?[26] To the extent that accountability responses, in order to have a point as a form of communication, require their targets to have the capacity for quality of regard, then yes. And it looks as if they do. In order to have a communicative point, my anger at you requires you to have a sense of your own agential identity, to be able to identify with your past or future selves. But that ability is just entailed by the ability to engage in agential empathy generally, and as it is hard to imagine someone able to identify with others but *not* with her past or future selves, it is a safe bet to infer that those who are impaired for self-empathy are just impaired for empathy full stop. And to be impaired for empathy generally is just to be impaired for quality of regard, and so to be impaired for (or exempt from) accountability.[27]

It looks, then, that given the empirical details of DSs' impairments, we can see how the tripartite theory delivers a fairly plausible story about why they have either no or seriously mitigated answerability and accountability. And yet it may still seem true of DSs that they express ill—or good!—will in some of their actions in some sense. In particular, it still seems that they may be, on occasion, mean, kind, generous, sour, pinched, or cheerful. Examples of positive behavior may initially be more resonant. Suppose that when I visit my moderately demented grandfather, he reaches for a chocolate in the candy jar and brings it over to me, despite the great physical effort it requires. My expressing real gratitude to him at that point has no communicative point (it may well be highly confusing). He cannot remember what he just did, he will not remember how I respond to what he just did, he cannot identify with that moments-ago agent, and he cannot deliberate about the future (and so identify with some expected future self). He lacks the sense of his agential identity, and empathy generally, required to be accountable. Nevertheless, what he did was *kind*, and if he does this generally, it reflects on a trait of his character: *he* is kind. Such aretaic predications suggest that DSs may thus be *attributability*-responsible, that is, their dementia may not

[26] Thanks to Chad Van Schoelandt for raising this worry.

[27] What about those who, fully capable of agential empathy, behave immorally and then become demented? Are they any longer accountable? In a word, no. Of course, we mouth blaming language to such people all the time—"I blame my demented father for how he treated me," say—but blame language is capacious; that is, it may not presuppose accountability at all, and even if it does, such talk is often best understood as including a big counterfactual element, as in "IF my dad were not demented (and IF he met the conditions for quality of regard), I would be (fittingly) angry with him." Thanks to Katrina Sifferd and Michael McKenna for raising these issues.

necessarily undermine their ability to have a motivational structure that grounds various fitting attributions. Indeed, I think this is quite correct.

These sorts of predications are anything but unfamiliar to us. And these assessments are deployed more confidently when they are traits continuous with those from their pre-demented days. "She was always patient like this," we may say when watching our mothers with our own attention-deficient children. "He's still so considerate," we may say about my grandfather to another chocolate-receiving guest. Of course, matters are not always so rosy. Many demented parents and grandparents remain just as cranky or cantankerous as ever. Some are still stingy, callous, narcissistic, difficult, inconsiderate, or even cruel, displaying long-standing traits that have persisted through the dementia and continue to be expressed in actions and attitudes. But then here is how agential history may provide epistemic service once more: it can help us figure out whether the current expressions are indeed *remnants* of the agent's pre-demented character (because consistent with it), and so help us figure out whether the agent is still responsible for his or her attitudes in the attributability sense in virtue of still *having* such quality of character.

Indeed, of those psychological features relevant to our enterprise, character seems the last to go. Dementia, even advanced, may leave intact enough of who one was to ground a continuing, albeit limited, range of assessments of genuine responsibility. It is to these remnants of character that they attach, just as it is to these remnants of character that we—their children, friends, and caregivers—still cling. While DSs may no longer be (full) members of the accountability or answerability community—we can no longer really make intelligible normative demands of them, nor can they make many rational decisions—they are not outside the world of responsibility altogether. And insofar as the attributability for which they are eligible may still inform and shape the ways in which we continue to respond (and not just react) to them, it could well constitute the last remaining threads of our interpersonal relationships with them.

The Meanness Objection

History, I have argued, need be relevant to DSs' attributability only epistemically, as an aid to discovering whether some attitudes are expressive of the agent's persisting character traits, and so whether they are attributable to her in a way that renders fitting various aretaic responses. After all, traits are dispositions expected to be expressed in roughly predictable ways across time, and so they leave patterned traces. When grandpa is kind, and he was always like that, then it makes sense to think of certain of his care-commitment clusters as having been preserved across the dementia.

But what if grandpa turns mean?[28] Perhaps he now lashes out with contempt at the petty flaws of others, whereas prior to his disease he was always patient and indulgent. Is this new meanness attributable to him? And if so, what does this say about the nature of character generally?

There seem to be three possible options here. Perhaps, first, grandpa developed a new character trait post-dementia. Call this the *new trait* option. If this is taken to involve the development of new cares and commitments, a development requiring the exercise of abstraction, planning, and anticipation abilities, then this option is unfeasible, given that we are supposing grandpa to have already undergone significant executive impairments that would tend to undermine the abilities in question. Perhaps, then, second, he was just mean all along but hid it, and we are only now seeing it because of his loss of control over his expressions. Call this the *masked (old) trait* option. I doubt this possibility too, as it would have required a kind of control throughout his life up until now that is beyond the range of most humans (and so the implausibility comes in thinking of just how many DSs display such "revealed" meanness in contrast to the likely numbers of those who could realistically exercise such control throughout their lives). It seems, then, that we are probably going to be stuck with a third option, namely, perhaps what happens in such cases is that dementia has just *ravaged* the agent's character, so that what behaviors now occur are just a function of "glitches" in their mental machinery or are first-order desire-based responses to stimuli, responses which then yield the sorts of immediate joys or frustrations associated with the simple desire satisfaction or dissatisfaction of young children and even some nonhuman animals. Call this the *deterioration of (old) traits* option. If this is the only plausible explanation for this familiar phenomenon, then a problem arises for my claim that DSs may be attributability-responsible, for if their so-called "meanness" isn't meanness at all, then why should we think that any other so-called traits persist either? Why not instead view their behavior as bearing only an accidental resemblance to their character-grounded behavior of old, not flowing from any deep self, simply because *no such self exists anymore*?

I think we can resist the objection posed by the *deterioration of (old) traits* option by developing a different, more plausible, version of the first, *new trait*, option. To do so, we need to widen what it might mean to develop a "new" character trait. I agree that it is unlikely that new cares and commitments could be formed post-dementia given impairments to executive capacities. But

[28] I am grateful to Angela Smith for pressing this important worry on me.

already-formed cares and commitments may not necessarily require executive capacities to persist, insofar as they are essentially dispositions, triggered by various thoughts and perceptions that can survive executive impairment. Threats to things one loves may spark fairly immediate and direct protective action, with little or no need for any real deliberation. When a loved one is in peril, the impulse to save him or her tends to move one fairly automatically, unmediated by executive thinking or planning.

It is thus possible that some cares and commitments may persist through several stages of dementia. Many cares and commitments may not do so, though. Obvious candidates will include commitments whose objects or appropriate response behaviors require certain abstraction or planning capacities. Religious commitments, prudential caring, and certain moral commitments may fall by the wayside with the onset or advancement of dementia, insofar as they require an ability to conceive a very abstract object of devotion (see Jaworska 1999, 24).[29] But one does not have to be able to theorize about morality to be a morally good person. Kindness, say, does not require thoughts about either the nature or the demands of kindness; it may at times simply require an exquisite emotional sensitivity and responsiveness to the plight of others (cf. Arpaly 2003). At issue, then, is how to make sense of the "new" meanness in DSs who were never mean, on the assumption that it is not as a result of their having formed new cares and commitments.

My suggestion is that, when such behavior is not merely expressed frustration or a function of glitches in the mental machinery, it may flow from remnants of care-commitment *clusters*—character traits—some of whose members dementia has destroyed. Loss of a tempering commitment, say, could serve to unleash new volitional possibilities from some clusters in a way that would strike us as mean. But such volitions would not be flowing from new cares or commitments; rather, they would be flowing from old, persisting, care-commitment clusters, just with fewer members. On this view, "new" traits are really *altered* traits, an alteration produced by the deterioration or loss of some individual cares or commitments. And these deteriorated or lost cares or commitments would most likely be those requiring the executive capacities typically ravaged by dementia, namely, the abilities to abstract and plan.

In illustration, consider a real-life case of someone who was both deeply religious and loved his wife dearly. Pre-dementia he never would have considered

[29] Jaworska talks here in terms of values, and she also notes the ways in which some values may *persist* through dementia (see her n. 41 on p. 124), but her notion of values and my notion of the cares and commitments constituting character traits are importantly similar in many respects.

suicide (viewing it as seriously immoral), but post-dementia, when his wife died, he repeatedly expressed the wish to die (Jaworska 1999, 107). To the extent that he lost his religion to the dementia, the restrictions were removed on the scope of acceptable behavior in response to the loss of his remaining object of care. Or consider another real-life case, a man who was financially responsible pre-dementia, but post-dementia went out and bought the fancy truck he had always wanted, a purchase that would require great financial sacrifices for him and his family (Jaworska 1999, 107). To the extent that he may have lost his ability to engage in prudential planning, the prior restrictions on buying his dream vehicle were removed. But his caring about having the dream vehicle remained.

What I am suggesting is that a story along these lines may sometimes explain a DS's mean turn as well. This would most likely be true for those who were previously nothing but kind primarily due to a religious or moral commitment. Once the abstraction abilities necessary to religious or moral understanding were lost as part of their executive impairments, the restrictions on some formerly unthinkable behavior were also lifted. Crucially, that is not to say that they were mean all along and just hiding it (the *masked (old) traits* option); rather, changes in the membership of care-commitment clusters can change *the nature of the traits* they constitute. Caring about truth-telling is typically tempered by a commitment to protect the feelings of others. Losing that tempering commitment may produce true but hurtful statements, which could count as meanness. Or caring about comfort may produce a kind of belligerent demandingness if not tempered by a certain sort of respectful attitude (something that may well be lost in light of executive impairments), and again, this may count as meanness.

Meanness often consists in hurting the feelings of others. Whenever the feelings of others cease to matter, therefore, meanness may erupt, and this predicate may truly apply regardless of the target's executive incompetence or inability to understand any answerability or accountability responses, and regardless of the historical source of any such inability, just as long as some character traits—care-commitment clusters—are being expressed in the process. Meanness may be attributable to one, even if one is no longer answerable or accountable for being mean.

Agential history thus matters, but not in any constitutive metaphysical way. Instead, a DS's care-commitment history, as well as the history of her precise impairments, will help reveal to us whether she is "mean" with or without the scare quotes. These are difficult matters to discover, though, and "better safe than sorry" may counsel suspension of aretaic responses altogether. But, crucially, that is not to say that the attributability rendering them fitting does not still obtain, and it is also not to say that the history informing whether they are fitting is itself anything more than an epistemic guide. *If* grandpa is attributability-responsible for his "new" meanness, it is in virtue solely of his *currently* poor quality of character. His history may help us see *that* he still has a quality of character, though, vindicating our ambivalence and revealing a lingering source of interpersonal engagement to which we may ferociously cling.

Conclusion

In this chapter, I have discussed the possible role of agential history in responsibility by, again, discussing some marginal cases. The plea of poor formative circumstances may be thought by some to be exempting, allegedly motivating additional (non-quality-of-will) requirements for the tripartite theory to explain the exemption. I argued instead that, in both versions of poor formative circumstances—moral deprivations and childhood abuse—they may not be exempting at all. At most, they may be mitigating, but even when they are, additional (non-quality-of-will) requirements are not motivated thereby; rather, the history in both cases plausibly plays merely an epistemic role, informing us of the actual nature of the target's *current* quality of will.

I then turned to explore the interesting role history may play in dementia cases. While those in its moderate stages tend to be neither answerable nor accountable (for different reasons), they may still be attributability-responsible, expressing their remaining character traits in various ways. Their history here may reveal the *fact* of their responsibility, the fact that they still have a quality of character, without contributing to any of its conditions. This conclusion may also offer some solace to caregivers, vindicating certain kinds of ambivalence felt toward their charges. While angry responses to those in their care will tend to be unwarranted, some responsibility responses—admiration, pride, veneration, disdain, or even contempt—may indeed still be fitting to those with dementia, reflecting their persisting membership in at least some of our interpersonal communities.

Conclusion

My aim in this book has been to build a robust quality of will theory of responsibility, one intended to fulfill Strawson's hope of recovering "from the facts as we know them a sense of what we mean, i.e. of *all* we mean, when, speaking the language of morals, we speak of desert, responsibility, guilt, condemnation, and justice" (Strawson 2003, 91; emphasis in original). To do so, in Part I, I developed the tripartite theory as a response to the fact of our ambivalence in the marginal cases, and in Part II, I tested the theory by revisiting the marginal cases to see whether, in combination with the relevant empirical details about them, it yielded plausible verdicts about the precise nature of our ambivalence. In this concluding chapter, I will retrace in some more detail the path we have taken, discuss some possible gaps or limitations of the enterprise, and then suggest some additional virtues of the theory.

Retracing the Dialectic

We start by reminding ourselves how we got here. A theory of responsibility should explain (or at least explain away) our entire set of responsibility responses, those emotional responses we have to various expressions of practical agency. Strawson identified quality of will as the unifying object of these responses, primarily basing his story on a considered examination of the triumvirate of resentment–indignation–guilt and when these attitudes tend to be suspended. But his theory stumbles over the fact that there are agents among us—children, the insane—who, while exempt from the triumvirate, still seem to express quality of will in some sense. While different monistic *Pure Quality of Will* theories drawing from different interpretations of "will" (including "character," "judgment," and "regard") could be developed to handle these cases, none individually could account for the fact of our ambivalence toward a variety of marginal cases. Instead of abandoning the general quality of will approach for an unwieldy amalgam of conditions on responsibility agency, however (as others have done), I combined these three distinct monistic approaches to quality of will into a single theory that incorporates three distinct *qualities* of will, which give birth to three distinct *types* of responsibility. Why?

Our ambivalence in the marginal cases consists in our feeling that marginal agents tend to be eligible for some responsibility responses but not others. But when we take an honest look at the responses both suspended and deployed in such cases, we can see that there are a whole lot more in play then merely the resentment–indignation–guilt triumvirate. They include admiration, disdain, contempt, disgust, regret, disappointment, disapproval, shame, pride, embarrassment, gratitude, hurt feelings, and many more (see *The Tripartite Profile: A Chart*, p. 35). I argued that among these many responses there are three basic sentimental syndrome pairs (the agential versions of disdain/admiration, regret/pride, and anger/gratitude) that best reveal to us the boundaries of three types of responsibility. Agential disdain/admiration evaluates quality of character, agential regret/pride evaluates quality of judgment, and agential anger/gratitude evaluates quality of regard. By exploring these emotional syndromes in detail, we were able to articulate their unique fittingness conditions, the different types of responsibility they pick out, and so the different agential capacities their fitting deployment requires.

As investigation into the familiar syndrome of agential admiration reveals, its fittingness depends on the target's volitional structure. An admired attitude (or dependent action) is, we think, *admirable*—meriting admiration—to the extent that it expresses one's deep self, which consists in one's cares (emotional dispositions), commitments (evaluative stance), or care-commitment clusters, contrary to prior Humean *or* Platonic theories of the deep self. Typically, one's character traits are a function of one's clusters, revealed in diachronic patterns. Agential admiration evaluates such traits—such qualities of character—as good. Agential disdain, the relevant negative counterpart, evaluates quality of character as bad. When fitting, these responsibility responses correctly attribute some attitude to the agent's deep self, and agents generally eligible for such responses are *attributability*-responsible. To be eligible for such responses is to have the capacity for quality of character, which consists in (a) the having of a deep self, and (b) the ability to have one's attitudes express[1] that deep self.

We tested the plausibility of this theory in Part II of the book by exploring its predictions and explanations about our ambivalence in several marginal cases (in combination with the relevant empirical details). In our discussion of clinical depression, mania, and Alzheimer's dementia, we got a more detailed

[1] Recall that the expression relation is one of both causal dependence and content harmony.

understanding of character and how it might be altered through the course of these disorders. What these disorders may do, in different ways, is cut the tempering tethers of various care-commitment clusters, and so alter what specific character traits are expressed. But that is not to say that these disorders undermine *attributability* as such; indeed, for some depressed, manic, and demented patients, some aretaic predications about them may still be true: they in fact *are* certain ways, albeit altered. We also saw, in our discussion of scrupulosity, both how important the specific details of these disorders are for identifying the proper target of our attributability-responses (and so revealing the source of our ambivalent responses as well), and why attributability is about agents' *objective* volitional structures, obtaining (or not) independently of what agents think about the attitudes in question. While the scrupulous individual attributes all sorts of attitudes to her own deep self, the disorder actually seems to undermine her ability to discriminate which of those attitudes actually belong and which do not. Still, a *moral orientation* may be attributable to the scrupulous individual: the fact that she does care that others avoid pain and such may be sufficient to render fitting a certain limited range of aretaic responses and predications to her. And these implications of the tripartite theory are all intuitively plausible, I think.

Answerability is also an objective, structural relation, between various of one's attitudes and one's evaluative judgments. Specifically, as long as the targeted attitudes (and dependent actions) are sensitive to one's judgments about the worth of the relevant "instead of" reasons, one is answerable for them. Agential regret is the paradigm sentimental syndrome revealing the contours of answerability. It evaluates one's own quality of judgment as poor, and it motivates policy change. As agential regret targets judgmental quality, it is fitting (and so one's judgment—or lack thereof—was *regrettable*) to the extent that the attitudes in question were indeed sensitive to one's judgment about "instead of" reasons, and so are things for which one can in principle *answer*. Third-person responses like disappointment, disapproval, approval, and various forms of praise and criticism also often have quality of judgment in their sights. To be eligible for such responses is to have the capacity for quality of judgment, then, which involves the ability to (a) recognize "instead of" reasons, and (b) form judgments about such reasons. The latter includes two critical stages (following Scanlon 1998): making judgments that some facts that appear to be reasons really are reasons, and making judgments as to the worth of those reasons relative to others. Importantly, answerability (along with attributability and accountability) ranges more widely than just the moral domain. What makes for moral answerability is, in part, whether the reasons recognized or weighed are a function of one's antecedent *evaluational regard*. But then there is nothing about answerability per se that grounds moral blame.

We tested the plausibility of this account by investigating psychopaths and adults with mild intellectual disability (MID). The theory predicts that if the psychopath is incapable of regard, and so is unable to perceive any facts about others' normative perspectives as (even appearing to be) reasons, then he cannot be answerable for his judgment that others' interests are worthless, in virtue of the fact that he has no access to the relevant "instead of" regard-based reasons. This result holds even if his general rational and judgmental capacities are fully functional. Nevertheless, he could be answerable in a more restricted sense in such cases, insofar as he may at least have access to the self-interested "instead of" reasons to *refrain from coming to verdicts at all* about the treatment of some others. By contrast, my theory of answerability implies that adults with MID may lack (or have impairments in) the capacity to make certain sorts of judgments or apply some abstract evaluative standards to concrete cases, and so may lack answerability in those cases (even though they may be fully accountable to a restricted range of others). My theory of answerability is sufficiently nuanced to explain how both psychopaths and adults with MID have mitigated (or no) answerability in two different ways: psychopaths tend to have serious difficulty with the first, recognitional, capacity listed above, whereas adults with MID tend to have serious difficulty with the second, judgmental, capacity. And once again, these implications of the theory for these marginal cases are quite intuitively plausible.

Accountability is a matter of one's eligibility for fittingly being held accountable, the only one of our types of responsibility to implicate motivations for confrontation from responder to respondee. The sentiment on which we leaned heavily here is agential anger, an emotional syndrome evaluating quality of regard as poor, and having a communicative motivational component, where the communicative aim is a demand for acknowledgment. Its positive sentimental analog is gratitude (which also has a communicative component). Other "cognitively sharpened" variations on these paradigm sentiments are familiar, and they include resentment, indignation, and guilt, and other emotions in the family include hurt or warm feelings. Regard is in its pure form a function of identification, which consists in at least one of two types of empathy: evaluational or emotional. Evaluational empathy typically enables one to come to perceive facts about others' normative perspectives as seeming to be simpatico reasons in one's own deliberative perspective. Emotional empathy typically enables one to feel at least a simulacrum of what the other feels in certain respects, a function of one's shared cares (or at least the "trying on" of the other's cares). Anger is fitting for an insufficient degree of regard of either sort. But it may also be fitting for cases in which poor judgment and disregard overlap, both where one judges that certain sorts of facts about others' normative perspectives that seem to be reasons are not reasons, and where one judges that some reasons flowing from others' normative perspectives have insufficient worth. In these latter two cases, the agents in question are both answerable and accountable for the same attitude, rendering fitting not only anger but also answerability responses such as moral disapproval and regret.

Our exploration of the relation between psychopathy and high functioning autism was instructive for several reasons. First, we were able to see why previous attempts to draw from how psychopaths allegedly do on the moral/conventional distinction to a view of their responsibility were deeply flawed: "the" distinction, at least as it has been drawn, is chimerical, and the task designed to test facility with "it" actually tested for facility with a variety of orthogonal distinctions. Nevertheless, I argued, we might be able to learn something from one aspect of its early deployment on psychopaths, namely, that psychopaths may be impaired for recognizing agential authorizations as reason-giving. This is very likely a result of their impairments in identifying empathy, which is what would yield deficits in regard, and thus (at least) mitigated accountability, on my tripartite theory. Here we got a deeper glimpse into the nature of identifying empathy, which is complicated and requires some sophisticated skills. Psychopaths, it seems, have serious difficulty making the transition from a detached survey of another's normative landscape to seeing that person's projects as worthwhile from that person's perspective. But it seems like the psychopath also tends to have real difficulty seeing his *own* projects as worthwhile, and so he is even impaired for *self*-regard. Those with high-functioning autism, on the other hand, are complicated in a different way. While they seem to have significant deficits in emotional regard, they *may* have a mostly unimpaired ability to engage in evaluational regard via a nonstandard route. Unlike psychopaths, those with high-functioning autism do at least seem to have a full-fledged capacity for self-regard, for taking their own projects to have worth (and so they have ends). Nevertheless, I think that the available evidence, in combination with the tripartite theory, more plausibly suggests that those with high-functioning autism are not accountable. For one thing, it looks as if they may be more fixated on the rules for social order than on the concern or regard for other people that often grounds those rules, and for another, our emotional demands for acknowledgment sometimes seem completely pointless as forms of communication to those with high-functioning autism, again suggesting impairments in the regard capacities necessary for accountability.

All three types of responsibility are ahistorical, focusing exclusively on the agent's current quality of will. The appeal to poor formative circumstances has been thought to challenge this ahistoricity on two fronts, requiring either the addition of a non-quality-of-will capacity or the inclusion of an explicitly historical condition (that, for example, the agent's current quality of will had a non-poor-formative-circumstances history). I argued to the contrary that neither addition is plausibly motivated by the appeal to poor formative circumstances. History does matter, but only epistemically. It helps us to see, in the case of childhood moral deprivation, the *difficulty* the agent may currently have in perceiving various regard-relevant facts as putative reasons. In the case of childhood trauma, by contrast, the current agent's history may reveal to us how he actually has impairments in his regarding abilities, insofar as he may have had, say, the empathy nearly beaten out of him. Nevertheless, to the extent that such agents are not psychopaths, anger may still be fitting in its forward-looking communicative role, as a way of attempting to reach such agents and bring them more fully back into the accountability fold. In addition, we saw from the case of Alzheimer's dementia a different, significant way in which agential history may matter, namely, as an aid to our figuring out whether a moderately demented agent still *has* a quality of character, the remnants of which may constitute the last tendrils of our interpersonal attachments. But this revelation of history is also merely epistemic.

Gaps and Limitations

I was motivated to construct the tripartite theory to account for the wide range of responsibility responses we have—responses revealed by our ambivalence in marginal cases—in terms of quality of will. But perhaps there are some responsibility responses it misses? Does the tripartite theory, in other words, meet Strawson's aim of actually recovering from the facts as we know them *all* that we mean by "desert, responsibility, guilt, condemnation, and justice"? In this section, I will explore some possible reasons to think not.

We may begin by noting the obvious: I have said nothing whatsoever about desert, condemnation, or justice. But some theorists insist that the most fundamental facts about responsibility are about desert (see, e.g., Pereboom 2004, 2007, 2008, 2014; and Smilansky 1996; for discussion, see McKenna 2012, Chs. 6–7); others focus on the relationship between responsibility and condemnation (Hughes 1958; Wertheimer 1998); and still others focus on the important relationships between responsibility and both distributive and retributive justice (Matravers 2007). So having said nothing about any of them, how could I have offered anything like a complete theory of responsibility?

As most people seem to assume there is at least a crucial link between responsibility and desert, I will focus on it here. Desert is a very large topic, with a very large literature, and I can unfortunately say only a very few things about its absence in my discussion. I have focused primarily on our emotional responses, what I have called our responsibility responses. So are these deserved? It depends on what "deserved" means, of course. If it just means "fitting," then in cases where the fittingness conditions are met, the answer would be 'yes' on the sentimentalist version I have advanced (see also King 2012). If it means something different, then perhaps the answer would be no; I cannot comment unless I know what sense we would be dealing with. But it is hard to see desert as referring to anything other than fittingness for any type of responsibility but accountability, and that is because accountability is the only type whose paradigmatic sentimental responses motivate *confrontation*. In other words, while it may make sense to say that my agential admiration of you is not deserved, or that my approval of my son's good decisions is deserved, the only thing I can see that would render these sensible ways of talking is that they are really just about fittingness. For example, on my account the only thing that could render my agential admiration for you from afar undeserved is if I admire you for some perceived trait that is not actually attributable to you (an expression of your deep self). Or what renders my private approval of my son's decisions deserved is his actually having formed good judgments with respect to them. And as neither response requires expressing these emotions to their targets, there is nothing about them that might raise any additional questions of desert.

Agential anger, though, is another story, as one's response does not count as such unless one has the associated motivational impulse to communicate it to the angersome party. Now as a feeling alone, agential anger gets the same "desert = fittingness" treatment as the attributability and answerability emotions. But as a *communicated* feeling, it brings us into new territory, for it may be thought to raise the worry of whether the targeted party deserves to be the brunt of someone's anger. I suggested in Chapter 3 one response to this concern when talking about the fairness of angry responses: these responses are emotionally dramatic demands that the target acknowledge his slight via taking up the perspective of the victim. *Suffering* is not a necessary aim of such communication, though; rather, like any other telling of what one takes to be a hard truth, the question of desert only enters into the *manner* of the telling. If I think the meal you have cooked for me is terrible, my telling you this would communicate (what I take to be) the truth (that you should acknowledge the badness of your meal), but we might nevertheless say, after you have run off in tears afterwards, that you did not deserve that. But what didn't you deserve? To hear the truth? No; instead, you did not deserve to be *told* it with my harsh manner, or with my poor timing or clunky delivery. But my words still "fit" the situation, as they were true, and they demanded what you probably ought to acknowledge, at least if you hope to have a successful dinner party in the future. So too with the communication of agential anger: its communication fits disregard, but the manner in which it is communicated may be subject to worries about desert. But—and this is the key point—the *manner* in which one communicates one's agential anger is quite different from one's being motivated to communicate it. The former falls under the rubric of morality, and perhaps additional concerns about desert; the latter only falls under the rubric of fittingness, where desert seems to play no *distinctive* role.

And this leads to a more general point: My hunch is that desert has been thought to be crucial for responsibility primarily because of the close and necessary association that has been thought to obtain between responsibility and *harsh treatment*. But we might well think instead, building on the theory I have constructed, that harsh treatment (or, in the positive case, rewards or pleasant treatment) is really a response *to* agential responsibility, that it *builds on* antecedent responsibility assessments, which themselves imply nothing about harsh (or pleasant) treatment. As I said, agential admiration and approval, third-person positive emotional responses to, respectively, attributability and answerability, imply no treatment of the assessed agent whatsoever. And the motivation for communication necessary to agential anger implies no *particular* form of communication, so no particular form of treatment either. One's agential anger may be communicated simply by one's pursed lips or a quiet shutting of the door. But these may constitute the *entire* responsibility response. What one does *on top of* such responsibility responses, therefore—doling out sanctions, punishment, or rewards—may implicate additional concerns about desert, but these concerns will be distinctively *moral* concerns—"wrong kinds of reasons" concerns—about what we may or may not permissibly do to those who have responsibly offended against us.[2]

I have no doubt I will get significant pushback on this point, especially from people wanting to point to the *practices* of responsibility even Strawson seems to

[2] And while there may be various sorts of evolutionary explanations of our responsibility responses that make reference to their selective value in being closely associated with harsh treatment (e.g., their aiding in the enforcement of group norms), this explanation may just be irrelevant to their current *fittingness* conditions. Compare to humor. A plausible evolutionary explanation for amusement and laughter may be its role in group bonding. This explanation is just irrelevant, though, in a diagnosis of what makes amusement a fitting response to some behavior or string of words. So too may the fittingness of anger, say, float free of any particular evolutionary role in norm enforcement.

license (practices built around the reactive attitudes), wherein someone's offense seems to make it permissible to withdraw one's good will and treat him in various harsh ways, ways it certainly would have been impermissible to treat him in the absence of his offense (see, e.g., McKenna 2012 for this practice-based approach to responsibility). Nevertheless, I want to insist on the crucial distinction (a distinction I believe has long been overlooked) between the fittingness of various sentimental responsibility responses and the appropriateness of harsh treatment of offenders. The latter is a distinctively moral response and it simply does not bear at all on whether we have reasons of fit for the former. The latter does of course bear on whether we have all-things-considered reasons to respond to people in certain ways, where these are a weighted function of reasons of fit and moral reasons (along with other sorts of reasons, perhaps, e.g., prudential reasons). The real question, then, is whether the practices of harsh treatment to offenders are also necessarily and essentially *responsibility* responses, alongside the sentiments I have discussed. But I cannot see that they are, once this distinction has been highlighted. I have already noted how we do not think being guilty of an offense necessarily calls for any harsh treatment at all (as in the pursed lips and quiet withdrawal cases). But note also that we seem to think it quite permissible to reward or sanction (e.g., shun) people for all sorts of *non*responsibility states of affairs: for their type or degree of body odor, for their sense of humor, for their aesthetic taste, for who their parents are or where they come from, and so forth. Many of these in their poorer instantiations fall under the rubric of the *shameful*, and as we all know, being shameful has been, and still is, what grounds many shunning or sanctioning responses, despite having nothing to do with responsibility (see Justin D'Arms and Daniel Jacobson, *Rational Sentimentalism* [unpublished manuscript]). Here we may well wonder whether people, say, *deserve* to be shunned in light of their shameful parents (assuming shame is fitting for such a thing), but now this is clearly neither a question about responsibility nor a question about shame's fittingness (which we have stipulated obtains); rather, it is explicitly a question about what is *morally* appropriate in light of the shameful. My view in the responsibility domain is analogous: granting that (clear-cut responsibility responses like) agential disdain, disapproval, or anger are fitting, the question of whether people deserve sanctions in light of the fittingness of these responses is a question about the moral appropriateness of harsh treatment that is not itself necessarily about responsibility.

Relatedly, talk of "blame" has also been absent from my discussion. But blame, it may be thought, is surely a matter of responsibility which involves harsh treatment and implicates desert. My response is that blame is an incredibly capacious concept (see Coates and Tognazzini 2013 for many different and conflicting accounts of blame). Objects of blame range from the living to the dead, from agents near to those far, and, crucially, from quality of will to the purely causal non-agential contribution (as in, "I blame the hair dryer for tripping the circuit breaker"). I have a hard time seeing how these instances are at all unified. But more importantly, even if they are, or even if we can somehow (non-arbitrarily) carve out a relevantly unified subset, I cannot see how that subset could necessarily implicate *any* distinctive sort of treatment, let alone harsh treatment, and so implicate desert. This is for the very simple reason that any plausible account of blame will have to include under its rubric *private* blame, the blame that remains secret to all but the blamer. We have all, I presume, experienced this at one time or another, perhaps a quiet, simmering resentment toward someone that has absolutely no effect on one's treatment of that person. Perhaps the resented person is one's boss, and one really needs the job. But at any rate, to the extent that this still counts as blame, I fail to see how blame necessarily implicates either harsh treatment or desert, and so my leaving it out of the discussion has not somehow buried a key instantiation of desert. (See also Hieronymi 2004; Scanlon 2008; and Smith 2013.)

Finally, I have also not said anything here about *free will*. There may be two worries about this omission. The first is that I might be trying to get compatibilism on the cheap by suggesting that the deterministic challenge to free will and responsibility is just moot, given our emotional construction. This, recall, was more or less the second of Strawson's attempted argumentative aims in "Freedom and Resentment." But it is also the argument I have deliberately and explicitly set aside in this book, and I wish to continue to do so here. I take no stand whatsoever on whether responsibility as I have construed it is compatible with determinism, or whether it requires free will that itself is compatible with determinism. Of course, as I suggested in the Introduction, free will, in at least a minimal sense, may be implicated on any plausible quality of will theory (as noted by, e.g., McKenna 2005). But nothing that I have said here *requires* that it is, or that its instantiation must have any special relation with determinism or indeterminism.

But this brings us to the second worry: By omitting even a mention of free will to this point, my claim to have accounted for all we mean when talking about responsibility is threatened. For surely, it might be thought, "free will" is among those terms that is crucial to such talk (as Strawson likely thought as well). In response, I must first confess that I am unsure whether there is a clear and unified understanding of the term, so my ignorance has in part governed my omission. However, one understanding of it that has gained traction in recent years is that "free will" just refers to whatever ability a person has to *control* her actions in the sense necessary for moral responsibility (see, e.g., Fischer and Ravizza 1998, e.g., 28–34; Mele 2006; McKenna 2006, 24; and 2012, 10). But if we put the concern in terms of control, then I *have* discussed it a bit, when laying out the theory of accountability in Chapter 3. There I tried to make clear that there are a number of ways in which something might be "up to us," being something over which we have "control." The favorite way of talking for most free will theorists has been in terms of *volitional* control, wherein one governs one's actions with one's will. Angela Smith has emphasized a second form of control, namely, *rational* control (Smith 2005), where one's attitudes are governed by one's evaluative judgments (i.e., they are judgment-sensitive). To these I have added a third, *empathic* control, where either one's seeing facts about others' normative perspective as putative reasons or one's responding in a simpatico emotional fashion to others is governed by one's identification with them (i.e., these perceptions or responses are empathy-sensitive). I have no doubt that this form of control will strike many as insufficiently robust to count as a form of *responsibility*-control. But to the extent that empathy-based regard is indeed the target of our accountability-responses, it is nevertheless all the control that is necessary for it. Further, if we focus on what I think are the fundamental responsibility sentiments in this realm—agential anger and gratitude—and we again recognize that "harsh treatment" and so forth is not a necessary constituent of these responses, then perhaps the motivation to seek out a more robust conception of control will just diminish.

Ultimately, then, I admit that there are several missing *terms* in the account, including desert, blame, and free will, as well as condemnation and justice. But in each case, at least where I can understand the terms in question, I doubt that the missing term reveals a *gap*; rather, either what the term refers to has already been incorporated, or what it refers to is unnecessary.[3] Of course, this response is merely suggestive. Again, I recognize that there is a large and sophisticated literature on these questions that I am setting aside here, so take what I say with however big a grain of salt one needs.

Lagniappe

I have presented the tripartite theory as a project within the Strawsonian framework, taking seriously his appeal to the moral sentiments and the broad explanatory

[3] I have not made this case for "condemnation" and "justice" for reasons of space, but I think the need to do so is at least less pressing for them, and anyway, I suspect the resolution will go along the same lines as the others I have discussed.

power of quality of will. As the theory is now complete, I intend in this final section to discuss three possible independent virtues of the theory, (mostly suggestive) considerations non-Strawsonians might also find attractive about it.

First, I think the tripartite view may help dissolve a long-standing dispute about what a theory of responsibility is supposed to be about. Very roughly, there have been two different traditions articulated and developed over the last 40 years: the *deep self* approach and the *reasons-responsive* approach (see Sripada Forthcoming). The former—represented most straightforwardly in the contemporary literature by Harry Frankfurt (see several of the essays in Frankfurt 1988), Gary Watson (to some extent; see Watson 2004), and Susan Wolf (again, to some extent; see Wolf 1987), but having its historical roots in Aristotle and Hume—puts forward the basic idea that agents are responsible only for those actions or attitudes that express their deep selves, a privileged subset of their psyche representing the core of their practical identities. If an action or attitude does not reflect the real *me*, it is thought, how could *I* be responsible for it? The leading contemporary advocates of the latter, reasons-responsive approach have been Fischer 1994 and Fischer and Ravizza 1998, but others who adopt some form of the view include Wallace 1994; Haji 1998; McKenna 2006; Nelkin 2011; Brink and Nelkin 2013; and McGeer and Pettit Forthcoming. The basic idea is that agents are responsible for certain actions or attitudes only to the extent that they (or their agential mechanisms) are appropriately sensitive to the reasons pertaining to those actions and attitudes. How could I be responsible for some action, it is thought, if I could not recognize or respond to the reasons for or against performing it?[4]

One might suggest that both approaches would affirm the statement that "I cannot be responsible for Φ unless I am in control of Φ," but deep self theorists put heavier emphasis on the *I* and reasons-responsive theorists put heavier emphasis on the *control*. There is, however, an important sense in which these theorists are engaged in a clear dispute, namely, over whether certain *modal capacities* are important to one's being responsible. Deep self theorists require no such capacities (although they certainly require others), that is, to the extent that

[4] Some theorists, like Scanlon 1998; and Smith 2005 and 2008, likely see themselves as representing both traditions (and so bridging the purported divide), holding that responsibility is about what relates an agent to an attitude, and then claiming that this relation obtains just in case the latter expresses the former's deep self, which occurs only when the agent was reasons-responsive with respect to its formation. For reasons that will become clear in the text and in footnote 8 below, I locate such theorists squarely on the deep self side of the divide. They would just have a very different understanding of reasons-responsiveness than the dominant one in the contemporary literature.

one's action or attitude in fact expresses one's deep self, one is responsible for that action or attitude, *regardless* of whether one could have brought about any other attitude or action. Reasons-responsive theorists, however, do require such capacities (and it is in their specification that matters typically get very complicated), that is, one's responsibility for Φ is (roughly) a function of one's capacity to respond to reasons to do *other* than Φ in the specified circumstances.[5]

Now both of these sets of theorists are focused on what makes a non-exempt agent responsible for something in some specific set of circumstances,[6] whereas I have been focused on what makes some *agent* non-exempt (generally eligible) for responsibility responses in the first place. But we can take both sets of theorists to be advancing conditions for agential capacities as well. So think of the deep self theorist as saying that responsible agency is a function of one's capacity for having one's actions/attitudes be governable by one's deep self, and think of the reasons-responsiveness theorist as saying that responsible agency is a function of one's capacity for being, in general, sensitive to reasons. The dispute thus remains at the level of responsible agency.

There is something quite important in both approaches: one emphasizes the importance of *revealing one's self* in one's responsible actions and attitudes, and the other emphasizes the importance of *exercising one's agency* in one's responsible actions and attitudes. The first virtue of my tripartite account should therefore be obvious, as it could dissolve the dispute by providing both approaches their own distinctive zone of application. The deep self theory, we might say, best fits attributability, whereas the reasons-responsive theory best fits answerability. The former is the type of responsibility in which one subset of responses is fitting for agents who express their deep selves, their characters; the latter is the type in which a different subset of responses is fitting for agents whose decisions are govern*able* by their judgments about the worth of various "instead of" reasons.[7] In the former, then, the availability of alternatives does not matter,

[5] Importantly, this is not to say that reasons-responsive theorists believe in the so-called Principle of Alternate Possibilities, that one has to be able to do otherwise (because one is able to choose otherwise) in order to be responsible for what one did. Instead, reasons-responsiveness is typically adopted by compatibilists who believe that one is responsible for what one did given the actual sequence of events—that one either did or did not in fact respond to the relevant sorts of reasons—but where one's responding to the reasons one did was a function of one's (or one's reasons-responsive mechanism's) *responsiveness* to a certain range of reasons generally, such that one *would have* responded otherwise had different reasons presented themselves (see McKenna 2006, 25).

[6] And so, as Eddy Nahmias points out, they are all presenting, noncoincidentally, theories of free agency/free will.

[7] Notice that neither view, in its basic formulation, makes any nonderivative reference to *regard*, which I have argued is the basis of accountability.

whereas in the latter, it does.[8] On my pluralistic view, both accounts are tracking something important, namely, distinctive *types of responsibility*.[9]

A second virtue of the tripartite view is that it may offer a better explanation of certain phenomena that have, for other theorists, been thought to ground relativism, or a general skepticism, about responsibility. These theorists appeal to the fact that different cultures seem to have very different views of responsibility. In honor cultures, for instance, the victim of violence is strongly expected to be the one who retaliates, not the state, and it is far less important that the responder do so to the actual individual who victimized him; instead, retaliation to other members of the victim's group may suffice. Failures to respond in this way are often viewed as shameworthy (Sommers 2012, Ch. 2; see also Williams 1993). In more collectivist cultures, like Korea or Japan, shame is taken to be appropriate with respect to the untoward actions of members of one's group or culture, as many Korean-Americans were ashamed when a young Korean shooter killed 32 college students at Virginia Tech in 2007 (Sommers 2012, 1–3). The basic idea, then, is that these different cultures simply have different—rival—conceptions of responsibility, and these different conceptions are simply the product of different ways of life or different ecologies and social structures (Williams 1993, 55; Sommers 2012, 95). These different frameworks thus give rise to different responsibility responses: Someone's responsibility responses in a Western, individualist society are just going to be very different from someone's responsibility responses in a non-Western shame or honor culture. To the extent that each set of responses arose simply because of evolution or social ecology, goes the argument, there is no non-arbitrary reason to prefer one over the other. So as "we cannot rationally adjudicate between the rival accounts of moral responsibility each tends to generate..., we should regard our preferred theory as unjustified" (Levy 2013, 90, in summarizing Sommers' argument). But the same will go for the preferred theory of *any* responsibility theorist. Consequently, "there are no universally true conditions for moral responsibility" (Sommers 2012, 108).

[8] This way of viewing the matter might surprise the Scanlonians who embrace answerability but also seem to deny the importance of alternatives (Scanlon 1998, 179–98). I think Smith's 2008 admission that she is a deep self theorist is quite telling, as it is really actual self-expression that seems to matter to her, not any counterfactual capacities.

[9] Of course, both deep self and reasons-responsive theorists take themselves to be exclusively grounding *all* of our responsibility responses, but I think this is just false. The expression of a deep self alone implicates neither fitting anger nor fitting gratitude, nor does the grasping of and responding to a specific set of moral reasons (or not). So both theorists will not only have to be understood as holding forth on distinct and exclusive types of responsibility, they will also have to make do with being able to account for only a subset of our responsibility responses.

Nevertheless, for all that these phenomena reveal, we should embrace *pluralism* about responsibility, not relativism. Note first that there is nothing at all about these cases suggesting that non-Western cultures do not also share several features of responsibility in common with Western cultures. Agential anger (or gratitude) in response to poor (or high) quality of regard, for example, remains abundantly present in both honor and shame cultures. And the other paradigm sentimental pairs I have discussed—agential admiration/disdain and regret/pride—are also abundantly universally present (that is why they are deemed human *sentiments*, after all). Second, the cultural differences ostensibly motivating relativism/skepticism are easily accounted for on the tripartite theory. The non-Western emphasis on shame and honor is about *attributability*; what the instances bring out in particular is a focus on character. Honor cultures place a premium on failures to respond personally and violently to offenders (or their kin), but these are still expressions of character as Westerners understand it (they just are not aretaic features some Westerners typically care so much about). And what of cases of retaliation against non-offenders who are nevertheless members of the offender's group? The better explanation in such cases is that there are just different *communicative mores for accountability* in play: among the range of acceptable options for communicating the demand for acknowledgment to the offender is harming the offender's brother, say. Now whether this is a morally permissible communicative tactic is not my concern;[10] rather, all I need to defend is the likelihood that these are all examples of *holding to account*, that is, of expressing angry demands for acknowledgment, and it seems fairly clear that they are.

What this relativist/skeptical challenge brings out is the second distinct virtue of the tripartite view, namely, its *emphatic flexibility*. While it is a universal theory of responsibility, it can still account for the different cultural emphases about which the responsibility relativists and skeptics make hay. It puts forward three types of responsibility that obtain universally, as they are revealed or carved out by pan-cultural responsibility sentiments. But the account is flexible in allowing that different societies or cultures may emphasize some types of responsibility over others. For example, some cultures (e.g., many Western cultures) may put heavier weight on accountability and answerability, with agential anger and disapproval being dominant, whereas other cultures (e.g., some non-Western

[10] Nevertheless, it is a distinct virtue of my pluralistic approach that it is quite comfortable with there being better and worse communicative practices, and even with there being legitimate criticism of some cultures whose ecologies and social histories channeled them into unfitting sentiments and sentimental expressions. Thanks to Eddy Nahmias for noting this point.

cultures) may put heavier weight on attributability, with agential admiration, disdain, or shame being dominant. But, crucially, the fact that they put heavier weight on one or two types of responsibility over others does not mean the less-emphasized types are non-existent in the culture; it just means that the members of these cultures perhaps *care less* about some qualities of will than they do others.[11]

The final virtue of the tripartite theory is perhaps more of a provocative suggestion than a persuasive consideration. The thought is that the theory may go some ways toward explaining the persisting appeal of the three main competing normative ethical theories: virtue ethics, consequentialism, and Kantian deontology. What I want to suggest is that there are important features of each theory being targeted in one way or another by the three types of responsibility. To the extent that the three types are concerned with *moral* responsibility, then, the fact that they target different features distinctive of different normative ethical theories may help explain why the competing theories remain attractive, namely, they each contain *some* feature to which we are responsibility-committed. Let me explain.

The easiest case to make, of course, is with respect to virtue ethics. The basic persisting idea of this theory is that one ought to cultivate various virtues, such that one's actions and attitudes are expressions of virtuous traits. The emphasis, then, is on the cultivation of a good character. What reveals or carves out our first type of responsibility, attributability, are aretaic sentimental responses like agential admiration, which are precisely responses to expressed character traits. Character indeed *matters* to us, so it is no wonder that an ethical theory urging the development of character would persist as it has.

The case regarding the other two theories is a bit more complicated. Start with consequentialism, which, in its purest form, counsels agents to maximize the good. While the "good" may be specified in a variety of ways, the most famous ancestor of consequentialism—utilitarianism—specified it in such a way that all of its plausible descendants must take on board as at least *one* of the relevant goods pleasant states of consciousness. Utilitarianism's focus on pleasure gave rise to an important methodological tool, namely, appeal to the sympathetic impartial spectator. In order to figure out the right thing to do, one was to take up the affective perspective of all affected parties as if they were one's own and then

[11] There are other important differences between the cultures that may be relevant to the tripartite theory, however, including the fact that what falls under the rubric of *slights* may differ from culture to culture. So even if agential anger fits slights in every culture, what specific actions or attitudes render it fitting may differ. Thanks to Angela Smith for noting this point.

(impartially) determine from that agglomeration what the maximum balance of pleasure over pain would be. Notice, though, the two-step procedure here: (a) the taking up of various affective perspectives as one's own, and (b) the weighing of the various interests recognized from the perspectives. One might thus fail in two ways, either by failing to take up the affective perspectives or by failing to properly weigh the relevant interests. But such failures would express poor *quality of emotional regard* and poor *quality of judgment*, which on the tripartite theory are the realms of, respectively, accountability and answerability. To the extent that contemporary consequentialism deploys some aspect of this methodology or preserves its relevant features—namely, emotional regard and judgment about the worth of various reasons—it will persist in resonating with us in virtue of our sentimental responsibility commitments to those features.

Kantian deontology (as well as its more heteronomous cousins like contractualism) requires that one respect humanity in others by treating them never merely as means, but always as ends. Various decision procedures have been urged to enable us to identify the deontological right-maker, but they all typically consist in some kind of universalization maneuver: What, they ask, could be consistently willed, or agreed to, by all rational or reasonable agents? Answering this question thus requires taking up the normative viewpoint of others *qua* rational or reasonable agents, that is, seeing others' own ends as worthwhile from their perspective, and so as appearing to be (simpatico) reasons from one's own perspective. One must then decide whether to include these reasons in one's deliberative mix as well as how one is to judge as to their worth. But again, we should see this is a two-stage process whose failures express, respectively, poor qualities of *evaluational regard* and *judgment*, and so implicate central aspects of both accountability and answerability. Rather than identifying with others emotionally (as is suggested by the utilitarian strand of consequentialism), we are to identify with others evaluatively, as committed to the worth of various ends. These are the ends which often ground our demands for *respect*. Failure to take them seriously is inconsiderate, a form of disregard, and renders agential anger fitting.

It seems, then, as if, while virtue ethics has central features implicating quality of character, both consequentialism and deontology have central features implicating both quality of judgment and quality of regard, albeit differing over the strand of regard they emphasize. What I have been insisting on from the beginning of the book is the importance to us of *all three* qualities of will. If I am right, it is no wonder that, to the extent that such qualities play distinctive roles in multiple normative ethical theories, those theories persist in being attractive, as they each capture something essential to our interpersonal lives.

What the tripartite theory may do, then, is explain—and predict—the persistence of these competing normative ethical theories in perhaps a surprising but resonant way.

In conclusion, there are at least three possible independent (non-Strawsonian) virtues of the tripartite theory. These may be no more than promising suggestions, though. Perhaps others will deliver on those promises. My main aim in the book has been to construct the most plausible version of a quality of will theory I could muster, one motivated by our ambivalent responses to the marginal cases, and as that aim at least has been accomplished, my work here is done.

Bibliography

Aarts, Henk, et al. 2010. "The Art of Anger: Reward Context Turns Avoidance Responses to Anger-Related Objects into Approach." *Psychological Science* 21: 1406–10.

Abramowitz, Jonathan S. 2008. "Scrupulosity." In Jonathan S. Abramowitz, Dean McKay, and Steven Taylor, *Clinical Handbook of Obsessive-Compulsive Disorder and Related Problems* (Baltimore, MD: The Johns Hopkins University Press), Ch. 11.

Adams, Robert Merrihew. 1985. "Involuntary Sins." *Philosophical Review* 94: 3–31.

Aharoni, Eyal, Sinnott-Armstrong, Walter, and Kiehl, Kent A. 2012. "Can Psychopathic Offenders Discern Moral Wrongs? A New Look at the Moral/Conventional Distinction." *Journal of Abnormal Psychology* 121: 484–97.

Alexander, G. and Crutcher, M. 1990. "Functional architecture of basal ganglia circuits: Neural substrates of parallel processing." *Trends in Neurosciences* 13: 266–71.

Algoe, Sara B. and Haidt, Jonathan. 2009. "Witnessing Excellence in Action: the 'Other-Praising' Emotions of Elevation, Gratitude, and Admiration." *Journal of Positive Psychology* 4: 105–27. Citations from online version: <http://www.ncbi.nlm.nih.gov/pmc/articles/PMC2689844/pdf/nihms108473.pdf>.

American Psychiatric Association. 1994. *Diagnostic and Statistical Manual of Mental Disorders, Fourth Edition, DSM-IV*. Washington, DC.

American Psychiatric Association. 2013. *Diagnostic and Statistical Manual of Mental Disorders, Fifth Edition, DSM-5*. Washington, DC.

American Psychiatric Association. 2000. *Diagnostic and Statistical Manual of Mental Disorders, Fourth Edition, Text-Revision, DSM-IV-TR*. Washington, DC.

Anton, Raymond F. 2000. "Obsessive-Compulsive Aspects of Craving: Development of the Obsessive Compulsive Drinking Scale." *Addiction* 95: 211–17.

Aristotle. 1985. *Nicomachean Ethics*. Transl. by Terence Irwin. Indianapolis, IN: Hackett Publishing.

Aristotle. 1954. *The Rhetoric and the Poetics of Aristotle*. Transl. by W. Rhys Roberts. New York: The Modern Library.

Arpaly, Nomy. 2006. *Merit, Meaning, and Human Bondage*. Princeton and Oxford: Princeton University Press.

Arpaly, Nomy. 2003. *Unprincipled Virtue*. Oxford: Oxford University Press.

Arpaly, Nomy and Schroeder, Timothy. 1999. "Praise, Blame, and the Whole Self." *Philosophical Studies* 93: 161–88.

Barrios, G.E. and Gili, M. 1995. "Abulia and Impulsiveness Revisited: A Conceptual History." *Acta Psychiatrica Scandinavica* 92: 161–7.

Barry, John W., Dasen, Pierre R., and Saraswathi, T.S., eds. 1997. *Handbook of Cross-Cultural Psychology*, Second Edition. Boston: Allyn and Bacon.

Batson, C. Daniel, Early, Shannon, and Salvorani, Giovanni. 1997. "Perspective-Taking: Imagining How Another Feels vs. Imagining How You Would Feel." *Personality and Social Psychology Bulletin* 23: 751–8.

Batts, Shelley. 2009. "Brain Lesions and Their Implications in Criminal Responsibility." *Behavioral Sciences & the Law* 27: 261–72.

Blackburn, Ronald, and Lee-Evans J. Michael. 1985. "Reactions of Primary and Secondary Psychopaths to Anger-Evoking situations." *British Journal of Clinical Psychology* 24: 93–100.

Blair, James, et al. 1996. "Theory of Mind in the Psychopath." *Journal of Forensic Psychiatry* 7: 15–25.

Blair, R.J.R. 2007. "The Amygdala and Ventromedial Prefrontal Cortex in Morality and Psychopathy." *Trends in Cognitive Science* 11: 387–92.

Blair, R.J.R. 1996. "Brief Report: Morality in the Autistic Child." *Journal of Autism and Developmental Disorders* 26: 571–9.

Blair, R.J.R. 1995. "A Cognitive Developmental Approach to Morality: Investigating the Psychopath." *Cognition* 57: 1–29.

Blair, R.J.R. 2012. "Considering Anger from a Cognitive Neuroscience Perspective." *Wiley Interdisciplinary Reviews: Cognitive Science* 3: 65–74.

Blair, R.J.R. 1997. "Moral Reasoning and the Child with Psychopathic Tendencies." *Personality and Individual Differences* 22: 731–9.

Blair, R.J.R. 2010. "Psychopathy, Frustration, and Reactive Aggression: The Role of Ventromedial Prefrontal Cortex." *British Journal of Psychology* 101: 383–99.

Blair, R.J.R. 1999a. "Psychophysiological Responsiveness to the Distress of Others in Children with Autism." *Personality and Individual Differences* 26: 477–85.

Blair, R.J.R. 1999b. "Responsiveness to Distress Cues in the Child with Psychopathic Tendencies." *Personality and Individual Differences* 27: 135–45.

Blair, R.J.R., et al. 1995. "Is the Psychopath 'Morally Insane'?" *Personality and Individual Differences* 19: 741–52.

Blumberg, Hilary P. 2012. "Euthymia, Depression, and Mania: What Do We Know About the Switch?" *Biological Psychiatry* 71: 570–1.

Bora, Emre, Gökçen, Sezen, and Veznedaroglu, Baybars. 2008. "Empathic Abilities in People with Schizophrenia." *Psychiatry Research* 160: 23–9.

Bratman, Michael. 1999. *Faces of Intention.* Cambridge: Cambridge University Press.

Bratman, Michael. 2002. "Hierarchy, Circularity, and Double Reduction." In Buss and Overton 2002, pp. 65–85.

Bratman, Michael. 2007. *Structures of Agency.* Oxford: Oxford University Press.

Brink, David and Nelkin, Dana. 2013. "Fairness and the Architecture of Responsibility." In Shoemaker 2013a, pp. 284–313.

Brooks, Robert and Goldstein, Sam. 2001. *Raising Resilient Children: Fostering Strength, Hope, and Optimism in Your Child.* Lincolnwood, IL: Contemporary Books.

Buss, Sarah. 2012. "Self-Determination in the Passive Mode." *Ethics* 122: 647–91.

Buss, Sarah and Overton, Lee, eds. 2002. *Contours of Agency.* Cambridge, MA: MIT Press.

Caparulo, Frank. 1991. "Identifying the Developmentally Disabled Sex Offenders." *Sexuality and Disability* 9: 311–22.

Castles, Elaine. 1996. *"We're People First": The Social and Emotional Lives of Individuals with Mental Retardation.* Westport, CN: Praeger.

Chevalier, G. and Deniau, J. 1990. "Disinhibition as a basic process in the expression of striatal functions." *Trends in Neurosciences* 13: 277–80.

Clark, Hilary Anne, ed. 2008. *Depression and Narrative: Telling the Dark*. Albany, NY: SUNY Press.

Cleckley, Hervey. 1976. *The Mask of Sanity*, Fifth Edition. St. Louis: C.V. Mosley.

Coates, D. Justin and Tognazzini, Neal, eds. 2013. *Blame: Its Nature and Norms*. New York: Oxford University Press.

Cohen, A. and Leckman, J. 1992. "Sensory Phenomena Associated with Gilles de la Tourette's Syndrome." *Journal of Clinical Psychiatry* 53: 319–23.

Cooke, D.J., Kosson, D.S., and Michie, C. 2001. "Psychopathy and ethnicity: Structural, item and test generalizability of the Psychopathy Checklist-Revised (PCL-R) in Caucasian and African-American participants." *Psychological Assessment* 13: 531–42.

Corwin, Miles. 1982. "Icy Killer's Life Steeped in Violence." *Los Angeles Times* (May 16).

D'Arms, Justin. 2013. "Value and the Regulation of Sentiments." *Philosophical Studies* 163: 3–13.

D'Arms, Justin and Jacobson, Daniel. 2006b. "Anthropocentric Constraints on Human Value." In Russ Shafer-Landau, ed., *Oxford Studies in Metaethics* 1. Oxford: Oxford University Press, pp. 99–126.

D'Arms, Justin and Jacobson, Daniel. 2000. "The Moralistic Fallacy: On the 'Appropriateness' of the Emotions." *Philosophy and Phenomenological Research* 61: 65–90.

D'Arms, Justin and Jacobson, Daniel. 2006a. "Sensibility Theory and Projectivism." In David Copp, ed., *The Oxford Handbook of Ethical Theory*. Oxford: Oxford University Press.

D'Arms, Justin and Jacobson, Daniel. 2003. "The Significance of Recalcitrant Emotions (or, Anti-Quasijudgmentalism)." Reprinted in Anthony Hatzimoysis, ed., *Philosophy and the Emotions*. Cambridge: Cambridge University Press.

Dadds, Mark R., et al. 2009. "Learning to 'Talk the Talk': the Relationship of Psychopathic Traits to Deficits in Empathy Across Childhood." *Journal of Child Psychology and Psychiatry* 50: 599–606.

Darwall, Stephen. 2006. *The Second-Person Standpoint*. Cambridge, MA: Harvard University Press.

Darwall, Stephen. 2002. *Welfare and Rational Care*. Princeton, NJ: Princeton University Press.

David, Robert. 1989. *My Journey into Alzheimer's Disease: Helpful Insights For Family and Friends*. Wheaton, IL: Tyndale House.

de Oliveira-Souza, Ricardo, et al. 2008. "The Antisocials Amid Us." In Sinnott-Armstrong 2008, pp. 151–8.

de Vignemont, Frederique and Frith, Uta. 2008. "Autism, Morality, and Empathy." In Sinnott-Armstrong 2008, 273–80.

Deigh, John. 1995. "Empathy and Universalizability." *Ethics* 105: 743–63.

Deigh, John. 2011. "Reactive Attitudes Revisited." In Carla Bagnoli, ed., *Morality and the Emotions*. Oxford: Oxford University Press, pp. 197–216.

Doi, T. 1973. *The Anatomy of Dependence*. New York, NY: Kodansha International.

Dorsey, Dale. 2013. "Consequentialism, Cognitive Limitations, and Moral Theory." In Timmons 2013, pp. 179–202.

Driver, Julia. 1992. "The Suberogatory." *Australasian Journal of Philosophy* 70: 286–95.

Duff, R.A. 2007. *Answering for Crime*. Oxford: Hart Publishing.

Duff, R.A. 2009b. "Legal and Moral Responsibility." *Philosophy Compass* 4/6: 978–86.

Duff, R.A. 1977. "Psychopathy and Moral Understanding." *American Philosophical Quarterly* 14: 189–200.

Duff, R.A. 2009a. "Strict Responsibility, Moral and Criminal." *Journal of Value Inquiry* 43: 295–313.

Eatough, Virginia and Smith, Jonathan. 2006. "'I Was Like a Wild Person': Understanding Feelings of Anger Using Interpretive Phenomenological Analysis." *British Journal of Psychology* 97: 483–98.

Eckman, Paul. 1992. "Are there basic emotions?" *Psychological Review* 99: 550–3.

Eckman, Paul. 2003. *Emotions Revealed.* New York: Henry Hold and Co.

Eid, Michael and Diener, Ed. 2001. "Norms for Experiencing Emotions in Different Cultures: Inter- and Intranational Differences." *Journal of Personality and Social Psychology* 81: 869–85.

Eisenberg, Nancy and Strayer, Janet, eds. 1987. *Empathy and Its Development.* New York, NY: Cambridge University Press.

Eshleman, Andrew. 2009. "Moral Responsibility." *The Stanford Encyclopedia of Philosophy*, Edward N. Zalta, ed., <http://plato.stanford.edu/entries/moral-responsibility/>.

Eshleman, Andrew. 2004. "Responsibility for Character." *Philosophical Topics* 32: 65–94.

Evans, Daryl Paul. 1983. *The Lives of Mentally Retarded People.* Boulder, CO: Westview Press.

Faraci, David and Shoemaker, David. 2014. "Huck vs. JoJo: Moral Ignorance and the (A) Symmetry of Praise and Blame." *Oxford Studies in Experimental Philosophy* 1: 7–27.

Faraci, David and Shoemaker, David. 2010. "Insanity, Deep Selves, and Moral Responsibility." *Review of Philosophy & Psychology* 1: 319–32.

Feshbach, N.D. 1979. "Empathy Training: A Field Study in Affective Education." In S. Feshbach and A. Fraczek, eds., *Aggression and Behavior Change: Biological and Social Processes.* New York: Praeger.

Feshbach, N.D. 1983. "Learning to Care: A Positive Approach to Childtraining and Discipline." *Journal of Clinical Child Psychology* 12: 266–71.

Feshbach, N.D. and Feshbach, S. 1982. "Empathy Training and the Regulation of Aggression: Potentialities and Limitations." *Academic Psychology Bulletin* 4: 399–413.

Fessler, Daniel M.T. 1999. "Toward an Understanding of the Universality of Second-Order Emotions." In A. Hinton, ed., *Beyond Nature or Nurture: Biocultural Approaches to the Emotions.* New York: Cambridge University Press, pp. 75–116.

Fine, Cordelia and Kennett, Jeanette. 2004. "Mental Impairment, Moral Understanding, and Criminal Responsibility: Psychopathy and the Purposes of Punishment." *International Journal of Law and Psychiatry* 27: 425–43.

Fingarette, Herbert. 1967. *On Responsibility.* New York: Basic.

Finkel, Norman J., Harre, Rom, and Rodriguez Lopez, Jose-Luis. 2001. "Commonsense Morality Across Cultures: Notions of Fairness, Justice, Honor and Equity." *Discourse Studies* 3: 5–27.

Fischer, John Martin. 1986. "Introduction." In John Martin Fischer, ed., *Moral Responsibility.* Ithaca, NY: Cornell University Press.

Fischer, John Martin. 1994. *The Metaphysics of Free Will.* Oxford: Blackwell Publishers.

Fischer, John Martin. 2004. "Responsibility and Manipulation." *The Journal of Ethics* 8: 145–77.

Fischer, John Martin and Ravizza, Mark, eds. 1993. *Perspectives on Moral Responsibility*. Ithaca, NY: Cornell University Press.

Fischer, John Martin and Ravizza, Mark. 1998. *Responsibility and Control*. Cambridge: Cambridge University Press.

Fischer, John Martin and Tognazzini, Neal. 2011. "The Physiognomy of Responsibility." *Philosophy and Phenomenological Research* 82: 381–417.

Foot, Philippa. 1978. "Hume on Moral Judgment." In *Virtues and Vices*. Berkeley: University of California Press.

Frankfurt, Harry. 1988. *The Importance of What We Care About*. Cambridge: Cambridge University Press.

Frankfurt, Harry. 1999. *Necessity, Volition, and Love*. Cambridge: Cambridge University Press.

Frankfurt, Harry. 2004. *The Reasons of Love*. Cambridge: Cambridge University Press.

Frankfurt, Harry. 2002. "Response to Michael E. Bratman." In Buss and Overton 2002, pp. 86–90.

Frijda, Nico. 1986. *The Emotions*. Cambridge: Cambridge University Press.

Fulford, Daniel, Johnson, Sheri L., and Carver, Charles S. 2008. "Commonalities and Differences in Characteristics of Persons at Risk for Narcissism and Mania." *Journal of Research in Personality* 42: 1427–38.

Gacono, C.B., and Hutton, H.E. 1994. "Suggestions for the Clinical and Forensic Use of the Hare Psychopathy Checklist-Revised (PCL-R)." *International Journal of Law and Psychiatry* 17: 303–17.

Gao, Yu, and Raine, Adrian. 2010. "Successful and Unsuccessful Psychopaths: A Neurobiological Model." *Behavioral Sciences & the Law* 28: 194–210.

Glannon, Walter. 2008. "Moral Responsibility and the Psychopath." *Neuroethics* 1: 158–66.

Gordon, R.M. 1995. "Sympathy, Simulation and the Impartial Spectator." *Ethics* 105: 727–42.

Graybiel, A., et al. 1994. "The basal ganglia and adaptive motor control." *Science* 265: 1826–31.

Greene, Joshua and Haidt, Jonathan. 2002. "How (and Where) Does Moral Judgment Work?" *Trends in Cognitive Sciences* 6: 517–23.

Greene, Joshua D. 2008. "The Secret Joke of Kant's Soul." In Sinnott-Armstrong 2008, pp. 35–80.

Griffiths, Paul. 2004. "Is Emotion a Natural Kind?" In P. Cruse and D. Evans, eds., *Emotion, Evolution and Rationality*. Oxford: Oxford University Press.

Gruber, June and Johnson, Sheri L. 2009. "Positive Emotional Traits and Ambitious Goals Among People at Risk for Mania: The Need for Specificity." *International Journal of Cognitive Therapy* 2: 176–87.

Gruber, June, et al. 2008. "Risk for Mania and Positive Emotional Responding: Too Much of a Good Thing?" *Emotion* 8: 23–33.

Haapasalo, J. and Pulkkinen, L. 1992. "The Psychopathy Checklist and Non-Violent Offender Groups." *Criminal Behaviour and Mental Health* 2: 315–28.

Haidt, Jonathan. 2003a. "Elevation and the Positive Psychology of Morality." In C.L.M. Keyes and Jonathan Haidt, eds., *Flourishing: Positive Psychology and the Life Well-Lived*. Washington, DC: American Psychological Association, pp. 275–89.

Haidt, Jonathan. 2001. "The Emotional Dog and Its Rational Tail: A Social Intuitionist Approach to Moral Judgment." *Psychological Review* 108: 814–34.

Haidt, Jonathan. 2003b. "The Moral Emotions." In R.J. Davidson, K.R. Scherer, and H.H. Goldsmith, eds., *Handbook of Affective Sciences*. Oxford: Oxford University Press, pp. 852–70.

Haidt, Jonathan, Graham, Jesse, and Joseph, Craig. 2009. "Above and Below Left-Right: Ideological Narratives and Moral Foundations." *Psychological Inquiry* 20: 110–19.

Haidt, Jonathan and Seder, Patrick. 2009. "Admiration/Awe." In David Sander and Klaus R. Scherer, *The Oxford Companion to Emotion and the Affective Sciences*. Oxford: Oxford University Press, pp. 4–5.

Haji, Ishtiyaque. 2008. "Authentic Springs of Action and Obligation." *The Journal of Ethics* 12: 239–61.

Haji, Ishtiyaque. 1998. *Moral Appraisability*. New York: Oxford University Press.

Haji, Ishtiyaque. 2010. "Psychopathy, Ethical Perception, and Moral Culpability." *Neuroethics* 3: 135–50.

Hare, Robert. 2003. *Manual for the Revised Psychopathy Checklist*, Second Edition. Toronto, ON, Canada: Multi-Health Systems.

Hare, Robert D., Neumann, Craig S., and Widiger, Thomas A. 2012. "Psychopathy." In Thomas A. Widiger, ed., *The Oxford Handbook of Personality Disorders*. Oxford: Oxford University Press, pp. 478–504.

Harenski, Carla L. and Kiehl, Kent A. 2010. "Reactive Aggression in Psychopathy and the Role of Frustration: Susceptibility, Experience, and Control." *British Journal of Psychology* 101: 401–6.

Harpur, T.J., Hare, R.D., and Hakstian, A.R. 1989. "Two-factor conceptualization of psychopathy: Construct validity and assessment implications." *Psychological Assessment* 1: 6–17.

Hart, H.L.A. 1961. *The Concept of Law*. Oxford: The Clarendon Press.

Hart, H.L.A. 2008. *Punishment and Responsibility*, Second Edition. Oxford: Oxford University Press.

Hart, Stephen D. and Dempster, Rebecca J. 1997. "Impulsivity and Psychopathy." In Christopher D. Webster and Margaret A. Jackson, eds., *Impulsivity: Theory, Assessment, and Treatment*. New York: The Guilford Press, pp. 212–32.

Herpertz, Sabine C. and Sass, Henning. 2000. "Emotional Deficiency and Psychopathy." *Behavioral Sciences and the Law* 18: 567–80.

Heshusius, Louis. 1981. *Meaning in Life as Experienced by Persons Labeled Retarded in a Group Home*. Springfield, IL: Charles C. Thomas.

Hieronymi, Pamela. 2001. "Articulating an Uncompromising Forgiveness." *Philosophy & Phenomenological Research* 62: 529–55.

Hieronymi, Pamela. 2004. "The Force and Fairness of Blame." *Philosophical Perspectives* 18: 115–48.

Higashida, Naoki. 2013. *The Reason I Jump: The Inner Voice of a Thirteen-Year-Old Boy with Autism*. Trans. by K.A. Yoshida and David Mitchell. New York: Random House.

Hirsch, Irwin. 2011. "Narcissism, Mania and Analysts' Envy." *The American Journal of Psychoanalysis* 71: 363–9.

Hobbes, Thomas. 1994. *Leviathan*. Edited by Edwin Curley. Indianapolis, IN: Hackett Publishing Co.

Hobson, Peter. 1992. "Social Perception in High Level Autism." In E. Schopler and G. Mesibov, eds., *High Functioning Individuals with Autism*. New York: Plenum, pp. 157–84.

Hobson, Peter R., et al. 2011. "Autism and the Self." In Shaun Gallagher, *The Oxford Handbook of the Self*. Oxford: Oxford University Press, pp. 571–91.

Hobson, Peter R., et al. 2006. "Foundations for Self-Awareness: An Exploration through Autism." *Monographs of the Society for Research in Child Development* 71: 1–166.

Hollos, M., Leis, P., and Turiel, E. 1986. "Social Reasoning Children and Adolescents." *Journal of Cross Cultural Psychology* 17: 352–74.

Holmgren, Margaret. 2012. *Forgiveness and Retribution: Responding to Wrongdoing*. New York: Cambridge University Press.

Holmgren, Margaret. 2014. "A Moral Assessment of Strawson's Retributive Reactive Attitudes." In Shoemaker and Tognazzini, 2014, pp. 165–86.

Horberg, E.J., et al. 2009. "Disgust and the Moralization of Purity." *Journal of Personality and Social Psychology* 97: 963–76.

Houk, J., David, J., and Beiser, D., eds. 1995. *Models of Information Processing in the Basal Ganglia*. Cambridge, MA: MIT Press.

Huebner, Bryce, Dwyer, Susan, and Hauser, Marc. 2009. "The Role of Emotion in Moral Psychology." *Trends in Cognitive Sciences* 13: 1–6.

Hughes, G.E. 1958. "Moral Condemnation." In A.I. Melden, ed., *Essays in Moral Philosophy*. Seattle, WA: University of Washington Press.

Hughes, Julian C., Louw, Stephen J., and Sabat, Steven R., eds. 2006. *Dementia: Mind, Meaning, and the Person*. Oxford: Oxford University Press.

Hughes, Paul M. 1995. "Moral Anger, Forgiving, and Condoning." *Journal of Social Philosophy* 26: 103–18.

Hume, David (1740/1975). *Treatise of Human Nature*, ed. L.A. Selby-Bigge. Oxford: Oxford University Press.

Huppert, Jonathan D., Kiev, Jedidiah, and Kushner, Elyssa S. 2007. "When Religion and Obsessive-Compulsive Disorder Collide: Treating Scrupulosity in Ultra-Orthodox Jews." *Journal of Clinical Psychology* 63: 925–41.

Jacobson, Daniel. 2011. "Fitting Attitude Theories of Value." In Edward N. Zalta, ed., *The Stanford Encyclopedia of Philosophy*, <http://plato.stanford.edu/archives/spr2011/entries/fitting-attitude-theories/>.

Jacobson, Daniel. 2012. "Moral Dumbfounding and Moral Stupefaction." In Mark Timmons, ed., 2013, *Oxford Studies in Normative Ethics* 2 (Oxford: Oxford University Press), pp. 289–316.

Jacobson, Daniel. 2013. "Regret, Agency, and Error." In Shoemaker 2013a, pp. 95–125.

Jaworska, Agnieszka. 2007. "Caring and Internality." *Philosophy and Phenomenological Research* 74: 529–68.

Jaworska, Agnieszka. 1999. "Respecting the Margins of Agency: Alzheimer's Patients and the Capacity to Value." *Philosophy & Public Affairs* 28: 105–38.

Johnston, Mark. 1997. "Human Concerns without Superlative Selves." In Jonathan Dancy, ed., *Reading Parfit*. Oxford: Blackwell.

Jolliffe, Darrick and Farrington, David P. 2004. "Empathy and Offending: A Systematic Review and Meta-Analysis." *Aggression and Violent Behavior* 9: 441–76.

Jolliffe, T., Lansdown, R., and Robinson, C. 1993. "Autism: a Personal Account." *Educare-London-National Bureau for Handicapped Students*: 8.

Jones, Alice P., et al. 2010. "Feeling, Caring, Knowing: Different Types of Empathy Deficit in Boys with Psychopathic Tendencies and Autism Spectrum Disorder." *Journal of Child Psychology and Psychiatry* 51: 1188–97.

Joyce, Richard. 2006. *The Evolution of Morality*. Cambridge, MA: MIT Press.

Kassinove, Howard, et al. 1997. "Self-Reported Anger Episodes in Russia and America." *Journal of Social Behavior & Personality* 12: 301–24.

Kelly, Daniel et al. 2007. "Harm, Affect, and the Moral/Conventional Distinction." *Mind and Language* 22: 117–31.

Kennett, Jeanette. 2001. *Agency and Responsibility*. Oxford: Oxford University Press.

Kennett, Jeanette. 2002. "Autism, Empathy, and Moral Agency." *Philosophical Quarterly* 52: 340–57.

Kennett, Jeanette and Fine, Cordelia. 2008b. "Could There Be an Empirical Test for Internalism?" In Sinnott-Armstrong 2008, pp. 217–25.

Kennett, Jeanette and Fine, Cordelia. 2008a. "Internalism and the Evidence from Psychopaths and 'Acquired Sociopaths'." In Sinnott-Armstrong 2008, pp. 173–90.

Khoury, Andrew. 2013. "Synchronic and Diachronic Responsibility." *Philosophical Studies* 165: 735–52.

Kiehl, Kent. 2008. "Without Morals: The Cognitive Neuroscience of Criminal Psychopaths." In Sinnott-Armstrong 2008, pp. 119–49.

Kilmann, Ralph H., O'Hara, Linda A., and Strauss, Judy P. 2010. "Developing and Validating a Quantitative Measure of Organizational Courage." *Journal of Business Psychology* 25: 15–23.

Kim, Sangmoon, Thibodeau, Ryan, and Jorgensen, Randall S. 2011. "Shame, Guilt, and Depressive Symptoms: A Meta-Analytic Review." *Psychological Bulletin* 137: 68–96.

King, Matt. 2012. "Moral Responsibility and Merit." *Journal of Ethics and Social Philosophy* 6, <http://www.jesp.org/PDF/moral_responsibility_and_merit_080912.pdf>.

Kirsch, Laura G., and Becker, Judith V. 2007. "Emotional Deficits in Psychopathy and Sexual Sadism: Implications for Violent and Sadistic Behavior." *Clinical Psychology Review* 27: 904–22.

Kremer, John F. and Dietzen, Laura L. 1991. "Two Approaches to Teaching Accurate Empathy to Undergraduates: Teacher-Intensive and Self-Directed." *Journal of College Student Development* 32: 69–75.

Landman, Janet. 1987. "Regret: A Theoretical and Conceptual Analysis." *Journal for the Theory of Social Behavior* 17: 135–60.

Lawson, Wendy. 2001. *Life Behind Glass: A Personal Account of Autism Spectrum Disorder*. London: Jessica Kingsley.

Leahy, Robert. 1999. "Decision Making and Mania." *Journal of Cognitive Psychotherapy* 13: 83–105.

Lerner, Jennifer S. and Keltner, Dacher. 2001. "Fear, Anger, and Risk." *Journal of Personality and Social Psychology* 81: 146–59.

Lerner, Jennifer S., et al. 2003. "Effects of Fear and Anger on Perceived Risks of Terrorism: A National Field Experiment." *Psychological Science* 14: 144–50.

Levy, Morgan L., et al. 1998. "Apathy Is Not Depression." *The Journal of Neuropsychiatry and Clinical Neurosciences* 10: 314–19.

Levy, Morgan L., et al. 2007. "The Responsibility of the Psychopath Revisited." *Philosophy, Psychology, & Psychiatry* 14: 129–38.

Levy, Neil. 2013. "Be a Skeptic, Not a Metaskeptic." In Gregg D. Caruso, ed., *Exploring the Illusion of Free Will and Moral Responsibility*. Plymouth, UK: Lexington Books, pp. 87–102.

Levy, Neil. 2007. "The Responsibility of the Psychopath Revisited." *Philosophy, Psychiatry, & Psychology* 14: 129–38.

Lippert-Rasmussen, Kasper. 2003. "Identification and Responsibility." *Ethical Theory and Moral Practice* 6: 349–76.

Locke, Don. 1975. "Three Concepts of Free Action: I." *Proceedings of the Aristotelian Society*, supp. Vol. XLIX: 95–112.

Logan, Linda. 2013. "Selfless." *The New York Times Magazine* (April 28): 54–60.

Lopez-Perez, Raul and Vorsatz, Marc. 2010. "On Approval and Disapproval: Theory and Experiments." *Journal of Economic Psychology* 31: 527–41.

Losoya, Sandra and Eisenberg, Nancy. 2001. "Affective Empathy." In Judith Hall and Frank Bernieri, eds., *Interpersonal Sensitivity: Theory and Measurement*. Mahwah, NJ: Lawrence Erlbaum Associates Publishers, pp. 21–43.

Lucas, John. 1993. *Responsibility*. Oxford: Oxford University Press.

Luria, A.R. 1975. *The Man with a Shattered World*. Harmondsworth, Middlesex: Penguin Education.

Lykken, D.T. 1995. *The Antisocial Personalities*. Hillsdale, NJ: Erlbaum.

Maibom, Heidi. 2008. "The Mad, the Bad, and the Psychopath." *Neuroethics* 1: 167–84.

Maibom, Heidi. 2007. "The Presence of Others." *Philosophical Studies* 132: 161–90.

Markus, H.R. and Kitayama, S. 1991. "Culture and the self: Implications for cognition, emotion, and motivation." *Psychological Review* 98: 224–53.

Marin, Robert S., Firinciogullari, Sekip, and Biedrzycki, Ruth C. 1993. "The Sources of Convergence Between Measures of Apathy and Depression." *Journal of Affective Disorders* 28: 117–24.

Matravers, Matt. 2007. *Responsibility and Justice*. Cambridge: Polity Press.

Matson, Johnny L. and Senatore, Vincent. 1981. "A Comparison of Traditional Psychotherapy and Social Skills Training for Improving Interpersonal Functioning of Mentally Retarded Adults." *Behavior Therapy* 12: 369–82.

Mauro, Robert, Sato, Kaori, and Tucker, John. 1992. "The Role of Appraisal in Human Emotions: A Cross-Cultural Study." *Journal of Personality and Social Psychology* 62: 301–17.

Macnamara, Coleen. 2013b. "Reactive Attitudes as Communicative Entities." *Philosophy & Phenomenological Research*. DOI: 10.1111/phpr.12075.

Macnamara, Coleen. 2013a. "'Screw You!' & 'Thank You!'" *Philosophical Studies* 165: 893–914.

McGeer, Victoria. 2014. "P.F. Strawson's Consequentialism." In Shoemaker and Tognazzini 2014, pp. 64–92.

McGeer, Victoria. 2008. "Varieties of Moral Agency: Lessons from Autism (and Psychopathy)." In Sinnott-Armstrong 2008, pp. 227–57.

McGeer, Victoria and Pettit, Philip. Forthcoming. "Capacity and Capacitation." In David Shoemaker, ed., *Oxford Studies in Agency and Responsibility* 3. Oxford: Oxford University Press.

McKenna, Michael. 2006. "Collective Responsibility and the Agent Meaning Theory." *Midwest Studies in Philosophy* 30: 16–34.

McKenna, Michael. 2012. *Conversation and Responsibility*. New York: Oxford University Press.

McKenna, Michael. 2008. "A Hard-line Reply to Pereboom's Four-Case Manipulation Argument." *Philosophy and Phenomenological Research* 77: 142–59.

McKenna, Michael. 1998. "The Limits of Evil and the Role of Moral Address: A Defense of Strawsonian Compatibilism." *The Journal of Ethics* 2: 123–42.

McKenna, Michael. 2013. "Responsibility & Globally Manipulated Agents." In Paul Russell and Oisin Deery, eds., *The Philosophy of Free Will: Essential Readings from the Contemporary Debates*. Oxford: Oxford University Press, pp. 342–61.

McKenna, Michael. 2005. "Where Frankfurt and Strawson Meet." *Midwest Studies in Philosophy* 29: 163–80.

McKenna, Michael and Vadakin, Aron. 2008. "Review of George Sher's *In Praise of Blame*." *Ethics* 118: 751–6.

Meffert, Harma, et al. 2013. "Reduced Spontaneous but Relatively Normal Deliberate Vicarious Representations in Psychopathy." *Brain* 136: 2550–62.

Mele, Alfred R. 1995. *Autonomous Agents: From Self-Control to Autonomy*. New York: Oxford University Press.

Mele, Alfred R. 2000. "Deciding to Act." *Philosophical Studies* 100: 81–108.

Mele, Alfred R. 2006. *Free Will and Luck*. New York: Oxford University Press.

Mele, Alfred R. 2008. "Manipulation, Compatibilism, and Moral Responsibility." *The Journal of Ethics* 12: 263–86.

Mele, Alfred R. 2009a. "Moral Responsibility and Agents' Histories." *Philosophical Studies* 142: 161–81.

Mele, Alfred R. 2009b. "Moral Responsibility and History Revisited." *Ethical Theory and Moral Practice* 12: 463–75.

Mele, Alfred R. 2013. "Moral Responsibility, Manipulation, and Minutelings." *The Journal of Ethics* 17: 153–66.

Mele, Alfred R. 1992. *Springs of Action*. New York: Oxford University Press.

Mendez, Mario, et al. 2005. "An Investigation of Moral Judgement in Frontotemporal Dementia." *Cognitive and Behavioral Neurology* 18: 193–7.

Mesquita, B., Frijda, N., and Scherer, K. 1997. "Culture and Emotion." In Barry, Dasen, and Saraswathi 1997, pp. 255–98.

Miller, C.H. and Hedges, D.W. 2008. "Scrupulosity Disorder: An Overview and Introductory Analysis." *Journal of Anxiety Disorders* 22: 1042–58.

Mink, J. 1996. "The basal ganglia: Focussed selection and inhibition of competing motor programs." *Progress in Neurobiology* 50: 381–425.

Mink, J. 2001. "Neurobiology of basal ganglia circuits in Tourette syndrome: Faulty inhibition of unwanted motor patterns?" In D. Cohen, C. Goetz, and J. Jankovic, eds., *Tourette Syndrome*. Philadelphia, PA: Lippincott Williams and Wilkins.

Morreall, J. 1983. "Humor and Emotion." *American Philosophical Quarterly* 20: 297–304.

Morrison, David and Gilbert, Paul. 2001. "Social Rank, Shame and Anger in Primary and Secondary Psychopaths." *Journal of Forensic Psychiatry* 12: 330–56.

Mullins-Nelson, Jana L., Salekin, Randall T., and Leistico, Ann-Marie R. 2006. "Psychopathy, Empathy, and Perspective-Taking Ability in a Community Sample: Implications for the Successful Psychopathy Concept." *International Journal of Forensic Mental Health* 5: 133–49.

Murray, John B. 1992. "Kleptomania: A Review of the Research." *The Journal of Psychology: Interdisciplinary and Applied* 126: 131–7.

Nelkin, Dana Kay. 2011. *Making Sense of Freedom & Responsibility*. Oxford: Oxford University Press.

Nelson, Elizabeth A., et al. 2006. "Scrupulosity in Patients with Obsessive-Compulsive Disorder: Relationship to Clinical and Cognitive Phenomena." *Journal of Anxiety Disorders* 20: 1071–86.

Newman, J.P. and Wallace, J.F. 1993. "Divergent Pathways to Deficient Self-Regulation: Implications for Disinhibitory Psychopathology in Children." *Clinical Psychology Review* 13: 699–720.

Newman, George E., Bloom, Paul, and Knobe, Joshua. 2013. "Value Judgments and the True Self." *Personality and Social Psychology Bulletin* 22: 1–14. DOI: 10.1177/0146167213508791.

Newman, George E., De Freitas, Julian, and Knobe, Joshua. 2014. "Beliefs About the True Self Explain Asymmetries Based on Moral Judgment." *Cognitive Science*. DOI: 10.1111/cogs.12134.

Nichols, Shaun. 2007. "After Incompatibilism: A Naturalistic Defense of the Reactive Attitudes." *Philosophical Perspectives* 21: 405–28.

Nichols, Shaun. 2001. "Mindreading and the Cognitive Architecture Underlying Altruistic Motivation." *Mind and Language* 16: 425–55.

Nichols, Shaun. 2002. "Norms with Feeling: Towards a Psychological Account of Moral Judgment." *Cognition* 84: 221–36.

Nichols, Shaun. 2004. *Sentimental Rules*. Oxford: Oxford University Press.

Nisan, M. 1987. "Moral Norms and Social Conventions: A Cross-Cultural Comparison." *Developmental Psychology* 23: 719–25.

Nucci, Larry P. and Herman, Susan. 1982. "Behavioral Disordered Children's Conceptions of Moral, Conventional, and Personal Issues." *Journal of Abnormal Child Psychology* 10: 411–26.

Nucci, Larry P. and Nucci, Maria Santiago. 1982b. "Children's Responses to Moral and Social Conventional Transgressions in Free-Play Settings." *Child Development* 53: 1337–42.

Nucci, Larry P. and Nucci, Maria Santiago. 1982a. "Children's Social Interactions in the Context of Moral and Conventional Transgressions." *Child Development* 53: 403–12.

Nucci, Larry P. and Turiel, Elliot. 1978. "Social Interactions and the Development of Social Concepts in Preschool Children." *Child Development* 49: 400–7.

O'Connor, Lynn E., et al. 2007. "Empathy and Depression: The Moral System on Overdrive." In Tom F.D. Farrow and Peter W.R. Woodruff, *Empathy in Mental Illness*. Cambridge: Cambridge University Press, pp. 49–75.

Oppenheimer, Catherine. 2006. "I am, thou art: Personal Identity in Dementia." In Hughes, Louw, and Sabat, eds. 2006, pp. 193–203.

Ortony, Andrew and Turner, Terence J. 1990. "What's basic about basic emotions?" *Psychological Review* 97: 315–31.

Oshana, Marina. 1997. "Ascriptions of Responsibility." *American Philosophical Quarterly* 34: 71–83.

Palumbo, D., Maughan, A., and Kurlan, R. 1997. "Tourette syndrome is only one of several causes of a developmental basal ganglia syndrome." *Archives of Neurology* 54: 475–83.

Parfit, Derek. 1984. *Reasons and Persons*. Oxford: Oxford University Press.

Parkinson, Brian, Fischer, Agneta H., and Manstead, Antony S.R. 2004. *Emotion in Social Relations: Cultural, Group, and Interpersonal Processes*. New York: Psychology Press.

Pereboom, Derk. 2014. *Free Will, Agency, and Meaning in Life*. Oxford: Oxford University Press.

Pereboom, Derk. 2007. "Hard Incompatibilism." In Pereboom, Fischer, Kane, and Vargas, *Four Views on Free Will*. New York: Blackwell, pp. 85–125.

Pereboom, Derk. 2008. "A Hard-line Reply to the Multiple-Case Manipulation Argument." *Philosophy and Phenomenological Research* 77: 160–70.

Pereboom, Derk. 2004. *Living Without Free Will*. Cambridge: Cambridge University Press.

Peterson, B. et al. 1998. "A functional magnetic resonance imaging study of tic suppression in Tourette syndrome." *Archives of General Psychiatry* 55: 326–33.

Pieters, Rik and Zeelenberg, Marcel. 2005. "On Bad Decisions and Deciding Badly: When Intention-Behavior Inconsistency is Regrettable." *Organizational Behavior and Human Decision Processes* 97: 18–30.

Pinderhughes, Elaine B. 1984. "Teaching Empathy: Ethnicity, Race and Power at the Cross-Cultural Treatment Interface." *American Journal of Social Psychiatry* 4: 5–12.

Prinz, Jesse. 2011b. "Against Empathy." *The Southern Journal of Philosophy* 49 (Spindel Supplement): 214–33.

Prinz, Jesse. 2011a. "Is Empathy Necessary for Morality?" In Peter Goldie and Amy Coplan, eds., *Empathy: Philosophical and Psychological Perspectives*. Oxford: Oxford University Press, pp. 211–29.

Prinz, Jesse. 2004. "Which Emotions Are Basic?" In D. Evans and P. Cruse, eds., *Emotion, Evolution, and Rationality*. Oxford: Oxford University Press.

Puka, Bill. 2002. "Foregoing Forgiveness." In Sharon Lamb and Jeffrie G. Murphy, eds., *Before Forgiving: Cautionary Views of Forgiveness in Psychotherapy*. New York: Oxford University Press, pp. 136–52.

Rawls, John. 1971. *A Theory of Justice*. Cambridge, MA: The Belknap Press of Harvard University Press.

Robert, P.H., et al. 2002. "The Apathy Inventory: Assessment of Apathy and Awareness in Alzheimer's Disease, Parkinson's Disease and Mild Cognitive Impairment." *International Journal of Geriatric Psychiatry* 17: 1099–105.

Roberts, Robert C. 2003. *Emotions: An Essay in Aid of Moral Psychology*. Cambridge: Cambridge University Press.

Rogers, John et al. 2006. "Autism Spectrum Disorder and Psychopathy: Shared Cognitive Underpinnings or Double Hit?" *Psychological Medicine* 36: 1789–98.

Roskies, Adina L. 2008. "Internalism and the Evidence from Pathology." In Sinnott-Armstrong 2008, pp. 191–206.

Rozin, P., Lowery, L., Imada, S., and Haidt, J. 1999. "The CAD Triad Hypothesis: A Mapping Between Three Moral Emotions (Contempt, Anger, Disgust) and Three Moral Codes (Community, Autonomy, Divinity)." *Journal of Personality and Social Psychology* 76: 574–86.

Russell, J.A. and Fehr, B. 1994. "Fuzzy Concepts in a Fuzzy Hierarchy: Varieties of Anger." *Journal of Personality and Social Psychology* 67: 186–205.

Russell, James A. and Mehrabian, Albert. 1974. "Distinguishing Anger and Anxiety in Terms of Emotional Response Factors." *Journal of Consulting and Clinical Psychology* 42: 79–82.

Russell, Paul. 2008. "Free Will, Art and Morality." *Journal of Ethics* 12: 307–25.

Russell, Paul. 1995. *Freedom and Moral Sentiments*. Oxford: Oxford University Press.

Russell, Paul. 2004. "Responsibility and the Condition of Moral Sense." *Philosophical Topics* 32: 287–305.

Russell, Paul. 2013. "Responsibility, Naturalism, and 'The Morality System'." In Shoemaker 2013a, pp. 184–204.

Russell, Paul. 1992. "Strawson's Way of Naturalizing Responsibility." *Ethics* 102: 287–302.

Ryberg, Jesper. 2014. "Responsibility and Capacities: A Note on the Proportionality Assumption." *Analysis*. DOI: 10.1093/analys/anu039.

Scanlon, T.M. 2008. *Moral Dimensions*. Cambridge, MA: Belknap Press of Harvard University Press.

Scanlon, T.M. 1988. "The Significance of Choice." In Sterling McMurrin, ed., *The Tanner Lectures on Human Values*, 8. Salt Lake City: University of Utah Press, pp. 149–216.

Scanlon, T.M. 1998. *What We Owe to Each Other*. Cambridge, MA: The Belknap Press of Harvard University Press.

Schroeder, Timothy. 2005. "Moral Responsibility and Tourette Syndrome." *Philosophy & Phenomenological Research* 71: 106–23.

Schroeder, Timothy. Forthcoming. "Obsessive-Compulsive Moral Scrupulosity." In David Shoemaker, ed., *Oxford Studies in Agency and Responsibility 3*. Oxford: Oxford University Press.

Searle, John. 1980. "Minds, Brains, and Programs." *Behavioral and Brain Sciences* 3: 417–24.

Serin, Ralph C. 1991. "Psychopathy and Violence in Criminals." *Journal of Interpersonal Violence* 6/4: 423–31.

Shabo, Seth. 2012. "Where Love and Resentment Meet." *Philosophical Review* 121: 95–124.

Shafran, R. and Rachman, S. 2004. "Thought-Action Fusion: A Review." *Journal of Behavior Therapy and Experimental Psychiatry* 35: 87–107.

Shamay-Tsoory, Simone G., Aharon-Peretz, Judith, and Perry, Daniella. 2009. "Two Systems for Empathy: A Double Dissociation Between Emotional and Cognitive

Empathy in Inferior Frontal Gyrus versus Ventromedial Prefrontal Lesions." *Brain* 132: 617–27.

Shamay-Tsoory, Simone G., et al. 2009. "Neuropsychological Evidence of Impaired Cognitive Empathy in Euthymic Bipolar Disorder." *The Journal of Neuropsychiatry and Clinical Neurosciences* 21: 59–67.

Shapiro, Johanna, Morrison, Elizabeth H., and Boker, John R. 2004. "Teaching Empathy to First-Year Medical Students: Evaluation of an Elective Literature and Medicine Course." *Education for Health* 17: 73–84.

Shoemaker, David. 2011b. "Attributability, Answerability, and Accountability: Toward a Wider Theory of Moral Responsibility." *Ethics* 121: 602–32.

Shoemaker, David. 2012a. "Blame and Punishment." In D. Justin Coates and Neal A. Tognazzini, eds., *Blame: Its Nature and Norms*. Oxford: Oxford University Press, pp. 100–18.

Shoemaker, David. 2003. "Caring, Identification, and Agency." *Ethics* 114: 88–118.

Shoemaker, David. Forthcoming-a. "Ecumenical Attributability." In Randolph Clarke, Michael McKenna, and Angela Smith, eds., *The Nature of Responsibility*. Oxford: Oxford University Press.

Shoemaker, David. 2014b. "Emotional Lobbying." *Georgetown Journal of Law and Public Policy* 12: 505–19.

Shoemaker, David. 2014c. "McKenna's Quality of Will." *Criminal Law and Philosophy*. DOI: 10.1007/s11572-014-9322-5.

Shoemaker, David. 2007. "Moral Address, Moral Responsibility, and the Boundaries of the Moral Community." *Ethics* 118: 70–108.

Shoemaker, David. 2011a. "Moral Responsibility and the Self." In Shaun Gallagher, ed., *The Oxford Handbook of the Self.* Oxford: Oxford University Press, pp. 487–518.

Shoemaker, David. 2013b. "On Criminal and Moral Responsibility." In Timmons 2013, pp. 154–78.

Shoemaker, David, ed. 2013a. *Oxford Studies in Agency and Responsibility* 1. Oxford: Oxford University Press.

Shoemaker, David. 2011c. "Psychopathy, Responsibility, and the Moral/Conventional Distinction." *The Southern Journal of Philosophy* 49, Spindel Supplement: 99–124.

Shoemaker, David. 2013c. "Qualities of Will." *Social Philosophy & Policy* 30: 95–120.

Shoemaker, David. 2014a. "Remnants of Character." In Justin D'Arms and Daniel Jacobson, eds., *Moral Psychology and Human Agency*. Oxford: Oxford University Press, pp. 84–107.

Shoemaker, David. 2009. "Responsibility and Disability." *Metaphilosophy* 40: 438–61.

Shoemaker, David. 2012b. "Responsibility Without Identity." *Harvard Review of Philosophy* XVIII: 109–32.

Shoemaker, David. 2014d. "Review of Derk Pereboom, *Free Will, Agency, and Meaning in Life*." Notre Dame Philosophical Reviews. <http://ndpr.nd.edu/news/50121-free-will-agency-and-meaning-in-life/>.

Shoemaker, David. Forthcoming-b. "The Stony Metaphysical Heart of Animalism." In Stephan Blatti and Paul Snowdon, eds., *Animalism*. Oxford: Oxford University Press.

Shoemaker, David and Tognazzini, Neal, eds. 2014. *Oxford Studies in Agency and Responsibility* 2. Oxford: Oxford University Press.

Sigman, Marian, et al. 1986. "Social Interactions of Autistic, Mentally Retarded and Normal Children and Their Caregivers." *The Journal of Child Psychology and Psychiatry* 27: 647–56.

Singer, Peter. 1981. *The Expanding Circle*. Princeton: Princeton University Press.

Sinnott-Armstrong, Walter, ed. 2008. *Moral Psychology, Volume 3: The Neuroscience of Morality: Emotion, Brain Disorders, and Development*. Cambridge, MA: The MIT Press.

Smetana, J. 1981. "Preschool Children's Conceptions of Moral and Social Rules." *Child Development* 52: 1333–6.

Smetana, J. 1985. "Preschool Children's Conceptions of Transgressions: Effects of Varying Moral and Conventional Domain-Related Attributes." *Developmental Psychology* 21: 18–29.

Smilansky, Saul. 1996. "Responsibility and Desert: Defending the Connection." *Mind* 105: 157–63.

Smith, Adam. 2006. "Cognitive Empathy and Emotional Empathy in Human Behavior and Evolution." *Psychological Record* 56. <http://opensiuc.lib.siu.edu/tpr/vol56/iss1/1>.

Smith, Angela. 2012. "Attributability, Answerability, and Accountability: In Defense of a Unified Account." *Ethics* 122: 575–89.

Smith, Angela. 2008. "Control, Responsibility, and Moral Assessment." *Philosophical Studies* 138: 367–92.

Smith, Angela. 2013. "Moral Blame and Moral Protest." In Coates and Tognazzini 2013, 27–48.

Smith, Angela. 2007. "On Being Responsible and Holding Responsible." *The Journal of Ethics* 11: 465–84.

Smith, Angela. 2005. "Responsibility for Attitudes: Activity and Passivity in Mental Life." *Ethics* 115: 236–71.

Smith, Craig A. and Lazarus, Richard S. 1990. "Emotion and Adaptation." In L.A. Pervin, ed., *Handbook of Personality: Theory and Research* (New York: Guilford), pp. 609–37.

Smith, Michael. 1994. *The Moral Problem*. Oxford: Blackwell Publishers.

Smith, Michael. 2008. "The Truth about Internalism." In Sinnott-Armstrong 2008, pp. 207–15.

Snyder, Lisa. 2006. "Personhood and Interpersonal Communication in Dementia." In Hughes, Louw, and Sabat 2006, pp. 259–76.

Soder, Marten. 1990. "Prejudice or Ambivalence? Attitudes toward Persons with Disabilities." *Disability, Handicap & Society* 5: 227–41.

Sommers, Tamler. 2012. *Relative Justice*. Princeton, NJ: Princeton University Press.

Sousa, Paolo. 2009. "On Testing the 'Moral Law'." *Mind & Language* 24: 209–34.

Sousa, Paolo, Holbrook, Colin, and Piazza, Jared. 2009. "The Morality of Harm." *Cognition* 113: 80–92.

Southwood, Nicholas. 2011. "The Moral/Conventional Distinction." *Mind* 120: 761–802.

Spielberger, Charles D., et al. 1983. "Assessment of Anger: The State-Trait Anger Scale." In James N. Butcher and Charles D. Spielberger, eds., *Advances in Personality Assessment*, Vol. 2. Hillsdale, NJ: Lawrence Erlbaum Associates, Inc.

Sripada, Chandra Sekhar. 2010. "The Deep Self Model and Asymmetries in Folk Judgments about Intentional Action." *Philosophical Studies* 151: 159–76.

Sripada, Chandra Sekhar. Forthcoming. "Moral Responsibility, Reasons, and the Self." In David Shoemaker, ed., *Oxford Studies in Agency and Responsibility* 3. Oxford: Oxford University Press.

Sripada, Chandra Sekhar. 2012. "What Makes a Manipulated Agent Unfree?" *Philosophy and Phenomenological Research* 85: 563–93.

Stein, Daniel J. and Hollander, Eric. 1993. "The Spectrum of Obsessive-Compulsive-Related Disorders." In Eric Hollander, ed., *Obsessive-Compulsive Related Disorders*. Washington, DC: American Psychiatric Press, Inc., Ch. 12.

Sterponi, Laura. 2004. "Construction of Rules, Accountability and Moral Identity by High-Functioning Children with Autism." *Discourse Studies* 6: 207–28.

Stipek, D. 1998. "Differences between Americans and Chinese in the circumstances evoking pride, shame, and guilt." *Journal of Cross-Cultural Psychology* 29: 616–29.

Stocker, Michael with Hegeman, Elizabeth. 1996. *Valuing Emotions*. Cambridge: Cambridge University Press.

Stormberg, David, et al. 1998. "Brief Communication: Pathological Narcissism in Bipolar Disorder Patients." *Journal of Personality Disorders* 12: 179–85.

Stout, Martha. 2005. *The Sociopath Next Door*. New York: Broadway Books.

Strawson, Galen. 1993. "On 'Freedom and Resentment'." In Fischer and Ravizza 1993, pp. 67–100.

Strawson, P.F. 2003. "Freedom and Resentment." In Watson 2003, pp. 72–93.

Street, Sharon. 2006. "A Darwinian Dilemma for Realist Theories of Value." *Philosophical Studies* 127: 109–66.

Styron, William. 1990. *Darkness Visible: A Memoir of Madness*. New York: Vintage Books.

Summers, Jesse S. and Sinnott-Armstrong, Walter. 2014. "Scrupulous Agents." *Philosophical Psychology*. URL: http://dx.doi.org/10.1080/09515089.2014.949005

Talbert, Matthew. 2012a. "Accountability, Aliens, and Psychopaths: A Reply to Shoemaker." *Ethics* 122: 562–74.

Talbert, Matthew. 2008. "Blame and Responsiveness to Moral Reasons: Are Psychopaths Blameworthy?" *Pacific Philosophical Quarterly* 89: 516–35.

Talbert, Matthew. 2012b. "Moral Competence, Moral Blame, and Protest." *The Journal of Ethics* 16: 89–109.

Talbert, Matthew. 2012c. "Praise and Prevention." *Philosophical Explorations* 15: 47–61.

Talbert, Matthew. 2014. "The Significance of Psychopathic Wrongdoing." In Thomas Schramme, ed., *Being Amoral*. Cambridge, MA: MIT Press, pp. 275–300.

Tangney, June Price, Wagner, Patricia, and Gramzow, Richard. 1992. "Proneness to Shame, Proneness to Guilt, and Psychopathology." *Journal of Abnormal Psychology* 101: 469–78.

Taylor, Charles. 1976. "Responsibility for Self." In Amelie Oksenberg Rorty, ed., *The Identities of Persons*. Berkeley, CA: University of California Press, pp. 281–99.

Taylor, Steven J. and Bogdan, Robert. 1989. "On Accepting Relationships between People with Mental Retardation and Non-disabled People: Towards an Understanding of Acceptance." *Disability, Handicap & Society* 4: 21–36.

Thomas, Sandra and Jefferson, Cheryl. 1996. *Use Your Anger: A Woman's Guide to Empowerment*. New York: Pocket Books.

Thomson, Judith Jarvis. 1990. *The Realm of Rights*. Cambridge, MA: The Harvard University Press.

Timmons, Mark, ed. 2013. *Oxford Studies in Normative Ethics* 3. Oxford: Oxford University Press.

Turiel, Elliot, Killen, Melanie, and Helwig, Charles C. 1987. "Morality: Its Structure, Functions, and Vagaries." In Jerome Kagan and Sharon Lamb, eds., *The Emergence of Morality in Young Children*. Chicago: The University of Chicago Press, pp. 155–243.

Van Kleef, Gerben A., De Dreu, Carsten K.W., and Manstead, Antony S.R. 2004. "The Interpersonal Effects of Anger and Happiness in Negotiations." *Journal of Personality and Social Psychology* 86: 57–76.

Van Kleef, Gerben A., et al. 2006. "Power and Emotion in Negotiation: Power Moderates the Interpersonal Effects of Anger and Happiness on Concession Making." *European Journal of Social Psychology* 36: 557–81.

Veling, Harm, Ruys, Kirsten, and Aarts, Henk. 2012. "Anger as a Hidden Motivator: Associating Attainable Objects with Anger Turns Them Into Rewards." *Social Psychology and Personality Science* 3: 438–45.

Velleman, J. David. 1992. "What Happens When Someone Acts?" *Mind* 101: 461–81.

Vihvelin, Kadri. 2013. *Causes, Laws, and Free Will: Why Determinism Doesn't Matter*. Oxford: Oxford University Press.

Wallace, R. Jay. 2014. "Emotions and Relationships: On a Theme from Strawson." In Shoemaker and Tognazzini 2014, pp. 119–42.

Wallace, R. Jay. 1994. *Responsibility and the Moral Sentiments*. Cambridge, MA: Harvard University Press.

Warmke, Brandon. 2011. "Is Forgiveness the Deliberate Refusal to Punish?" *Journal of Moral Philosophy* 8: 613–20.

Warmke, Brandon. 2013. "Two Arguments Against the Punishment-Forbearance Account of Forgiveness." *Philosophical Studies* 165: 915–20.

Watson, Amy C. and River, L. Philip. 2005. "A Social-Cognitive Model of Personal Responses to Stigma." In Patrick Corrigan, ed. *On the Stigma of Mental Illness: Practical Strategies for Research and Social Change*. Washington, DC: American Psychological Association, pp. 145–64.

Watson, Gary. 2004. *Agency and Answerability*. Oxford: Oxford University Press.

Watson, Gary, ed. 2003. *Free Will*, Second Edition. Oxford: Oxford University Press.

Watson, Gary. 2014. "Peter Strawson on Responsibility and Sociality." In Shoemaker and Tognazzini 2014, pp. 15–32.

Watson, Gary. 2013. "Psychopathy and Prudential Deficits." *Proceedings of the Aristotelian Society* 113: 269–92.

Watson, Gary. 2011. "The Trouble with Psychopaths." In R. Jay Wallace, Rahul Kumar, and Samuel Freeman, eds., *Reasons and Recognition: Essays on the Philosophy of T.M. Scanlon*. Oxford: Oxford University Press, pp. 307–31.

Wertheimer, Roger. 1998. "Constraining Condemning." *Ethics* 108: 489–501.

Wierzbicka, Anna. 1999. *Emotions Across Languages and Cultures*. Cambridge: Cambridge University Press.

Wiggins, David. 1987. "A Sensible Subjectivism?" In *Needs, Values, Truth: Essays in the Philosophy of Value*. Oxford: Blackwell.

Wiggins, David. 2003. "Towards a Reasonable Libertarianism." In Watson 2003, pp. 94–121.

Williams, Bernard. 1981. *Moral Luck*. Cambridge: Cambridge University Press.

Williams, Bernard. 1993. *Shame and Necessity*. Berkeley, CA: University of California Press.

Wispe, Lauren. 1987. "History of the Concept of Empathy." In Eisenberg and Strayer 1987, pp. 17–37.

Wolf, Susan. 1990. *Freedom Within Reason*. Oxford: Oxford University Press.

Wolf, Susan. 1987. "Sanity and the Metaphysics of Moral Responsibility." In Ferdinand Schoeman, ed., *Responsibility, Character, and the Emotions*. Cambridge: Cambridge University Press, pp. 46–62.

Wowra, Scott A. and McCarter, Robert. 1999. "Validation of the Empowerment Scale with an Outpatient Mental Health Population." *Psychiatric Services* 50: 959–61.

Zaibert, Leo. 2012. "On Forgiveness and the Deliberate Refusal to Punish: Reiterating the Differences." *Journal of Moral Philosophy* 9: 103–13.

Zalla, Tiziana, et al. 2011. "Moral Judgment in Adults with Autism Spectrum Disorders." *Cognition* 121: 115–26.

Zeelenberg, Marcel, et al. 2000. "On Bad Decisions and Disconfirmed Expectancies: The Psychology of Regret and Disappointment." *Cognition and Emotion* 14: 521–41.

Zeelenberg, Marcel, et al. 1998. "The Experience of Regret and Disappointment." *Cognition and Emotion* 12: 221–30.

Zimmerman, David. 1999. "Born Yesterday: Personal Autonomy for Agents Without a Past." *Midwest Studies in Philosophy* 23: 236–66.

Index